Resilience, Reciprocity and Ecological Economics

How did Northwest Coast peoples retain their wealth-producing relationship with their lands for more than 2000 years? Can the answer to this question inform the current debate about sustainability in today's' social–ecological systems? In his groundbreaking new monograph, Ronald Trosper addresses these questions through identification of key institutions – rules governing man's behavior – that characterized those societies.

The book explains why the institutions, through their interactions with each other and with the non-human components, provided both sustainability and its necessary corollary, resilience. Understanding the sources of resilience provides ideas about how key features of today's social–ecological systems can be changed to move toward sustainability, using some of the rules that proved successful on the Northwest Coast of North America. Trosper argues that the governance and exchange principles used on the Northwest Coast should be given serious consideration by those who desire the creation of resilient societies today.

Ronald L. Trosper shows how human systems connect environmental ethics and sustainable ecological practices through institutions. This book will be of interest to researchers and students of ecological economics, conservation, environmental economics, American Indian studies, First Nations studies and community development.

Ronald L. Trosper is Associate Professor of Aboriginal Forestry at the University of British Columbia in Canada.

Routledge Studies in Ecological Economics

Resilience, Reciprocity and Ecological Economics

Northwest Coast sustainability

Ronald L. Trosper

Routledge
Taylor & Francis Group

LONDON AND NEW YORK

First published 2009
by Routledge
2 Park Square, Milton Park, Abingdon, Oxon OX14 4RN

Simultaneously published in the USA and Canada
by Routledge
270 Madison Avenue, New York, NY 10016

Routledge is an imprint of the Taylor & Francis Group, an informa business

First issued in paperback 2011

© 2009 Ronald L. Trosper

Typeset in Times New Roman by
Value Chain International Ltd

British Library Cataloguing in Publication Data
A catalogue record for this book is available from the British Library

Library of Congress Cataloging in Publication Data
 Resilience, reciprocity and ecological economics : Northwest Coast
sustainability / Ronald L. Trosper.
     p. cm.
 Includes bibliographical references and index.
 1. Indians of North America—Northwest Coast of North America—
Government relations. 2. Indians of North America—Northwest Coast
of North America—Rites and ceremonies. 3. Potlatch—Northwest
Coast of North America. 4. Indians of North America—Northwest
Coast of North America—Government relations. 5. Indigenous
peoples—Ecology—Northwest Coast of North America. 6. Northwest
Coast of North America—Social life and customs. I. Title.
E78.N78I54 2008
979.5004´97–dc22
                                                              2008035731

ISBN10: 0-415-41981-6 (hbk)
ISBN10: 0-415-78252-X (pbk)
ISBN10: 0-203-88199-0 (ebk)

ISBN13: 978-0-415-41981-9 (hbk)
ISBN13: 978-0-415-78252-4 (pbk)
ISBN13: 978-0-203-88199-6 (ebk)

Dedicated to
Alexander Vernon, Jr.
Dorothy M. Trosper

In memory of
Thurman H. Trosper
1917–2007
Henrietta Blueye
1947–1982

Contents

Acknowledgements

I began on this book while on sabbatical from Northern Arizona University in 1997–98. The Pew Scholars Program in Conservation and the Environment supported the early research on the book. While on sabbatical, I received desk space and library access from both the University of British Columbia and the Newberry Library. I also received support from the Sustainable Forest Management Network, especially in the later stages of writing. I very much appreciate all of this assistance.

I was received warmly by the Nisg̱a'a Nation; special thanks go to Deanna and Harry Nyce for assisting me during my visits there. The board of the Wilp Wilx̱o'oskwhl Nisg̱a'a heard a presentation of the arguments of the book and approved my access to information about Nisg̱a'a history, culture, and governance. Many Nisg̱a'a elders answered my questions, which greatly increased my understanding of the Nisg̱a'a traditional system.

I thank the Confederated Salish and Kootenai Tribes for hiring me to assist in the Kerr Dam negotiations described in Chapter 8. The tribes gave me permission to write about the dispute after it was settled.

I received useful comments and criticism from anonymous reviewers for *Ecological Economics* and *Ecology and Society* on articles that presented the arguments of this book (Trosper 1998, 2002, 2003). Lisa Ambus provided excellent research assistance.

I thank Alex Vernon for continually insisting I move the book project to the front burner when other projects seemed to take precedence. His support and encouragement assured that eventually the manuscript would be completed. I would also like to thank Melikai (Mel) T. Vernon-Trosper for his help as I completed the manuscript.

Introduction

This book answers a new question. The societies on the Northwest Coast of North America exhibited great resilience over 2000 years: how did the humans organize themselves and their non-human neighbors into a social–ecological system that sustained itself? Lessons are available from an examination of the ways in which the societies on the Northwest Coast built their relationships with each other and with the world around them. Ecological economists and other students of sustainability need to examine examples of societies that have a track record of resilience. Examination of the Northwest Coast provides confirmation that some ideas about the causes of resilience are correct, and suggests new ideas that deserve serious examination.

The system relied upon common pool resources, primarily salmon, without creating a crisis that led to a change in the system. Even when European colonists challenged the societies, they changed and survived. Today the province of British Columbia faces major uncertainties in its land tenure system due to successful challenges from the indigenous peoples. In spite of losing access to their fisheries, indigenous communities on the coast have adapted. Their societies are sufficiently resilient to be able to transform themselves to deal with new circumstances.

The peoples of the Northwest Coast of North America were incorrectly classified by anthropologists as 'complex hunter–gatherers.' The social–ecological systems of the Northwest Coast, we now know, were based on the tending and care of plants, fisheries, and other resources. In a recently edited volume, Douglas Deur and Nancy Turner (2005) provide a set of chapters that show how the people had fields of perennial plants that provided food and consider how explorers and the early anthropologists managed to miss the fact. The simple answer is that cultivation of annual plants was evidence of agriculture. Cultivated perennials were simply invisible to people accustomed to viewing corn, beans, or squash as the evidence of agriculture in the Americas. Stephen Langdon (2007) has shown that the engagement of people with salmon began in what is now southeast Alaska over 3000 years ago, when they established new traps in the tidal zones of their rivers. Management of these traps increased the amounts of salmon harvested.

In the context of a belief in the evolution of societies from simple hunter–gatherers to complex industrialists, the Northwest Coast presented a puzzle. How could such complex societies, with fixed winter villages, large houses, dense populations, and a highly developed art come into existence without agriculture? The idea that 'wild' fish could be tended and cared for was also outside the explorers' experience.

The abundance of the coast was assumed to be a gift of nature, not the consequence of careful stewardship by the humans living there. The depopulation of the coast by disease also created a misleading situation: human population levels had fallen to levels that created an appearance of extraordinary marine resources.

In addition, by the time explorers reached the Northwest Coast, stereotypes about aboriginal people in North America were well developed. The ideology that such peoples did not improve land had been used to justify dispossession of that land, a theory popularized by John Locke (Arneil 1996). As explained in Chapter 2, a racist branch of anthropologists had succeeded in deploying the idea of the 'noble savage,' which challenged assumptions that indigenous peoples were civilized and complex. That they could have created a system that allowed them to utilize their landscapes in a highly productive manner was simply impossible to believe. Reconfigured as the 'ecologically noble savage,' the same imagery today remains a barrier to understanding the indigenous systems.

For these four reasons, few have started analysis of the Northwest Coast with the recognition that they did not fit the stereotypes. They were not merely hunters and gatherers; they tended, cared for, and enhanced their lands. They don't fit into an evolutionary scheme that places European civilization at the apex and every one else lower down. Depopulation due to disease changed circumstances. Civilizations can take many forms.

Now we know that Northwest Coast societies were complex. Archeologists have shown that the societies encountered in the nineteenth century were old. They may have the record in terms of longevity; no complex societies are reported to have survived that long in the survey provided by Joseph Tainter (1988). The level of complexity was not as great as in the classic civilizations surveyed by Tainter, as the Northwest Coast did not have a central government nor a system of writing. I argue in Chapter 6 that restraining the development of complexity below extreme levels contributed to the longevity of the system.

This book provides an initial explanation about how the institutions of the Northwest Coast contributed to the resilience of their systems. The research strategy was simple: look for features shared by all the societies and think about how those features could aid resilience. Many different groups, with different languages, resided on the coast from the Alaskan panhandle to northern California. Some of their institutions had been copied by interior peoples, particularly the various Athapascan and Salish peoples in central British Columbia. For instance, the oral history of the Lake Babine First Nation explicitly describes the reasons that they adopted the feasting and house system from the coast (Fisk and Patrick 2000).

While I assumed that the characteristics they shared had something to do with the mutually long track records, the second part of the research strategy was to determine how the various parts did plausibly fit together in a way that would provide resilience. This second step is invariably influenced by current ideas, such as the definition of resilience. While I tried to suspend biases based on present-day experience, other people may well detect aspects of the Northwest Coast systems that contributed in ways I have not understood. My own training is most extensive in economics, and for that reason I emphasize the parts of the systems that seem most relevant to economic issues.

The reader should be warned, however, that I left the economics fraternity a long time ago, unable to accept either the idea of *homo economicus* or the superiority of private property as a way to organize a territoriality system. I share the concern of others that much of economic theory presents barriers both to understanding how economic exchange actually works, and to understanding alternative ways of organizing it (O'Neil 2007; Marglin 2008). The Northwest Coast system rewards people for being generous, not selfish, and thus encourages generosity. Organizing exchange on principles of generosity creates a system that is quite different from modern markets.

While much of the early evidence comes from anthropologists, those investigators, particularly Franz Boas, were not interested in the exchange side of life. They were fascinated by issues of social organization and religion. They also had their vision clouded by the assumptions discussed above.

Fortunately, I did not have to rely on anthropological records. Because of current disputes over the control of land, the peoples themselves have set out to explain their territoriality systems. The Nisga'a went to court, succeeded, and initiated a treaty negotiation process. Their neighbors, the Gitxsan and Wet'suwet'en peoples, also went to court. Led by the holder of the title, Delgam Uukw, all the chiefs sued to have their title recognized under the laws of Canada. To demonstrate their control of the land, they explained their system, and the scholars who provided the documentation have written books (Mills 1994a, 2005; Daly 2005). The Nuu-chah-nulth of Vancouver Island joined in the defense of Clayoquot Sound and also explained their system to the Clayoquot Sound Scientific Panel when Richard Atleo, Chief Umeek, agreed to co-chair the panel (Scientific Panel for Sustainable Forest Practices in Clayoquot Sound 1995a). He later provided a monograph that explained the Nuu-chah-nulth world view (Atleo 2004).

By emphasizing the differences between their viewpoint and that of the dominant society in British Columbia, spokesmen such as Chief Umeek provide clear signs about what has to be examined in order to understand the aboriginal systems. He particularly emphasizes generosity. He also emphasizes that he learned from his great-grandfather, whose knowledge was acquired before significant contact with Europeans.

This book has a tension between explaining how the aboriginal systems worked and discussing how their institutions may or may not be useful in the modern era. Some characteristics of their systems are impossible today. For instance, they had slavery. That slavery existed provided a way for commoners to discipline titleholders, by cooperating in allowing their leaders to be captured and then refusing to pay the ransom. The principle that managers of land must be accountable for their actions we can use today; but the particular form of accountability is no longer feasible.

Another example of differences is the treatment of trespass as a capital offense. In many groups, a person could be killed by a head titleholder upon the third unapproved entry into the lands of the titleholder's house. While a feast was required to settle the matter with the house of the offender, the matter would end there. Few systems of private property have enforced trespass with such a severe sanction. Yet the principle that land managers need to be able to exclude those who do not follow the orders of the manager is a wise one that forms one of the justifications for private property analysis.

To learn from these examples, we need to separate the rule in question from its means of enforcement. This is not always easy. A similar problem exists with the idea of reincarnation. Clearly, people need to have a long time horizon in judging actions if they are to reach decisions that are sustainable. Do they need to believe they will exist in the landscape in the future in order to have such a long time horizon? If so, then people have to come to believe in specific forms of reincarnation, a prospect I regard as unlikely.

Rather than try to determine which of the features can be used today, I have simply tried my best to describe how the societies operated and why their rules contributed to resilience. I am uncertain that all of the rules were needed, or which were fundamental and which superfluous; but I make suggestions along these lines. I don't know which can be translated into present-day conditions. Full consideration of the usefulness of these ideas today is the topic of another investigation. Perhaps encouraging people to accept the need to be generous and to accept contracts in which they share in each other's profit is impossible, just as trespass is not likely to become a capital offense. I leave that judgment to readers; people today need to pick and choose what they find acceptable.

In considering which rules are useful now, one lesson from the Northwest Coast is that everyone should participate in discussions about social policy. The Nuu-chah-nulth insist that those with apparently strange ideas need to be heard; one does not know ahead of time to whom the spirits have spoken (Atleo 2004: 89). Making certain that everyone is heard and respected is a key rule that deserves to be heard. It is one often advocated today (O'Neil 2007).

Although I stress the complementarities among the components, I don't yet know what was essential and what was superfluous in the Northwest Coast systems. In Chapter 8, I provide an example that demonstrates how a little bit of contingent proprietorship provides some improvement in environmental management when it gives leverage to local people. Perhaps the various components can be combined in various ways, and are additive in effect.

I suspect that some of the rules are particularly important. The requirement to share net returns has excellent effects on incentives. The requirement that holders of land demonstrate their understanding and be accountable to their communities creates useful feedback loops. Sharing returns and public accountability improve social learning. Dropping the idea that society and nature are separate opens up new lines of inquiry that have been ignored until recently.

Readers may be curious about how this book came to be written. I came to this investigation as a member of one of the communities that existed on the periphery of the Northwest Coast. The Confederated Salish and Kootenai Tribes of the Flathead Indian Reservation, Montana, were influenced by some of the ideas from the Coast, but had not adopted a full house territory system as I describe in this book. We are more correctly classified as hunter–gatherers, although I don't like the classification system. My father was an enrolled member of the tribes, and my mother came from the neighboring town of Missoula, Montana. I grew up in a bicultural household. Because my father was one of the first members of his tribe to obtain a college education, he found employment in the US Forest Service to be preferable to anything available in Indian Country. He encouraged my education, and I obtained entrance to Harvard College for my undergraduate education. During my first week there, I went to the Peabody Museum, where there was a display of the Flathead Indians. Each of the descriptions was written in the past tense. I saw familiar beadwork described as artifacts of a people who no longer existed. This gave me good warning regarding what my education would entail. While at Harvard, I had the opportunity to do field work in Zinacantan, a Mayan community in the highlands of Chiapas. This experience with anthropological field work has influenced most of my research; I am an economist who likes to read anthropology.

When I went on to study economics in graduate school at Harvard, it helped to be half indigenous, because I could tolerate much of the cultural dissonance that was involved. I do not recommend the experience. Looking back, I don't know why I was as tolerant of the field as I was. I was aided by the open-mindedness of the faculty at the time. My dissertation advisor, Kenneth Arrow, encouraged me to study what obviously gave me great passion, the history and conditions of the Flathead Indian Reservation. My first and second topics did not lead to doable projects. In the end, I wrote about the land-tenure history of the reservation (Trosper 1974), a story that showed the dangers of a flawed application of the idea that people are aided if they are encouraged to adopt a private property system. I set out on a career studying economic affairs on reservations in the United States, which inevitably involved study of resource management as well. After a period of teaching in universities, I worked for a while with my tribe, assisting in economic analysis. I returned to academia to teach at the School of Forestry at Northern Arizona University, where I learned much about ecology from my colleagues.

Eventually, this experience led me to write an article, 'Traditional American Indian Economic Policy' (Trosper 1995), which then led to this project. That article appears to make generalizations about all American Indians, although it describes two forestry cases that are distinct applications of the proposed policy approach, and one grazing case that is not consistent with it. I have backed off of the desire to describe a pan-Indian approach, and prefer to examine particular examples. Even this project is a bit 'pan'-oriented, because I am generalizing about people who consider themselves distinct. But the geographic focus is narrow, the Northwest Coast; this book makes no claims about other indigenous peoples in North America. In the midst of the project, I was offered and accepted a job in the Faculty of Forestry at the University of British Columbia. Living in the region has been very important.

Chapter 1 provides the evidence that the social–ecological systems on the Northwest Coast maintained their key characteristics for more than 2000 years before contact with the explorers from the old world. The chapter also provides a brief summary of the arguments of the book. The second and third chapters present rebuttals to those who have claimed that indigenous peoples in North America have not taken care of their habitats. Chapter 2 deals with the concept of 'noble savage' and why it needs to be rejected. Chapter 3 deals with the role of beliefs in reincarnation in assisting both motivation and understanding regarding human interactions with non-humans and future generations. The cycles of life in ecosystems embody reincarnation and connect the past to the future.

Chapters 4–6 present the core of the results of this study. Chapter 4 explains how requiring reciprocity among fishermen removes the prisoners' dilemma that can lead to over-fishing. The famous potlatch feasts are key to this explanation: rather than being curiosities promoting status, as treated by many anthropologists, the exchanges in these feasts are fundamental to the economic structure of these successful societies. Chapter 5 deals with the territoriality system; the rules defining control of territories provide the requirement that fishermen share their wealth. These territoriality rules are needed to make the reciprocity system be a requirement for all who control resources. Chapter 6 explains how the processes of dispute resolution allowed leaders to deal with crises that otherwise would not be dealt with under the wealth transfer and territoriality systems.

Chapter 7 discusses ways in which the industrialization of the Northwest Coast might have been different if the settlers had joined the indigenous economic system, rather than pushing it aside. By telling this alternative history, this chapter should stimulate thought about how the rules used on the Northwest Coast might be applied to create resilience in today's systems that do not have resilience.

Chapters 8 and 9 present examples that show the entire system of the Northwest Coast isn't required for positive results: some of the ideas, by themselves, can be helpful. Relicensing of electricity production by Kerr Dam on my reservation shows how contingent proprietorship, a requirement that managers of a valuable piece of land respond to external accountability, led to a positive move in ecosystem management along the Flathead River. The successful resistance of the Nisga'a people to their displacement shows how excellent leadership principles can keep a people together, allowing them to establish a different but effective form of self-government even in the presence of a very hostile Canadian legal and political system.

The final chapter compares the results of Chapters 3–6 with the recommendations that are being developed by the Resilience Alliance. Some of the rules and attitudes on the Northwest Coast have been rediscovered, namely valuing the future in terms of the past, the importance of accountability for land managers to their communities, and the importance of considering humans as part of natural systems. But the Resilience Alliance has not given sufficient attention to reciprocity and to contingent proprietorship as principles of territorial systems. Further work is definitely needed to determine how these concepts can be applied today.

1 Sustainability needs tested ideas from the Pacific Northwest

'It's a strict law bids us dance.'

When European explorers first visited the Pacific Northwest Coast of North America, they encountered one of the richest aboriginal regions of the continent. The peoples of the coast lived in substantial wooden houses and had high population levels. Their stratified and complex society supported an elaborate artistic tradition. Their main source of wealth was the ocean, which produced salmon, halibut, shellfish and other products. They also cultivated root crops and managed berry production. They traded their surplus with each other and with other peoples in the interior. The Hudson's Bay Company found that they could not penetrate the economies on the coast, which were tightly controlled by the chiefs of the area.

Because disease decimated the people, and because the invading Europeans had superior military technology, the colonizing powers rather easily occupied the land and brought the aboriginal people under their control. They set up canneries and used the salmon resource as food for the developing industrial economies in other parts of the world. They cut the forests and dammed many rivers.

In utilizing the resources of the coast, the invaders completely misunderstood the origin of the wealth they encountered. The indigenous peoples had, over several millennia, developed a relationship between themselves and the fisheries which ensured abundance sufficient to support their high populations. They had tended the countryside to create productive landscapes. Having no idea that peoples who appeared to be mere hunters, fishers and gatherers had actually manipulated their environment to its high level of productivity, the new people thought the resources were a gift of nature, declared them open to everyone, and proceeded to decimate the fisheries.

In 1885, the conquerors outlawed what they called the potlatch, a set of ceremonies in which the leaders of the local communities would distribute wealth to their neighbors, appearing to impoverish themselves in the process. Such profligate generosity appeared wasteful. It appeared to give the wrong incentives, preventing accumulation of wealth. This action symbolizes the misunderstanding between the cultures encountering each other in this colonial period. I argue in this book that the potlatch system enabled people dependent upon a fishery to structure their relationship to the fish in such a way that the fish prospered and they prospered. By eliminating the potlatch and its associated institutions, and by substituting their own approaches, the settlers set up the conditions to destroy the fishery, a project that is almost complete.

Just after the potlatch was outlawed, the anthropologist Franz Boas began his first field work among the Kwakwaka'wakw people, known then as the Kwakiutl. Upon his arrival, one of the chiefs spoke at length to Boas, who did not yet understand the Kwakwala language. Ninety years later, the U'mista Cultural Centre of Kwakwaka'wakw people produced a video that provided text for the speech. According to the video, the chief asked the following of Boas:

> We want to know whether you have come to stop our dances and feasts, as the missionaries and agents who live among our neighbors try to do. We do not want to have anybody here who will interfere with our customs. We were told that a man-of-war would come if we should continue to do as our grandfathers and great grandfathers have done. But we do not mind such words. Is this the white man's land? We are told it is the Queen's land; but no! It is mine! Where was the Queen when our god came down from heaven? Where was the Queen when our God gave the land to my grandfather and told him, 'this will be thine?' My father owned the land and was a mighty chief; now it is mine. And when your man-of-war comes let him destroy our houses. Do you see yon woods? Do you see yon trees? We shall cut them down and build new houses and live as our fathers did. We will dance when our laws command us to dance, we will feast when our hearts desire to feast. Do we ask the white man, 'do as the Indian does?' No, we do not. Why then do you ask us, 'Do as the white man does?' It is a strict law that bids us dance. It is a strict law that bids us distribute our property among our friends and neighbors. It is a good law. Let the white man observe his law, we shall observe ours. Now, if you are come to forbid us to dance, leave us. If not, you will be welcome.
>
> (Shein and Wheeler 1975)

The chief did not explain why the 'strict law' is a 'good law.' This book argues that the chief was right. The 'strict law,' really a whole set of laws, guided a way of life that had persisted for at least two millennia, and that existed north and south of the land of the Kwakwaka'wakw people.

The U'mista Cultural Centre of Kwakwaka'wakw titled the video: 'Potlatch: A Strict Law Bides Us Dance' (*ibid.*). The video re-enacts the sentencing of those who participated in a December 1921 potlatch for Dan Cranmer, the father of the narrator, Gloria Cranmer Webster. It also shows a potlatch celebrated in 1974, a modern hamatsa, the very dance that upset the missionaries with its simulated cannibalism. Gloria demonstrates a valuable copper, and describes the old way of life as 'based on the giving away of wealth.' The quotation given above is read in its entirety. The movie makes clear what many others also have said: the feasts, dancing, and give-aways summarized as the 'potlatch' were fundamental to the governance of the societies of the Northwest Coast. The exact wording of the speech is probably provided by the movie-makers; Boas reported the following:

Finally, I noted that I had become the subject of their speeches, but naturally I had no idea what they wanted. At last they sent a young man who had been in Victoria for some time to interpret for me. I must add the natives were not too clear about why I was there and what I wanted, and that they were making all kinds of conjectures. At first they thought I was a priest, and now, because I had brought nothing, they thought I might be a government agent come to put a stop to the festival. The missionaries and the Indian agent have done this, but the Indians have refused to take orders and continued to celebrate. The agent said he would send a gunboat if they did not obey, but they did not believe him and were not going to pay attention to the warning.

(Boas and Rohner 1969: 33)

Boas's report in his diary indicates that some of the text in the movie overlaps with what he reports; but the key message, that the potlatch is a good law, Boas does not report. He was in the midst of watching a potlatch feast, and assured his hosts that he was not there at the behest of the Queen. He was interested in collecting stories, drawing pictures, and purchasing masks and other items for a museum collection; he reported 'there is a small or large potlatch almost every day, which of course interrupts my work' (*ibid.*: 38).

That the give-aways were outlawed, and that Boas found them to interrupt his work, illustrates the depth of misunderstanding. The settlers at the time came from a society that was in the midst of the industrial revolution that started in the eighteenth century. By the end of the nineteenth century, that society attributed its success to the private industriousness of its industrial leaders and to the willingness of people to work hard in the factories, on the farms and in the extractive industries. Giving away wealth was the opposite of the right message. In addition, spending weeks on feasts and dances meant work was not being completed.

A cannery was established at Alert Bay, and the Kwakwaka'wakw people were encouraged to move there as a work force. The men fished and brought salmon to the cannery for processing, and the women worked in the cannery preparing the fish. Mechanized boats harvested the fish in the ocean, and non-Indians persuaded the government to allow them into the fishery, gradually excluding the Indians. Eventually, the fishery crashed. Outlawing the potlatch and removing the authority of the chiefs to manage the fishery struck down a system of fishery management that had persisted for more than 2000 years. Within less than 100 years, the fishery was almost gone. Now, as all the fisheries in the world's oceans are either stressed or in greater trouble, the wisdom of ignoring the potlatch should be questioned.

Fisheries are not the only common pool good that is in trouble. At the largest scale, deposition of carbon dioxide and other greenhouse gases in the atmosphere is raising the atmosphere's temperature worldwide and changing the chemical balances of the oceans. At smaller scales, lakes and rivers suffer from pollution; that pollution often reaches the ocean, creating other problems. Use of the environment's ability to process wastes is a common pool problem of top priority. Modern humans address common pool problems with great difficulty; yet the peoples of the Northwest Coast had lived with a common pool resource for thousands of years. Understanding how they did so should provide some useful ideas for dealing with humanity's top concern now: how to be resilient when key components of their livelihood are environmental services threatened by unrestrained use. The Kwakwaka'wakw people's advice regarding their strict law needs to be investigated.

Sustainability is replacing growth as a social goal

The world is in the midst of a change in thinking about economic and social policy in general, and environmental policy in particular. Climate change is showing that the world depends upon a common pool resource, the atmosphere. Other common pool resources, such as fresh water and forests, are also important. Simply put, the world is discovering that people depend upon these common pool resources more than they believed. These common pool resources are much like fisheries, which are also in trouble throughout the world. How should people organize themselves when they depend upon a common pool resource? We need to study examples of peoples who have developed complex and productive systems using a common pool resource as the fundamental source of wealth. The peoples who lived with the salmon and other fisheries of the Pacific Northwest Coast of North America are such an example.

As I explain in this chapter, during a period between 3000 and 2000 years before today, the peoples in that region had developed a system that led them to prosper in their relationship with the fishery resources. Once developed, the system then persisted for two millennia, until it was displaced by the European settlers who arrived there in the nineteenth century. In some areas, the people survived and kept their knowledge of the systems they used to use. In other areas, particularly close to the cities that developed in the twentieth century, the people survived, but some of their practices did not.

Some may dispute the premise that these societies had reached a level of resilience that allowed them to persist in the face of unanticipated changes in resource productivity and in their own behavior. They also did not over-exploit the basis of their wealth. I argue in this chapter that we should accept the archeological evidence that their ways of life did persist for over 2000 years. Given this persistence, a good question is this: how were they successful at living well when their main source of food was a fishery? As we answer this question, we can also address a second: are any of the things that they did potentially useful today?

These two questions are significant because the dangers of ecological collapse are causing a shift in goals, from promoting a continual increase in human material welfare to ensuring that human welfare levels are sustainable. Because conventional analysis of economic policy was built to address the first goal, new ideas and new economic approaches are needed. This need provides a reason to examine peoples with a track record in sustainable resource management.

We know that for the goal 'promote a continual increase in human material welfare,' economic theory and modern economic practice have many familiar recommendations for institutional design. Among the most important has been to establish systems of transferable private property rights to land, capital, and commodities, enforced within a system of nation-states. If one wants to examine the rationale for this system, the literature of economics generally and development economics in particular explains it very well. A new subdiscipline in economics, 'the new institutional economics,' is actively investigating the ways privatization-oriented institutions create practices that achieve the desired goal. Douglass North received a Nobel prize for his contribution to this field. The Cambridge Series in Political Economy of Institutions and Decisions, published by Cambridge University Press, contains many of the contributions to this subdiscipline.

An alternative approach to the design of institutions has emerged from the 'new economics of information,' the results of which are usefully summarized by Nobel prize winner Joseph Stiglitz (1994) in his consideration of what recommendations should be provided to the formerly socialist countries of Europe and Asia. Rather than emphasize privatization, this literature emphasizes competition. Private ownership of property can in many circumstances support competition; but it can fail by allowing monopolization and other market failures. When private property systems impede competition, then government action may be needed to restore competition or to correct problems that competition cannot correct. For instance, monopoly may develop and need correction. A highly unequal distribution of the ownership of land may make agricultural markets inefficient due to incentive problems in labor contracts. The private information that people have about their health may make competitive medical insurance inefficient. In each of these cases, Stiglitz shows that markets cannot be left alone, thus disagreeing with those who think transferable property rights is the whole answer.

While scholars in these two fields emphasize different aspects of modern economies, and argue with each other, they share the priority given to maximizing the growth of human material welfare. The literature promoting equality in the distribution of wealth in modern economies also assumes that economic growth is a major goal. A recent book on realistic utopias features a debate about proposals that equalize the distribution of wealth and improve economic growth. Samuel Bowles and Herbert Gintis (1998) propose changes in the distribution of wealth which, by solving incentive problems identified by the economics of information, raise the level of output as well. Barry Bluestone and Bennett Harrison (2000) emphasize the external effects of technological discoveries, the public good character of basic investment, and the need for additional growth to provide the additional output that can be shared more equitably. Thus both those unconcerned about the distribution of income and those worried about it agree on the importance of economic growth.

The rising political importance of sustainability, however, suggests that the goal is changing. 'Maximize the present value of [justly distributed] human material welfare' is being replaced or augmented by 'Sustain human welfare.' If humans change the economic purpose of human organization in this way, the recommendations urged by generations of economists have to be re-examined. Institutions designed to cause growth have not adequately addressed sustainability: thus the need to deal with common pool goods and external effects.

But what changes should be made? This question is larger than simply managing common pool resources within existing institutions. This book also suggests that the institutions used on the Northwest Coast provide suggestions of ways to organize economic systems for sustainability.

Concurrent with the recognition of sustainability as a goal has been an improvement in the reputation of indigenous peoples. Chief Seattle, whether quoted correctly or not, is one icon who demonstrates the readiness of European and American audiences to idealize American Indians. Although the stereotype suggests that indigenous peoples have contributions to make to this discussion, discovering the contributions requires great care. I treat this topic in more detail in Chapter 2.

Observers can make another error: examination of only part of the system used by an indigenous group. The literature on indigenous peoples and the environment, however, has looked primarily at two types of idea: ethics and management practices. For instance, an ethical principle common in indigenous societies is that man is part of a community that includes animals, plants, and even mountains. An example of a practice common in indigenous systems is the creation of reserves where harvest is prohibited. To examine these types of ideas is to look at the goals and the practices of a social-economic system without examining important connections. A system of ethics defines desired outcomes. A set of management practices is a way to manage an ecosystem. What connects the ethics to the practices? How do members of such societies coordinate their actions in order to achieve sustainable welfare in practice?

Sympathetic observers, such as philosopher J. Baird Callicott (1989a,b, 1994) and ecologist Fikret Berkes (1999), recognize that institutions connect beliefs to actions. But they do not examine the connections. Callicott is interested in environmental ethics; Berkes is interested in management practices. This book is about institutions that connect environmental ethics to sustainable management practices.

Evidence from the Pacific Northwest regarding sustainable use

A first step in my presentation is to establish that the Pacific Northwest peoples are an example of resilience and sustainability. The proof has three parts. First, a demonstration that the peoples' ways of life did persist for a long time. The second is to demonstrate that the technology used for fishing could have been used to fish too intensely. The third point is that population levels were high in relation to the resource. If these three points are plausible, then investigation of the peoples' institutions should be worthwhile. I argue in this section that all three are quite believable.

The archeological record

Because nothing has endured forever, Costanza and Patten (1995) recommend that a definition of sustainability should contain a description of the time period that is reasonable. A society was sustainable that survived to old age, that persisted as long as other societies have lived in balance with their environments. To apply this standard, one needs to have a baseline for comparison. The peoples of the Northwest Coast of North America set a high standard for the criterion of persisting for a long time with an unchanged way of life. The archeological chapters of Volume 7 of the

Handbook of North American Indians (Suttles 1990) suggest that many of the cultures of that area established the patterns of their pre-contact cultures around 500 BC. Donald Mitchell, for instance, summarizes the Kwakiutl evidence as follows:

> In most important respects, this late (post-500 B.C.) culture type is recognizably like the way of life described for the Kwakiutl people.
>
> (Mitchell 1990: 355)

> Just to the south, the Strait of Georgia period is given the dates 400 A.D. to 1800 A.D., and in the Lower Fraser River Canyon area, the last culture type is given the time period 500–1800 A.D.
>
> (*ibid.*: 340–349)

On the Queen Charlotte Islands, the evidence shows an even longer period of continuity:

> The Graham tradition begins about 3000 B.C. and lasts until European contact, A.D. 1774 for the Queen Charlotte Islands …
>
> (Fladmark *et al.* 1990: 235)

Wessen (1990) reports that evidence from the Ozette site on the Olympic Peninsula suggests that cultural continuity extended over 2500 years.

The chapter on the Lower Columbia River reports the evidence as follows:

> Although the cultural chronologies for the Lower Columbia area clearly show stylistic change in artifact styles, as well as some probably functional additions or replacements of artifact classes, no fundamental change in the lifeway seems indicated for the last 3,000 years.
>
> (Pettigrew 1990: 522)

In their book reviewing the prehistory of the Northwest Coast, archeologists Ames & Maschner summarize as follows:

> Most archeologists working on the coast feel that the cultures of the Late Pacific [AD 200/500 to AD 1775] differed little, if at all, from those observed and recorded by the first European visitors to the coast. … As we have seen, there is reasonably strong evidence for cultural continuity on the coast overall for at least the last 3,000 years.
>
> (Ames and Maschner 1999: 95)

The archeological record reveals that the institutions in place upon contact with outside explorers were probably those that contributed to the long record of cultural continuity that has been observed. That this continuity can be identified with the current idea of 'sustainability,' however, requires attention to the size of the human economy in relation to the ecosystems of the area. If the people's population levels were low, then they did not challenge the capacity of their environment even if they were wealthy.

Some may doubt that the Indians of the Northwest Coast had the technology or the population levels necessary to make sustainability a serious policy issue for them; but recent evidence on both counts suggests that they had the technology to harvest more salmon that they did, and population levels high enough to make excessive harvest a possibility.

Fishing technology

Fishing technology consists of boats and fishing equipment, knowledge of the runs, and storage techniques. Much evidence exists that native technology was sufficient to lead to over-harvest if population and consumption levels were high enough. Along the Columbia River, in Puget Sound, along the Fraser River, on the coast of present-day Canada, and in Alaska, white settlers learned their fishing techniques from the natives. These were the techniques that the settlers (and natives they hired) used to exhaust the runs in the early twentieth century.

In his study of the fishing industry on the Columbia River, enthohistorian Courtland Smith describes the technical situation as follows:

> Having this assortment of gear, Native American fishers were well equipped to catch salmon in the various conditions of the river. In fact, their gear encompassed a range of variability comparable to that of the white fishers who exploited the salmon resources as a commercial enterprise.
>
> (Smith 1979: 11)

In her expert testimony for *United States v. Washington*, anthropologist Barbara Lane summarized the situation for the tribes that were party to the case:

> Traditional Indian fishing methods were highly efficient. These methods survived where Indians were allowed to maintain them; that is, where they were not outlawed or where Indians were not prevented access to areas where the methods were feasible.
>
> (Lane 1973a: 40–41)

Lane's report provides detailed information for each of the tribes that were party to this suit, which led to the well known 'Boldt Decision' that the treaty tribes of western Washington had rights to half of the salmon and steelhead fishery in that state (Cohen 1986). Robert Higgs (1996) describes how fishing in Washington State became less and less efficient as it moved away from the mouths of rivers into Puget Sound and eventually into the ocean. He argues that traditional Indian methods were the most efficient.

As with the Indians living on the Columbia River and living in what was to become western Washington State, Indians in British Columbia were also excellent fishermen:

The technology of commercial fishing was developed from the expertise of Indians, and it was their equipment that helped start and build the industry. Especially important was their knowledge of fish movement and small boat navigation in the uncharted tidal channels of the coast. Indian women were skilled in fish cleaning and preservation and needed little or no training to work in canneries ... and salteries.

(Kew 1990: 162–63)

In Alaska, use of a key technique by natives, the fish trap, was outlawed in 1889 and by the 1930s the use of fish traps by non-natives was the cause of excessive harvest:

In 1889 federal legislation was enacted that outlawed aboriginal traps and weirs. A few years later, legislation was adopted that permitted commercial fish traps to be placed in the mouths of salmon streams. ... The fish traps accounted for 70 percent of all salmon taken in southeast Alaska during 1925 to 1934. ... It was quite evident that the salmon stocks were decreasing and that fish traps were responsible for the decline. By 1953, President Dwight Eisenhower declared the fishing communities in southeast Alaska disaster areas.

(Worl 1990: 153)

The characteristics of gear and boats are not the whole story regarding fishing success. Fishermen need to know the locations and times that are most important, particularly for a migratory species. As Kew (1990) reports, the non-native fishermen who maintained an unsustainable harvest for the canneries of the early twentieth century did so using the knowledge gained from native fishermen. Many of the canneries, in fact, employed native fishermen. Non-Indians required more than ten years to learn how to employ reef nets successfully after finding that salmon traps taken from other regions did not work in the Strait of Juan de Fuca (Lane 1973d: 12–13). Reef nets are still in use today.

Canneries thrived on a preservation technique that allowed sale of salmon throughout the world. Native peoples had stored salmon in quantities that allowed preservation for their own use throughout the year. The native techniques were based on drying salmon rather than canning it, and are documented extensively by Hilary Stewart (1977) in her book on Indian fishing, and by Barbara Lane (1973a–d) in her expert testimony. Ames and Maschner (1999: 146) report that drying techniques have been used since at least 1800 BC.

Given that the technology existed to harvest and store fish in great amounts, what remains to be shown is that population levels on the Northwest Coast were great enough to cause potential stress on the fishery resources.

Population

The latest data on aboriginal population levels, combined with assumptions about levels of consumption, give estimated harvests for the Columbia River and the

Fraser River that are approximately the size of an estimated level of sustainable catch. The uncertainties are large, however, for all three components: population, consumption per capita, and the sustainable catch.

Boyd (1990) estimates that, conservatively, approximately 180,000 people were living on the Northwest Coast in 1774. Per capita levels of consumption matter for an accurate estimate of the impact a society places on its fisheries. All authors who have considered the issue have used 2000 calories per day as estimated human subsistence requirements. Weinstein and Morrell (1994) (following Schalk 1986) point out that fish were used to feed dogs, to provide oil for cooking, and to serve as trade goods with other Indian communities. For these reasons, estimates based only on human consumption are probably too small.

Smith (1979: 5) cites Hewes's (1973) estimate that the native population of the Columbia River would have harvested 18 million pounds of salmon a year. Smith gives pounds caught per year for all species from 1866 to 1973. The high seems to be 49.5 million in 1911; the modern low is 5.2 million in 1960. The harvest during the main canning period, 1874–1948, is 21 million to 45 million pounds per year (Smith 1979: Appendix B). It appears that the population estimated by Hewes was harvesting a substantial amount, which was less than the levels that led to decline in the salmon resource but greater than the modern lowest levels of harvest.

Terry Glavin (1996: 102–6) summarizes the literature regarding population levels along the Fraser River. He accepts an estimated aboriginal population of 60,000 people, a midpoint between high and low estimates. The pre-contact annual catch could have been as high as '12 million sockeye equivalents' in all salmon species. Since the actual sockeye catch plus spawning escapement has been between 3.3 million and 11.2 million fish during the period 1894–1986, the estimated pre-contact catch is in the same range as the post-contact catch that accompanied stock declines. The aboriginal catch would have been of all salmon species, however, and the resulting comparisons are insufficient because data on other species are not included. Other authors, such as Haggan *et al.* (2006), similarly have concluded that aboriginal people could have harvested salmon above sustainable levels.

Archeologists Virginia Butler and Sarah Campbell (2004) provide a different type of evidence. They examined salmon remains to determine if harvest pressure led to a decline in the proportion of bones from large fish. Prey-choice models suggest that over-exploitation of prey by humans leads to a decline in the proportion of large fish. Such models, applied to mammals, also suggest that the proportion of large mammals in archeological sites would decline if harvests lead to depletion of the larger prey. Butler and Campbell examined data from sites on the Pacific Coast and inland on the Columbia River. They found no decline either in salmon related to other fish or in large mammals (artiodactyls). Regarding salmon, they conclude as follows:

> Salmon, confirmed in its importance as the most abundant and widespread prey fish in both areas, was the target of focal fisheries for 10,000 years, yet there is no evidence of an impact leading to a shift in prey taxa. The fact that salmon were not depressed in either area supports a biological explanation,

that salmon populations are highly resilient due to their reproductive strategy and life cycle.

(*ibid.*: 390)

They conclude that the reason for no shift in relative abundance is due to the resilience of the salmon, not to management practices of the humans involved. Yet other evidence, reviewed above, suggests that humans were numerous enough and sophisticated enough technologically to over-exploit the resource had they wished to do so. Others also reject the idea that humans could have over-exploited the salmon runs (Singleton 1998: 52).

In summary, that the peoples of the Pacific Northwest could have lived in an unsustainable relationship with their environment is plausible, given their fishing technology and their population levels. Aboriginal harvests were of the same order of magnitude as modern levels, and if it had reached the high end for the ranges, the fisheries would have been seriously depleted. The archeological evidence suggests that they did not do so. Those who reject the possibility reduce their curiosity about the possible contributions of the potlatch to fisheries management, and seek other explanations for the existence of the potlatch and its associated institutions. The next section summarizes the rules that probably contributed to their record of sustainability.

Defining sustainability

Ecological sustainability occurs when the people living in an ecosystem, or a landscape of connected ecosystems, maintain that ecosystem in a condition of ecological health over many centuries. I mean to use ecological health in the broad sense of maintaining ecosystem composition, structure, and process, what others refer to as ecological integrity (Costanza *et al.* 1992). The maintenance of ecological health can be observed because the landscape remains constant enough for humans to continue to relate to it in a successful manner. The presence of humans in a landscape means that the characteristic composition, structure, and processes of the landscape are influenced by human presence. Man becomes part of the system. If the resulting patterns remain constant or improve for a long period (perhaps after an initial learning period), then there is sustainability of both the social and ecological systems, which are linked. If the patterns deteriorate over time, and as a consequence humans have to leave or reduce population as well, then ecological sustainability is absent.

Because, over a long period, external challenges can occur, such as long-term droughts or a mini-ice age, then sustainability needs to be augmented with an idea of resilience: a social ecological system that persists for a very long time has demonstrated resilience. A resilient social–ecological system maintains its key characteristics in response to extreme perturbations, either by resisting the onslaught or reorganizing and adjusting to it (Folke 2006).

As Costanza and Patten (1995) have pointed out, a modern claim of sustainability is a prediction, because we do not know where any of our current systems is headed. To find examples of sustained systems, we need to look to the history of mankind on the planet. I have selected the Northwest Coast of North America.

The Native peoples of the Northwest Coast of North America established a pattern of composition, structure, and process in their salmon-based economies, which remained unchanged for many millennia. Evidence from middens suggest that immediately after the end of the ice ages, salmon were not as important in the diet of humans as the fish eventually became. But once the salmon-based pattern was established, it persisted.

Research strategy

The archeological evidence suggests that the peoples of the Northwest Coast persisted in similar practices for approximately 2000 years. For some, the evidence is for a shorter time (AD 500–1775) and for others it is for a longer time. These peoples differ in many ways. They speak many languages. Some use matrilineal rules for the inheritance of titles and territory; others use patrilineal inheritance. My strategy is to ask this question: what characteristics did they share? I knew when I started this investigation that anthropologists had noted enough characteristics to define the region as one of the culture areas that deserved its own separate volume of the *Handbook of North American Indians*.

I also knew that one big similarity was the enormous public give-aways called the potlatch. Using economists' models of fisheries, one can easily show that the pooling or exchange of the surplus from the fishery through a give-away system solves the incentive problem known as the 'tragedy of the commons' (Hardin 1968). I provide this proof and discuss it in Chapter 4. If groups are in competition with each other, those that avoid depleting their fisheries will succeed in comparison with those who do not find solutions to the tragedy of the commons. The spread of the potlatch among the fishing tribes suggests that its advantages came to be widely recognized.

Potlatches, however, operate in the presence of other social practices, and these practices may also be part of the story. It is important, therefore, to look to other aspects of these societies to understand what they were doing. I also thought it important to talk to people in these societies today. The Nisga'a, in particular, had managed to keep their communities together and to resist the kind of changes that were being forced upon them. When the opportunity presented itself, they worked hard to generate conditions that would allow them to pursue a modern compromise with the settler societies. This they accomplished in 2000, a feat that is discussed in Chapter 9. A visit to one of their feasts revealed an important feature that I had not understood before – the fact that all the potlatch transactions were conducted in public, with the exchanges well publicized. This publicity provides accountability.

I am not going to spend much time on how these characteristics came to be common along the Northwest Coast. Students of evolutionary processes are currently developing models that provide plausible explanations of how group-beneficial characteristics can spread among human populations at the level of both groups and individuals. These scholars are reviving concepts of 'group selection' that Darwin originally suggested, but which fell out of favor within the community of scientists studying evolution. I refer in particular to the books by Robert Boyd and Peter Richerson (1985, 2002; Richerson and Boyd 2002), the recent survey by David Sloan Wilson (2007), and Christopher Boehm's important book on equality and hierarchy (Boehm 1999).

A look at the pattern of communities on the Northwest Coast easily suggests that group selection processes could have worked in the region. The mountains reach down to the sea, and create only a finite number of places along the shores that are suitable for villages. The oral histories and the archeological remains suggest that warfare existed between the groups, meaning that those who were able to generate a social surplus from their resources would be able to defend themselves better than other groups. Those who developed good relations with the salmon, meaning that their salmon runs were large, would have more surplus than others.

Once the complex of social rules that created a wealthy society had spread among the groups on the coast, a kind of equilibrium seems to have come into existence in which certain other traits could not develop. In particular, they developed no form of organization above that of an alliance among villages. No authority that spread over large areas developed. Perhaps unification of the fisheries in one or more of the large rivers would have provided a surplus large enough to support such a 'state'; but one did not emerge. I argue in Chapter 6 that the intersection of the territoriality systems and the rules for good governance prevented the emergence of leaders who could unify groups over a large area, limiting the ability of a state to emerge.

My first resource was Volume 7 of the *Handbook of North American Indians*. (Suttles 1990) Once I had discovered some of the common themes in that book, I looked further by reading ethnographies of some of the main groups. I was frustrated originally by the seeming lack of interest by the early anthropologists in economic issues. They seemed to assume that the abundance of salmon made such issues uninteresting. But some of the students of the first anthropologists became interested in the economic and ecological issues. The idea arose that the exchange of goods through the potlatch provided a kind of social insurance. That neighbors could be asked for support, knowing that such support would be returned, meant that groups could rely on their neighbors if their own salmon runs failed (Suttles 1960, 1987; Piddocke 1965).

The anthropologists, however, did not seem to be aware of the analyses being developed by economists to explain why fisheries would lead to a 'tragedy of the commons.' For this reason, the usefulness of the potlatch system in economic terms was probably not readily apparent. The chief quoted in the video, 'It is a strict law that makes us dance,' may have been aware of its worthwhile character. Chief Umeek, in his book explaining a Nuu-chah-nulth world view, praises generosity as follows:

> ... the law of generosity may be stated as follows: It is necessary to give in order to receive. According to this law, it is not better to give than to receive because both giving and receiving are equivalent and interactive values. Consequently generosity can be viewed as a natural law of reciprocity. The ancient Nuu-chah-nulth felt so strongly about the importance of the relationship

between generosity and the quality of life that the opposite of generosity was equated with death.

(Umeek 2004: 129)

Chief Umeek also may not be aware of the economic analysis that supports his assertion for a fishing people. But he believes in the importance of generosity enough to suggest it is a natural law.

Umeek goes on to assert that generosity improves the quality of life through giving a person a sense of personal well being. I'm not satisfied with Umeek's assertion. I want to know why generosity improves the quality of life. This may be true at an individual level, for people surviving in a region in which the economic life is organized with generosity. But why does it work at a group level, or for a whole system?

The description is based the *Handbook of North American Indians* and on the literature describing the Nuu-chah-nuulth, Kwakiutl, Nisga'a, Gitksan, and Wet'suwet'en. The Kwakiutl sources are Walens 1981, Johnsen 1986, Webster 1991, Weinstein 1994; these sources differ from earlier interpretations by Franz Boas. For the Gitksan, this description is based upon Adams 1973, Cove 1982, Copes and Reid 1995, Pinkerton and Weinstein 1995, Pinkerton 1998. The Wet'suwet'en are described by Mills (1994a) and Daly (2005). The Nisga'a provided me with materials they use in their schools (McKay 1982, McNeary 1994; Nisga'a Tribal Council 1995; Boston and Morven 1996) and also invited me to a major feast/potlatch. Many of these sources resulted from work done by experts in connection with the court case *Delgamuukw v. the Queen*. In this case, the Gitksan and Wet'suwet'en leaders sought to prove that they owned their land and to establish their right to self-government.

Summary of principles from the Pacific Northwest

The property, exchange, and leadership rules of the Pacific Northwest combined six types of idea into a system that provided incentives both to ordinary people and to leaders who supported sustainable resource use.

(1) First, rights of access and use of valuable lands and fishing sites were recognized as something similar to the European idea of property, meaning that individuals or groups could exclude others from using the valuable lands. To distinguish the idea from that of property, I shall call their territorial system one of proprietorship. The distinction is necessary because the person with the rights of proprietorship was not able to sell the land. He was also obligated to share some of the land's products. Neither of these conditions is typical of 'property' in the European sense.

(2) Second, proprietorship over territory was contingent on proper management of the territory. Not only did the chief of a house holding territory need to demonstrate he had been trained successfully for the job; he had to perform well as chief.

(3) Third, a system of ethics defined proper use; the ethical beliefs defined abuse of land in terms of reduction of its productivity for future generations.

(4) Fourth, systems of reciprocity defined economic exchange relationships among people, both individually and in groups. Reciprocity provided incentives that supported proper use of lands both by providing insurance against misfortune and by reducing the incentive to harvest too much.
(5) Fifth, enforcement of reciprocity rules was totally public.
(6) Sixth and finally, rules about the behavior of chiefs provided a system of governance that could maintain the other five elements and allow modifications as needed.

Proprietorship

The peoples of the Pacific Northwest had a system of territoriality I shall call 'pro-prietorship' to distinguish it from a system of 'property.' The system was similar to property systems in that the group connected to each territory had the right to exclude strangers from it, and as a result could use the land themselves. But the kinship connections limit the right of exclusion. The holders of the land were obligated to share what they produced from the land. Sale of land for a price was unknown, although transfers could occur when mutually agreed to. These characteristics made their system differ from the modern concept of 'property' or 'ownership of property.'

Proprietorship on the Northwest Coast was organized through systems of 'houses' – each of the language groups on the coast was organized by the use of houses. A house consisted of a number of related families who lived under the direction of a head titleholder. The leadership of the house had a series of titles, ranked, whose occupants carried on the business of the house. Each house has a territory containing fishing sites, berry-picking sites, gardens, and other sites that produced food or plant material for use of the house. Every place in the entire territory of a society belonged to a house. Even areas of the ocean near land were assigned to houses. The name for these houses are *wilp* among the Nisga'a and Gitxsan; the Nuu-chah-nulth call the traditional territory of a chief a *hahuulthi*.

Recently, legal philosopher J. E. Penner (1997) has argued that the 'bundle of rights' idea which defines private property in the English and American legal system is too broad. A narrower definition of property focuses upon the separate character of the object owned, and the right of exclusive use. For Penner, property is:

> the right to determine the use or disposition of a separable thing (i.e. a thing whose contingent association with any particular person is essentially impersonal and so imports nothing of the normative consequence), in so far as that can be achieved or aided by others excluding themselves from it, and includes the rights to abandon it, to share it, to license it to others (either exclusively or not), and to give it to others in its entirety.
>
> (*ibid.*: 152)

This definition applies to persons or to groups of persons. Penner explicitly excludes from his definition 'the power to sell property or otherwise dispose of it by contract.' (*ibid.*: 154) The idea of a contract defines the power to sell. The rules that govern contracting are also the rules that allow for owners of property to dispose of property through market exchanges. But 'none of the kinds of property we generally observe are conceptual creatures of markets. Rather, they are conceptual creatures of economies, and economies do not have to be based on contractual exchanges' (*ibid.*). In making this distinction, Penner departs from the usual definition of property, which includes the right to sell.

Penner's definition differs from the Pacific Northwest in two main ways. First, the connection to the land was not entirely impersonal. Particular corporate groups, the houses, were connected to the land through kinship with others who had lived on the land. Second, the 'right to share' was actually an 'obligation to share,' not an option held by the group holding the land.

Supplementing Penner, anthropologist Bruce Rigsby (1998) argues, further, that the use of property rules of some sort are a characteristic of all human societies, whether the societies succeeded in pursuing sustainable land-use policies or not. Any system of land use and governance needs to be able to maintain itself by enforcing both exclusion rules, to keep out people and influences that will undermine the system, and inclusion rules, which specify under what conditions new community entrants are allowed. I would differ from Rigsby by not using the word 'property' to describe the general characteristic of 'territoriality.' The term property brings in the specific other assumptions that Penner identifies, and thus misleads in describing territorial systems in general.

In an attempt to distinguish different abilities of people with access to a common property resource, Schlager and Ostrom (1992) have distinguished five types of powers a group may have over its resource. A proprietor may enter, remove items, manage, and exclude others. An owner may do everything a proprietor may do, plus sell the property to others. In Penner's terminology, Schlager and Ostrom err in assigning an owner the right to sell. The most common use of the word owner, however, is that which Schlager and Ostrom describe. In terms of Penner's analysis, the person with the property is a proprietor as described by Schlager and Ostrom. This paper will use the word proprietor to emphasize that the inability to sell does not mean an inability to exclude others.

The term proprietor, however, does not capture the duty to share as part of its normal use in English. Therefore a different term is needed; in Chapter 10 I use the term trustee-proprietor.

Contingency

By 'contingency,' I mean that the person in charge of a house territory had to comply with community standards in order to obtain and keep the position of head titleholder. These standards included complying with requirements to share. It also meant complying with community standards of preserving the productivity of the land. I describe these standards in the next categories.

As many have pointed out, English-style private property systems of ownership have some features that can help in ecosystem management. If the common-law rule that owners are not allowed to create nuisances for their neighbors is strictly enforced, then any single property owner can use a court system to protect his land against actions by neighbors that harm his land. (Brubaker 1998: 89) Much of the development of property law in the nineteenth century in the United States, in fact, increasingly limited the ability of owners to protect themselves against nuisance, in the interest of promoting economic growth (Horwitz 1992; McEvoy 1998)

The English common-law maxim 'Use your own property so as not to harm another's' certainly addresses external effects, depending upon the definition of 'harm.' The idea of the police power, a principle of law in the United States, would seem similar to the ability of a chief to impose some conditions on the actions of the weir operators in his territory. Again, the amount of control depends on the definition of the breadth of the police power (Sax 1971, 1993).

But the rule applied by the Northwest Coast systems goes further than the idea of nuisance prevention or the police power: it asserts a right on the part of other community members to punish the titleholder for harming the land or its streams and rivers. This is most similar to the modern idea of a lease: a person who rents land from another can be subjected to conditions on the use of the land by the terms of the lease. Most leases provide for protection of the inherent productive capacity of the property that is rented. But the proprietor of a territory in the Northwest Coast system was not leasing land from others who had rights to share in the income flowing from the land.

Environmental ethics

The idea of a contingent proprietorship allows a chief to enforce the community's concept of harm against any member of the house to whom the titleholder has assigned responsibility for a portion of the house's territory, or against the chief himself. The definition of harm becomes important and is a third component of the Northwest Coast system. Many North American aboriginal societies had a system of ethics and beliefs about the natural world that supported the idea of sustainable land use. The world views of societies in the Pacific Northwest stress three main ideas: the unity of man and nature, the importance of restraint in consumption, and the presence of a long time horizon.

Unity of man and nature

Stanley Walens provides a specific example from the Northwest Coast in describing Kwakiutl beliefs:

> The Kwakiutl believe that animals and spirits lead lives that are exactly equiv-alent to those of humans. They live in winter villages, perform dances, wear masks, marry, pray, and perform all other acts that humans perform. ... In fact, since animals are considered to be human beings who have donned the masks and costumes that created their animal forms, people are united with the animals by virtue of the fact that they are all actually human beings.

The opposite is also true – that people and animals are related because humans are really animals, but animals who have removed their masks and costumes to return to their human state.

(Walens 1981: 23)

This quotation demonstrates that the Kwakiutl did not see a separation of man from nature; man is part of the system. This view, shared with many other Native American world views, provides little support for the idea that man has a right to dominate nature; rather, man has a responsibility to conduct himself properly in order to maintain his place as a predator along with other predators.

Restraint in consumption

Walens, in his analysis of the Kwakiutl world view, emphasizes the importance placed on food, on controlling hunger, and on the cycling of food back and forth between animals and humans.

For the Kwakiutl the animal world, like the human world, is predicated on two opposing principles: the principle of hunger – the need and desire for food, which drives humans and animals alike to kill; and the principle of sociality – the principle by which humans and animals consciously suppress their hunger for the benefit of their associates.

(Walens 1981: 98)

The story of Transformer presents the Kwakiutl explanation for the origins of morality. Walens provides a lengthy analysis of the myth, in which Transformer 'transforms the world from its past, amoral, hunger-dominated condition to its present, moral, hunger-controlling state.' (Walens 1981: 125) Among the beings that he kills is a *sisiutl*, a giant serpent with two heads and a face in the middle of its body. A *sisiutl* is evil for two reasons: it has a voracious appetite, and it has no anus through which to excrete the animals it eats, preventing them from being reborn. Although not expressed as such, the *sisiutl's* inability to excrete waste also could be seen as bad because it interrupts the cycling of nutrients through an ecosystem.

At meals, Kwakiutl treat food respectfully, take small bites, and demonstrate that they have hunger under control by leaving food in their dishes at the end of the meal (Walens 1981: 87–93).

Long time horizon

Part of the problem with the *sisiutl* is interruption of the cycle of rebirth. The importance of concern for the far future is based on a belief in reincarnation, that after death a person's spirit spends some time in the spirit world, but later becomes a descendant of the person who died. The rebirth will occur specifically in the same lineage. For a titleholder in the Pacific Northwest, for instance, there would be specific ideas about which of the ancestors he or she had been in an earlier life.

Pacific Northwest houses are assumed to last forever, with people occupying leadership positions in the houses during their lifetimes. Most of the tribes believe in reincarnation. The belief is so specific among the Wet'suwet'en that elders determine which children are reincarnated previous chiefs. A chief, therefore, may know who he or she was in a prior life, and may expect to be reincarnated into a position in the tribe, if not in the very house in which the person now resides (Mills 1994a: 118–19). Other Northwest Coast tribes were also specific in their knowledge of the identities of reincarnated souls (Walens 1981: 17; Mills and Slobodin 1994). This provides a direct, sacred, spiritual continuity with the land, and is a basis for the concept of concern for the future generations. Decision-makers today are directly affecting their own future, after reincarnation.

The idea of reincarnation connects to the unity of man and animals:

> The entire economic system of the Kwakiutl is predicated on the idea that animals (and, to some extent, plants) are captured only because they are willing to be captured, and that they are willing to be captured only if they are treated in the proper manner. … Animals are willing to die for one reason: without death there can be no rebirth in the eternal cycle of life. Without death, animals and humans grow old, feeble, senile, and powerless. They must die so that they can be reborn.
>
> (Walens 1981: 72)

A belief in reincarnation can support sustainable use by increasing the weight given to future income. Even in the presence of a belief in reincarnation, chiefs could give lower weight to their own future income, based on uncertainty about the future. One might expect believers in reincarnation, however, to give greater weight to the future than would non-believers.

Taken together, these three components of Kwakiutl belief comprise an environmental ethic quite similar to others that Baird Callicott (1994) has identified among indigenous people. Man has a proper place in nature, he has to control his appetite, and he cares about the condition of the land forever.

Reciprocity

The contingent control of a house's territory by a chief depended on another key requirement: that a chief be generous with the products of a territory. The peoples of the Pacific Northwest Coast are well known for their system of potlatching. The requirement that titleholders share the surplus available from the use of their land's resources with other titleholders meant that reciprocity dominated the organization of economic exchange. A reciprocity system makes sense for a society based upon fisheries, because reciprocity creates the correct incentives for fishery management. This idea is explained fully in Chapter 4.

Although the terminology may vary, economists have realized recently that reciprocity provides incentives to deal with problems in managing common-pool resources, externalities, public goods, production of knowledge, and with market provision of insurance (Arnott and Stiglitz 1991; David 1998; Kolm 2000a, b). Evidence from laboratory experiments with human subjects has shown that simple models of self-interest are not consistent with the behavior of participants, further demonstrating the need to investigate reciprocity (Hoffman *et al.* 1998).

The potlatches, involving redistribution of wealth, are one part of the public ceremonies in Pacific Northwest societies. A portion of the year, usually the winter, is designated for feasts, which can occur for many reasons, usually having to do with birth, marriage, and death. Although many different things happen at feasts, my interest is in the giving away of property, speeches, and group decisions.

One common event is that a new chief of a house holds a funeral feast for his predecessor. His side of the village hosts the feast, and his house pays the primary expenses of the feast: food for everyone, and gifts for the other side of the village. The higher the rank of the house hosting the feast, the greater is the amount of gifts expected by the guests and the more villages that are invited. Several years after the funeral, the new chief will hold another feast, to raise a totem pole in his predecessor's honor. Both the funeral and pole-raising feasts require saving up wealth for several years; the wealth comes from the lands of the house through the labor of members of the house, who live from food taken from the lands and the fishing sites. The chief shows his worthiness by generating the surplus required for the feast, and the guests acknowledge his position when they accept the gifts.

Public accountability

When I visited the Nisg̱a'a while working on this book, a family invited me to one of their modern feasts. I was surprised to observe that every one of the transactions of cash during the feast was announced publicly. There was a large wooden bowl in the front of the room. Early in the process, money went into that bowl as each contribution was announced. Later in the feast, the money was distributed to key people in the room. The general distribution of goods that one normally associates with a potlatch occurred later, when even visitors such as myself received some things. These gifts were not announced.

Having observed the importance placed on public revelation of all the exchanges of cash during a feast among the Nisg̱a'a people, I looked at the reports of other feasts to see if the publicity aspect was also very evident. In his reports of feasts and gift-giving, provided to Franz Boas, Hunt (1905–08) often reports that 'tally keepers' are called upon by chiefs to keep track of the blankets and other items being distributed (Boas and Hunt 1905, 1908: 57–59, 207–13, 229–31, 279, 291). Chief and ethnologist William Beynon (2000) also carefully lists the exchanges given at the many feasts he observed in the winter of 1945, that confirm my observations at Nisg̱a'a: potlatch contributions are counted publicly.

Leaders as facilitators

A discussion of the benefits of reciprocity rules makes one look to questions of higher structures that enforce those rules and make adjustments to processes when conditions change. Our understanding both of current economic theory and of eco-logical theory shows that issues of public decision-making must be addressed when we seriously consider ecosystem management. Neither complete decentralization nor complete centralization can provide answers to the governance problems (Sah and Stiglitz 1988, 1991; Stiglitz 1994). Of particular importance is the interaction of rules for chiefly behavior and the other five areas explored here.

Because the feast hall was the central forum for settling disputes and reaching agreements, it was also the main system of governance at large scale:

> The feast hall ... is a forum in which people can express their different points of view and their grievances, and where they can find either an immediate or a slow resolution to a recognized conflict. While many of the issues to be settled involve territory, other matters are resolved as well. The head chiefs guide the resolution of differences because they have been acknowledged as the correct leaders through their succession to the highest names, all of which have been validated by the feast itself.
>
> (Mills 1994a: 71)

While much of the anthropological literature on the potlatch emphasizes recipro-cal exchange and either recognition or achievement of status, the potlatch system was also a system of governance. During a feast, guests are invited to speak, and any public business that needs attention can be placed before the assembly. Sides take turns speaking, there is no limit placed on the time for any speaker, and any decision is reached by consensus of the chiefs present. If no consensus is reached, the matter will be postponed to another feast. If other villages need to be involved, a feast will be scheduled to invite them to discuss the matter.

Gifts, chiefs and contingency

The position of a titleholder was inherited; people who were not in line for leader-ship could not be 'elected' or selected by any system similar to that in other tribes. The chief of a house controlled access to the lands of that house, and obtained a considerable share of the harvest from the lands. Yet these rulers were constrained by the ethical system, which required that they be stewards of their resources. Fail-ure to manage the salmon properly, as shown by a failure of the salmon to return, would threaten the leadership position of a titleholder. His duty to the salmon included a duty to be generous, and to sponsor winter ceremonies.

The idea of contingent proprietorship, which a chief could award to a member of his house, also applied to the chief's ability to hold onto his title if he failed to carry out his duties.

> Having a chief's name is an honour and a responsibility, requiring the holder to act correctly and with decorum. ... Those who desire to receive feast names know that they have to earn them and maintain them through proper conduct; in the same way, those who are worthy of names must be treated with the

respect due to such titles. … If someone given the honour and responsibility of being a chief does not live up to expectations, the title may be taken away.

(Mills 1994a: 136)

The duty to be generous created ways for commoners and other chiefs to constrain the actions of a particular titleholder. Commoners had options regarding which titleholder they would actually support. Although constrained by kinship ties, those ties were flexible enough to give choice. A husband and wife, for instance, had four different ways to trace their descent, from the father's parents or the wife's parents. (Weinstein 1994; Donald 1997) Thus they could move to another house if a titleholder was a poor manager.

The rulers were also constrained by the need to seek acceptance and approval from other titleholders. A person claiming a title had to demonstrate worthiness by conducting potlatches, in which he gave away wealth to other titleholders. Johnsen (1986) points out that providing goods to neighboring titleholders was probably a cheaper way to protect proprietorship than was investment in defensive military action. The accumulation of the wealth for a potlatch required support from a claimant's relatives, thus also providing 'commoners' with influence regarding which of those with claim to a title would receive their support. It appears that in some tribes there was open competition for titles in this way, while in other tribes the rights of the eldest children were more secure.

These titleholders had to be knowledgeable about their resource management, they had to know and lead in the system of sacred ceremonies, and they had to distribute their wealth. The presence of animals to harvest is due to the ritual powers of chiefs. As a result, harvest failures can have fatal effects for chiefs:

Since the active part of food collection is totally the responsibility of the commoners, and the analogic [sacred] part the responsibility of the chiefs, it is not surprising to read of a numaym [Kwakiutl house] whose members consider murdering their chief when food harvests are poor … , for they believe that if they perform their work correctly, the failure in the food-collecting process must be that the chief is not performing his ritual obligations. His death and replacement by a more responsible person are necessary if everyone else is to survive.

(Walens 1981: 81)

This heavy requirement for chiefs to retain their position brings this short description of the Northwest Coast rules full circle: not only did chiefs enforce contingent tenure; their own position was contingent on complying with the needs of their community.

Sustainability and resilience

In his description of the Pacific Northwest Coast system, economist Bruce Johnsen (2001) advances a startling hypothesis: the secure tenure held by titleholders enabled them to discover and apply evolutionary selective principles to affect the timing of runs and the size of salmon in those runs. This hypothesis is consistent with the idea, common in the area, that chiefs held important knowledge as well as spiritual power regarding salmon. The hypothesis also suggests a way in which salmon runs and the system of governance co-evolved, each supporting the strength of the other, through learning by titleholders. Johnsen omits the role of reciprocity in encouraging titleholders to share discoveries with each other. Because all share in each other's harvests, improving the harvests generally benefits everyone. Thus the knowledge learned by one chief, if shared with a neighboring chief, would in the end benefit both.

The principles of governance and exchange on the Northwest Coast fit together into a system in which the principles supported each other. Chiefs had to abide by the environmental ethics of the community, to show respect for the ability of land to provide for humans. Chiefs showed their respect for salmon by giving away their wealth; such generosity was required in order to assure that salmon would offer themselves in sufficient quantity for people to harvest. Houses held the territory controlled by the titleholders of the houses, and other titleholders showed their recognition of the territorial rights of the houses by accepting gifts when younger members of the elite acquired the titles upon the elders' deaths. All business at feasts and potlatches was conducted in public, with amounts given and received announced to all. Chiefs were expected to mediate disputes through the feasting process.

Contingent proprietorship provided a way to buffer human-caused disturbance by changing those making decisions. Environmental ethics defined the basis for judgement of good management. Feast hall discussions supplemented this need to deal with such developments. Potlatching to define proprietorship provided a way for the system to self-organize, without a higher-level governmental system to define ownership of lands. Potlatching provided a way for new proprietors to convince neighbors that they were worthy of holding lands without resort to military force (although this did occur). Finally, reciprocity provided incentives for titleholders to share knowledge about salmon management, and the system of inheriting titles provided ways for knowledge to pass among generations.

Non-utopian models

A substantial literature has developed examining 'alternatives to capitalism'; some of this literature treats ecological issues. In the introduction to one of these books, *Alternatives to Capitalism*, Jon Elster and Karl Ove Moene provide the following comment in a footnote after they contrast market and command economies:

> Mention should be made of a third mode of economic organization, distinct from both the market and central planning. K. Polanyi has argued (*The Great Transformation* [Boston: Beacon Press, 1957]) that reciprocity – giving and receiving according to need – has been the dominant mode of exchange in

many traditional societies. S.-C. Kolm (*la Bonne economie* [Paris: Presses Universitaires de France, 1984]), argues that it could and should also be made the dominant principle for complex industrial economies. In the absence of a sketch of the institutions that would embody the principle, the argument remains utopian.

(Elster and Moene 1989: 3)

This footnote creates a challenge: to provide a 'sketch' of the institutions that would utilize reciprocity, sufficiently detailed to avoid the charge of being utopian. Elster and Moene use a narrow definition of reciprocity, however. Anthropologists define reciprocity in two ways: 'generalized reciprocity,' which is close to the idea used in the above quotation, and 'balanced reciprocity,' in which giving and receiving is equalized and is not necessarily related to need in any way, which is more applicable to the Northwest Coast. This work accepts this challenge, and adds, in addition, institutions that complement reciprocity of both types.

I want to provide more than a sketch of the institutions that would embody reciprocity, and this book provides a survey of a system that worked for thousands of years. Chapter 7 responds to Ester and Moene, providing an alternative history to show how the Northwest Coast system might have changed the industrial system had the new entrepreneurs been required to fit into the Northwest Coast system.

Elster and Moene's use of 'utopia' as an epithet meant to debunk S.-C. Kolm reminds me of other uses of epithets to debunk ideas that have their origin in the original societies of the New World. Chapter 2 examines another examples, through a review of the literature which 'debunks' the idea that Native Americans were 'environmentalists.'

2   The 'noble savage' spin game

In a chapter in which he argues that nature is part of God's work, and that many religions support the idea of taking care of the Earth, Al Gore presents a quotation he attributes to Chief Seattle, without citing the source in his endnotes. Gore states that the power of Seattle's speech 'has survived numerous translation and retellings.' Here is Gore's quotation of Chief Seattle in full:

> How can you buy or sell the sky? The land? The idea is strange to us. If we do not own the freshness of the air and the sparkle of the water, how can you buy them? Every part of this earth is sacred to my people. Every shining pine needle, every sandy shore, every mist in the dark woods, every meadow, every humming insect. All are holy in the memory and experience of my people ...
>
> If we sell you our land, remember that the air is precious to us, that the air shares its spirit with all the life it supports. The wind that gave our grandfather his first breath also received his last sigh. The wind also gives our children the spirit of life. So if we sell you our land, you must keep it apart and sacred, a place where man can go to taste the wind that is sweetened by the meadow flowers.
>
> Will you teach your children what we have taught our children? That the earth is our mother? What befalls the earth befalls all the sons of the earth.
>
> This we know: the earth does not belong to man, man belongs to the earth. All things are connected like the blood that unites us all. Man did not weave the web of life, he is merely a strand in it. Whatever he does to the web, he does to himself.
>
> One thing we know: Our God is also your God. The earth is precious to Him and to harm the earth is to heap contempt on its Creator.
>
> (Gore 1992: 259)

This text emphasizes the following ideas: the Earth is sacred, it is our mother, man's connection to the Earth means what he does to the Earth he does to himself. Al Gore's chapter argues for these points using a variety of sources, not just Chief Seattle's speech. His use of the speech, however, creates a special vulnerability.

Author and science popularizer Matt Ridley found the quotation, and he quotes a selection of it in a chapter in which he argues 'there is no instinctive environmental ethic in our species. He keeps the key phrases, 'What befalls the earth befalls all the sons of earth,' and 'All things are connected like the blood that unites us all.'

Then he notes that if the speech is correct, his own analysis is wrong:

> If such eco-optimism is well founded, then the argument of this book falls, and people are not calculating machines designed to find cooperative strategies only when they assist enlightened self-interest. So if Chief Seattle really did live by his own philosophy of universal brotherhood with nature, I have a big explaining job to do. Ecologically noble savages – to borrow Rousseau's term – are inconsistent with the picture I have painted.
>
> (Ridley 1996: 214)

In the next paragraph, he delivers a rhetorical thunderbolt:

> The chief's prescience, alas, is illusory. Nobody knows what he said that day. The only report, made thirty years later, was that he praised the generosity of the great white chief in buying his land. The entire 'speech' is a work of modern fiction. It was written for an ABC television drama by a screenwriter and professor of film, Ted Perry, in 1971. Though many environmentalists, Gore included, like to pretend otherwise, Chief Seattle was not a tree-hugger. Among the few things we do know about him are that he was a slave owner and had killed almost all his enemies. As the case of Chief Seattle illustrates, the entire notion of living in harmony with nature is built on wishful thinking.'
>
> (Ridley 1996: 214–15)

That a speech is attributed incorrectly does not prove its contents to be false; but the rhetorical trick is effective. It gains its power partly from the fact that any falsification strikes at an argument's entire structure. Ridley follows up with an attack on Chief Seattle, providing no proof of his charges. He doesn't cite documentation that Seattle had killed his enemies, or that he held slaves. Both raiding among houses and slavery did occur in the Pacific Northwest; but to attribute them to Seattle needs proof. Both Gore and Chief Seattle are debunked by this strategy.

Others have played the game as well. Economist Terry Anderson, for instance, in an article on 'Conservation – Native American Style,' begins by quoting others quoting Chief Seattle, and argues that 'Appealing as this image of a Native American environmental ethic is, it is not accurate … By focusing on this myth instead of reality, environmentalists patronize American Indians, disparaging their rich institutional heritage which encouraged resource conservation' (Anderson 1997: 770). Anderson wants to undercut the ethical argument so that he can argue that American Indian property rights institutions are what explain their conservation. He reveals also that the quotations from Chief Seattle are from Ted Perry. Unlike Ridley, however, Anderson supports the idea that some North American Indians took care of their lands. Ridley follows his debunking with a series of examples purporting to show indigenous lack of respect for the environment. Thus

Anderson's variant is explicitly pro-Indian, while Ridley's is explicitly negative. Environmentalists are debunked in both examples.

Recent political developments in the United States have emphasized the role of 'spin' in distorting events for public consumption. Spin occurs in public debate, and represents a rhetorical artifice. A prize should be awarded for the most resilient case of spin. A strong candidate is the use of the idea that Rousseau believed in a 'noble savage' to debunk Rousseau, indigenous people, environmentalists, and advocates of indigenous people. This chapter explains the assumptions used in this spin, which occurs in several variants. This book needs to treat this question because the noble savage rhetorical techniques will be deployed to debunk its arguments. That any humans ever managed to live in a resilient relationship with their ecosystem has to be attacked by those who do not want to humans to make an attempt now to achieve such a goal.

The noble savage spin game has five components. (1) Identify an idea or image that is internally contradictory and vaguely connected to an idea that is to be debunked; (2) attribute the manufacture or use of the idea to a famous person or movement (aided if a famous person does use the idea); (3) show the image to be false; (4) draw the conclusion that the famous person or movement is wrong; and (5) present the argument to an audience inclined to agree with it.

The technique is an elaboration of the 'straw man' strategy, in which an argument is distorted and then shown to be false. The elaboration is that the straw man is connected to an actual person. Sometimes the person cooperates, as Al Gore did by quoting Ted Perry speaking for Chief Seattle. Sometimes the connection is mythical, as in the case of Rousseau, who never claimed the peoples of the New World were both noble and savage.

This use of Ted Perry's rewriting of Chief Seattle's speech removes Indians from control over their messages in three ways. First, non-Indians put words into Indian mouths, which pre-empts what Indians might have said. Second, other non-Indians expose the fact that the words are not legitimate, establishing an aura of falsity and inauthenticity about the words. Third, when and if Indians finally say what they want, if it has any resemblance to the distorted message, it can be dismissed easily as another example of a falsified myth.

Matt Ridley's quotation above baldly constructs exactly this chain of argument. He begins by establishing the speech is fabricated. He ends by dismissing the idea of living in 'harmony with nature.' He also disparages Chief Seattle as a slaveholder and warlike – someone 'savage' – without proof.

Another variant on the argument is to emphasize not the false attribution of the ideas of conservation, but that indigenous people have accepted the false idea as true. In his introduction to his book, *The Ecological Indian: Myth and History*, anthropologist Shepard Krech has this complaint about the stereotype:

> Yet as its simplistic, seductive appeal works its charm, the Noble Indian persists long beyond memory of when or how it entered currency. At first a projection of Europeans and European–Americans, it eventually became a self-image. American Indians have taken on the noble Indian/ecological

Indian stereotype, embedding it in their self-fashioning, just as other indigenous people around the world have done with similar primordial ecological and conservationist stereotypes. Yet its relationship to native cultures and behavior is deeply problematic.

(Krech 1999: 27, citing Lears 1985; Keesing 1989; Sahlins 1993)

In this statement, Krech joins others who claim that indigenous peoples have invented their culture from components learned from the colonizing powers. In doing so, he extends the principle of noting Ted Perry's authorship: he seeks to debunk any statement by indigenous people by implying they have adopted stereotypes of themselves. As Darren Ranco (2007) has discussed, Krech mistakenly cites Marshall Sahlins (1993) in the above passage. Sahlins' article is a refutation of the idea that native peoples of the Pacific invented their cultural practices as a result of contact with colonizing powers. Krech also asserts that the Cree learned conservation from the Hudson's Bay Company, and Harvey Feit has refuted that. When the Hudson's Bay Company attempted to restore beaver populations on Charlton Island in 1836, they were taught how to do so by the Cree. By 1856, the leadership of the company had learned the basics of beaver population dynamics (Feit 2007: 72–80).

Krech sets out to answer the question 'To what extent have Native North Americans been ecologists or conservationists?' (Krech 1999: 27) Note that he does not ask what was the relationship between Native North Americans and their world; he sets up two standards taken from modern times – ecology and conservation. He begins his quest with a question that requires an answer from within his own intellectual framework.

As with Ridley and Anderson, Krech cites the fraudulent Chief Seattle speech. He saves the tactic for his concluding chapter (p. 214), where he refers to a number of Indians making pro-environment statements. He ends the list with Chief Seattle, pointing out that his words were written by a freelance writer. He then connects the image of the ecological Indian to a 'rich tradition whereby the noble Indian – including the ecological Indian – is a foil for critiques of European or American society.' When American Indians say something that sounds like the noble Indian/ecological Indian stereotype, they join Al Gore as the object of the rhetoric, and are also debunked.

Krech can perhaps be excused for not knowing when the noble savage tactic was first used. Two years after the publication of Krech's book, Ter Ellingson (2001) published *The Myth of the Noble Savage*, in which he revealed the result of his search for the first use of the image, which was not by Rousseau (1984 [1755]). The first recorded use of this strategy was in 1859 by John Crawfurd. His context was different, however. Before the term 'ecologically' became attached, indigenous alternatives to European political processes had provided a basis for praise. Crawfurd set out to debunk ideas of respect for indigenous peoples, which he associated with Jean Jacques Rousseau. As Ter Ellingson shows, Rousseau never asserted the existence of noble savages. John Crawfurd, however, attributed the idea to Rousseau. Others followed; the tactic was so successful that the originator sunk from sight while his spin triumphed. Ellingson had to perform major detective work in order to find the original statement of the myth.

When Crawfurd was an incoming president of the Ethnological Society in London, he laid out the myth in an inaugural presentation. He was a leader of a group of racists who had managed to take control of an early anthropological association in England. After presenting the reasons why the white people of London were superior to other races, and especially the natives of Tierra del Fuego, he attributed the idea of noble savage to Rousseau after misquoting a poem by Dryden which used the noble savage term. Then Crawfurd attributed the concept to Rousseau. Here is the conclusion to the passage that Ellingson found:

> Such savages as I have now been describing, are the men whose condition was envied by a very eloquent but very eccentric philosopher of the last century; but I imagine a week's residence – even a night's lodging with the Fuegians would have brought Jean Jacques Rousseau to a saner conclusion. Meanwhile, I think I may safely congratulate you that you are not the red men of Terra [sic] del Fuego, but civilized white men and accomplished women, the humblest amongst you having the power of enjoying more of the comforts and pleasures, physical and intellectual, of life, than the proud lords of a horde of ten thousand barbarians.
>
> (Ellingson 2001: 294, citing Crawfurd 1859)

Ellingson summarizes the power of what he describes as a 'devastating weapon against any opposition to the racist agenda':

> The myth of the Noble Savage, if we examine it closely, is constructed so as to assert the existence of what it purports to critique, the existence of a belief in the absurd juxtaposition of the incompatible attributes of nobility and savagery. By projecting the absurdity of the construction itself onto a figure such as Rousseau, selected as the emblematic representation of more serious ideas (and their advocates) that are the real targets of the attack, the myth operates by oblique and obfuscatory symbolic manipulations to attain its intended purpose, the creation of a self-authenticating, and self-perpetuating rhetorical program for the promotion of racial superiority and dominance.
>
> (Ellingson 2001: 297)

Crawfurd used the five spin components listed above. First, the image is internally contradictory, hence memorable: nobility is juxtaposed with savage. It appears to praise those it describes, but it actually demotes them to the level of savage. Those who appear to praise indigenous people are accused of promoting them to the level of nobles – the upper classes in feudal Europe, when in fact they are lower than the lowest, namely, savages. Second, the idea is attributed to Rousseau. Third, the idea is shown to be false. Fourth, Crawfurd debunks Rousseau for even suggesting such an absurdity. His idea that practices representing individual autonomy, and the peoples who had such practices, should be emulated provided the germ of truth that makes the spin work and itself gets debunked. Fifth, he presented the idea to an audience of upper-class Englishmen who are benefiting from the expropriation of indigenous peoples, and hence ready to believe the argument.

Because his audience was people interested in anthropology, the claim also charges an early anthropologist with believing his objects of study have become noble. At the time of deployment, colonialism was in full movement, and the English and Americans developed racist beliefs about native peoples. The noble savage terminology provided a useful way to critique those native peoples and any anthropologist who seemed to look favorably upon them.

Ellingson argues that anthropology adopted the ritual of stating disagreement with Rousseau as a kind of systemic protection. Even Franz Boas, a great proponent of equal treatment of all societies, felt the need to state he was not agreeing with Rousseau [Boas 1989a [1889], 1989b [1904], cited by Ellingson: 299]. The real power of the anthropologists' society and times was the colonial governments that were displacing indigenous peoples from their lands. Anthropology needed to protect itself from that power; ritual citing of Rousseau's error provided that defense by assuring others that anthropology had not really changed sides (Ellingson 2001: 387).

Crawfurd was so successful in his formulation that the spin survived while credit for the idea was lost. Ellingson deserves great credit for realizing that finding the origin of the myth would be important. He and others who had searched in Rousseau's writing for a statement that indigenous peoples were noble had found no such statement; yet that assertion had become extremely prevalent in anthropology.

In the modern incarnation, the ecologically noble savage, both the environmental movement and indigenous people are the target of the rhetoric. Because the racist component, 'savage,' is not needed, authors such as Krech (1999: 17) drop it. Instead, he says 'Ecological Indian', with 'ecological' playing the role of 'noble.' (This rewording does not work in Canada, where 'Indian' has acquired connotations of 'savage.') With this step, Krech has added a sixth useful component to the spin. By denying a racist agenda, he can attack his own critics as racist. After noting that 'the harshest and most unforgiving critics happen also to be either environmentalists or American Indians,' he charges them with 'playing the race card' in order to have 'the fear of being branded racist' pre-empt further discussion (Krech 2007a: 5–6). Some of Krech's critics help him by explicitly calling him racist. He falsely claims he is being silenced by the charge. He positions himself as a defender of Indians, charging that users of the image of the Ecological Indian 'are ultimately dehumanizing,' because they deny the existence of variation (Krech 1999: 26).

The following quotations show that for Krech, the main target is not Indians. In his introduction, after reviewing many positive portrayals of Indians as examples of the ecologically noble Indian (whether they actually used the term or not), Krech points out that during 1963–73, the period of the birth of the environmental movement,

> New Ecological Indians exploded onto the scene. As critics linked many current global predicaments to industrial society, spoke openly of earlier less

complex times as being more environmentally friendly, and castigated Christianity for anthropocentrism, they marshaled Ecological Indians (as deployment of the Crying Indian makes clear) to the support of environmental and antitechnocratic causes. ... In their conscious antitechnocratic critique of Western society, Rousseau was reborn.

(ibid.: 20)

In his epilogue, he observes:

Those who despair at the pace and extent of the environmental change at the end of the millennium, are blind to the environmental impacts of pre-industrial societies, and adhere to the notion that native or indigenous people have always represented a kinder, gentler way of relating to the environment will no doubt be disturbed by this book's conclusions – despite the pains taken to acknowledge their ambiguities and limitations.

(ibid.: 227)

Claiming to acknowledge ambiguities might be added as a seventh part of the strategy; in spite of ambiguities, he maintains his main conclusion remains valid: indigenous peoples were not ecologists or conservationist.

Ellingson points out that the rhetorical virtues of the myth of the Noble Savage work also when deployed in ecological debate:

Ecological Noble Savage rhetoric ... tends to globalize and moralize [valid issues] into an indistinguishable blur, where the generic 'savage' can be interchangeably exemplified at one moment by the desert hunter and at the next by the rain forest agriculturalist, and the most isolated particular of environmental transgression by either becomes part of the global moralizing proof of the ignobility of all.

(Ellingson 2001: 357)

Ellingson's observation of the blurring effect of the rhetoric describes Krech's book. By using many particular environmental transgressions given with incomplete analysis of the ecosystems in question, Krech leaves the impression that North American aboriginal people *never* succeeded in caring for their environments, although what he actually says is that they didn't *always* do so. The individual examples are added together, and reviewers praised the resulting book for debunking an idea that is framed in the modern noble savage formulation as ecological Indian. Krech (2007a) conveniently provides citations. The publisher uses the formulation on the book jacket as a sales device.

Ellingson also points out that those who wrap their arguments in the rhetoric of confronting the image of the ecological Indian often formulate their hypotheses rather carelessly, and fail to connect the specific results to the general assertion. This also applies to Krech, whose examples draw mainly from cases of frontier contact (Hunn *et al.* 2003: S81). Krech does not consider the effects of the colonial contact situations on the responses of Indians; in particular, he does not consider the impact of the loss of control over the resources, and the need to compete in an open access environment. In those situations, the test for the Indians to be ecologically noble is that they discontinue harvest while others continue.

In the original noble savage image, Indians are savages, meaning either the lowest type of human or not human at all. For the ecological Indian image, the point is that Indians are people like everyone else, and hence cannot be looked to for further advice. This promotion might seem to be good. In examining the treatment of Native Americans by historians, Richard White (1998: 217–18) has characterized an older attitude as follows:

> Most American historians, like most modern Americans, are pious about Native American peoples, but they do not take Native Americans very seriously. ... In both popular culture and the academy, Native Americans are people who either have no significant history or exist outside history.

Popular understandings make Native Americans ahistorical by reflexively granting Native Americans a certain 'spiritual' or 'traditional' knowledge. This knowledge is timeless; it seemingly appeared whole at some point far in the past and now can only erode. It cannot be added to. In this formulation, Native Americans do not learn; they only forget and disappear.

> This inherited spiritual knowledge serves to make Native Americans nearly identical with nature itself. When Native Americans speak, nature speaks. So, in yet another version of the old western story of savagery – noble and ignoble – Native Americans merge with nature.

(Richard White 1998: 217–18)

As White recognizes, this view of Indians can be either complementary or damning: noble or ignoble. In both cases, it removes Indians from the category of 'human' by making them 'nearly identical with nature itself.' Unlike nature, however, Indians can speak. Thus Chief Seattle speaks, and advocates protection of nature. He has an authoritative voice. When Ted Perry writes a speech for him, Chief Seattle did not have the option of not obtaining credit. Sometimes other Indians like the credit, and like the role of speaking for nature. Furtwangler (1997) points out that the first transcription of Chief Seattle's speech was by a Seattle resident who was being displaced by further immigrants; he also found Seattle to be a useful authoritative voice.

Further evidence that being identified with nature has a great danger is illustrated by a view provided by political scientist John Dryzek. In his search for examples of people with rational ecological policies, he decides not to examine 'traditional societies such as preliterate anarchies.' Although he does not explicitly refer to North America, he describes their interaction with nature as follows:

> Often, people in such societies had to adjust their behavior to the natural forces – substantially outside of their control – to which they were subject. The

payment of respect to those forces (for example, by ascribing 'spirit' to animals, plants, or environments) is an understandable extension of this situation. While behavioral change in response to feedback signals could and did occur in such societies, there was no necessary period of extensive thought between failure and correction. ... Moreover, unnecessary (and potentially destabilizing) behavioral changes were ruled out by myth, superstition, tradition, or taboo (though within certain bounds experimental adaptation to the environment could take place ...). Therefore ecologically sound behavior could be the indirect result of actions with very different conscious motivation.

(Dryzek 1987: 220, citations omitted)

Thus his complaint here is a lack of self-consciousness, as well as an inability to adjust behavior when good reasons present themselves. Survival, as ecologically sound behavior, was an epiphenomenon: an accident that occurred for reasons not based on a desire to survive. The epiphenomenon explanation occurs widely (as summarized and debated by Hunn *et al.* 2003).

Such lack of self-consciousness is just the first problem. Dryzek continues,

If a locally self-sufficient form of social choice – indeed, any form of social choice – is to be resilient, then it must be governed by reason (either instrumental or practical) rather than tradition or myth. Preliterate anarchies (or for that matter, Rousseau's ideal rustic republic) could do without reason, but we cannot.

(Dryzek 1987: 220)

Thus the condition of such societies must have resulted from an evolutionary path, as in nature, rather than from a historical path, as in human societies. For without reason, how could the leaders of these preliterate societies do otherwise? As White has warned, this bias leads directly to the denial of humanity. Dryzek provides a signpost of his thinking by referring to Rousseau, a muted invocation of the noble savage. Rousseau, however, thought that humans in North America had moved beyond being identical with nature, and had developed societies (Ellingson 2001: 84).

Dryzek, unfortunately, thus exhibits a narrow, even stereotypical view of 'traditional' cultures. He is operating in a framework in which one cannot ask a member of such a society why he acts in a way that preserves his ecosystem because, lacking reason, the informant would be unable to provide an answer. In light of this attitude, one would be very surprised to find that Dryzek had read any secondary literature on the details of aboriginal political systems in North America, or the ways in which those systems adapted to change through the conscious decisions of leaders of those societies. I find this unfortunate, because Dryzek is one of a group of political scientists who are dealing seriously with the political side of the ecological crisis.

Another aspect of identification of Indians with nature is an implicit identification of North America prior to contact with the Bible's Garden of Eden. The Garden of Eden was a wonderful place to live, with abundant food. Since man was thrown out of Eden because of acquiring knowledge, it makes sense to identify traditional cultures with the pre-original sin category, and hence as peoples without reason.

Rousseau did not assume, as do the historians cited by White, or imply, as does Dryzek, that peoples of the new world were not human. This position generated the ire of racists such as Crawfurd. While he never used the term noble savage, he did present a concept of savage, and he did examine peoples of the New World.

His concept of 'savage' was a speculative model about what humans were like before they created societies. In that condition, they were 'wild,' not noble. In the state of nature, Rousseau located savage man between animals and humans with society (Ellingson 2001: 82). The wild or natural man did not have ideas or songs; he was mute. Neither was such a man capable of cruelty. Rousseau argues that the development of society coincides with the development of cruelty:

> Thus, revenge became terrible, and men grew bloodthirsty and cruel. This is precisely the stage reached by most of the savage peoples known to us; and it is for lack of having sufficiently distinguished between different ideas and seen how far these peoples already are from the first state of nature that so many authors have hastened to conclude that man is naturally cruel.
>
> (Rousseau 1984 [1755]: 114–15, cited by Ellingson 2001: 84)

Clearly, these 'savage peoples' weren't noble, they were cruel because they already had departed from the original state of nature. Rousseau's target was the notion from Hobbes that in the state of nature life was brutish and short, and man was evil, thus necessitating that men be governed, by a king or other state entity. Rousseau locates the source of difficulty in his contemporary society, not in man in a state of nature.

For Rousseau, man as savage was not corrupted by society. He was not cruel, but neither was he noble, since he was mute and could not sing. There is a germ of the idea later transformed into noble, in that Rousseau's savage was not evil; rather he was an empty slate.

Although Rousseau was not praising these other societies – he saw them as cruel – he also treated them as other humans. Ellingson attributes to Rousseau the presentations of ideas that would lead to open-minded anthropology, which later was just what Crawfurd and his associates sought to discredit with use of the noble savage spin. After listing the names of some great thinkers, he asked what would happen if they traveled the world and looked upon what they saw without bias:

> Suppose that these new Hercules, on their return from these memorable journeys, then wrote at leisure the natural, moral and political history of what they had seen, we ourselves would see a new world spring from under their pens, and we should learn thereby to know our own world.
>
> (Rousseau 1984 [1755]: 161; Ellingson 2001: 90)

This statement occurs in the midst of complaints about travelers reporting characteristics of their own culture on their travels, of failing to see clearly without biases resulting from their own characteristics. Rousseau imagined learning about 'a new world.' What did he mean by the word 'world'?

Rousseau's complaint that reading the reports of travelers did little more than tell him about European society can be applied to the use of the ecological Indian by both its proponents and its opponents. The image projected onto indigenous peoples reveals the thinking of those who use it. The debate over Indians is really a debate about Euro-American images of nature and man's correct relationship to nature. These debates begin with a concept, 'nature,' which has its own baggage.

This book began by presenting evidence that the original peoples of the Northwest Coast of North America had a high living standard and had kept their wealthy system going for more than 2000 years. In order to understand how they accomplished this, one naturally examines their institutions and tries to explain them. In doing so, one has to utilize concepts and theories that are readily available to the English reader. But great care has to be taken in describing the processes because of the danger that the concepts as generally used do not apply cross-culturally.

A number of words are particularly dangerous: sacred, respect, reverence, and nature are among the most troublesome. Also difficult are the ideas associated with property, reciprocity, and governance.

For instance, what is a gift (Mauss 1967)? The word normally means something that is freely given to another person. It does not have a connotation or denotation that such gifts require something in return. If something was required in return, then the gift would not be a gift. Most children in North America treat the requirement that something be returned as 'Indian giving.' If a child gives something to another child, and then asks for it back, he or she has committed 'Indian giving,' and will be teased for doing so. The definition of Indian giving catches the idea, common in North America, that a relationship between individuals or groups of individuals can be understood as a balanced or unbalanced exchange of goods and other things. When a chief on the Northwest Coast hosted a feast and its associated give-away, or potlatch, those who attended the feast and received the gifts also received obligations for later exchanges, or provided the chief with status and recognition of his position. Chapters 4–6 explain these complications in more detail.

Because of difficulties with the word 'sacred,' Keith Basso (1996) refuses to use it as he describes the importance of land to Apaches in *Wisdom Sits in Places*. One reason land is important for the Apaches of the White River is that stories containing important moral lessons occurred in specific places. A reference to the place provides a reference to the ethical or moral rules embodied in a story. The rule, in turn, applies to human behavior. When Fikret Berkes (1999) entitled his book *Sacred Ecology*, he was making a point about the importance of ecosystems to indigenous people. But sometimes indigenous people kill animals that they have designated as 'sacred.' An Athapaskan explained to Paul Nadasdy that shooting a wolf is 'not the same as shooting Saint Peter.' Nadasdy goes on to explain:

> Shooting a wolf is not blasphemy or sin. On the contrary, First Nations people's concept of respect is based on the need to kill animals. As long as hunters behave properly toward wolves and their remains, killing them can be a perfectly sensible and respectful act.

> (Nadasdy 2005: 320)

Nadasdy's comment also deals with difficulties in the meaning of 'respect.' To respect a wolf means to fear its power as well as to appreciate its existence.

Salmon are treated as sacred by the First Salmon Ceremony held by many Northwest Coast Tribes. One point of the ceremony is to show respect to, and to thank, salmon. This occurs before massive harvest. Anthropologist Stephen Langdon (2007), searching for a word to describe the relationship between Tlingit people and salmon, uses 'engagement.' The Tlingit engage salmon in a complicated way, and to use other terms, such as 'management,' is to distort the relationship. In fact, if asked 'Do you manage salmon,' many would say 'no.' They would say that because to manage salmon means to deal with salmon as the Department of Fisheries and Oceans does. Since that form of management is disliked, a chief might say, 'we did not manage salmon.' But if asked, did he take care of salmon spawning streams, the chief might well answer 'of course.' The Nisga'a have a story to explain the recent eruption of a volcano on their lands. The volcano erupted because young children, failing to listen to their elders, played with spawning salmon in a stream. Such behavior is extremely disrespectful. It disturbs salmon in their homes, doing important things to perpetuate their families. Other First Nations peoples disapprove of catch-and-release fishing, saying that it is disrespectful to play with one's food. Catch-and-release fishing is regarded as an excellent conservation policy for fish, yet it also is strongly disapproved of by indigenous people. Are they not conservationists because they oppose such fishing?

In his frustration with the difficulties of language (whether English or French), sociologist Bruno Latour baldly claims that indigenous people never lived in harmony with nature. In saying this, he is not agreeing with Shepard Krech that the concept of the ecological Indian is a myth. Rather, he is objecting to the meaning of 'nature.' He says, 'Non-Western cultures *have never been interested* in nature; they have never adopted it as a category; they have never found a use for it' (Latour 2004: 43). He means by this that the very idea of nature as separate from society is a Western concept. To understand how key the idea of nature is, try to think of a way to describe the world without using the word 'nature.' If one has no nature, and therefore no harmony with nature, then what does one have instead? And if non-Western people have not used the idea of nature, then how are those peoples to explain themselves to Westerners?

In his frustration with words such as nature, Bruno Latour has proposed new words and strange uses for old words. In place of the words nature and society, he proposes to use the 'common world.' He then recognizes the possibility of different common worlds, and proposes to label that phenomenon 'multinaturalism,' meaning that the planet is made up of not one nature and many cultures, but many worlds, each distinguished from others to create multinaturalism. If one is determined to hold on to the idea of nature, then Latour would insist that it be a plural word, the existence of 'natures' (Latour 2004: 29). But contemplating the idea of natures, one asks how can that be? Isn't 'mother nature' one thing, who should not be displeased? If nature does not exist, then the question is not well posed.

If one continues to use the idea of nature, then another difficult word is 'harmony.' How can one tell if a group of persons is in a relationship of harmony? The usual answer seems to be that a person in harmony with nature has not changed nature's characteristics very much. One has a 'light touch.' Implicit in this idea is that nature's natural condition is the standard to determine what is 'best.' This idea creates a major problem, however, since humans have been active on Earth for so many millennia that observations of what occurred before humans were present is difficult. Those who mistakenly thought the Americas prior to European settlement provided an example of pure nature have been very disappointed to learn that the indigenous peoples of the Americas had engaged with their environment to such a degree that conditions at contact can't be used to judge what would occur in the absence of humans.

The image of the ecological Indian utilizes the idea that there exists a separate entity, nature, and that science has a privileged relationship to nature. With their objectivity, scientists are able to describe and explain nature to every one else. Even the philosopher of environmental ethics, J. Baird Callicott (1994), who is very appreciative of indigenous thought, places science in the highest position. He assumes only science is 'self-consciously self-critical' (Callicott 1994: 191).

The ecological Indian becomes an oxymoron because ecology, a science, understands nature better than any other system of knowledge. By stepping away from the ecological Indian rhetoric, one drops the assumption of a separate nature, and the assumption of different types of humans or human cultures that are ranked in their ability to understand or care for nature.

But what ideas can replace nature? Bruno Latour has devoted much effort to this question, and has proposed an alternative I find both appealing and useful to describe how many of the societies of the Northwest Coast distinguished themselves from others. Latour suggests that combinations of humans and non-humans create one or more 'collectives.' Each collective consists of all the entities that are part of the common world the collective has created. The common world has an interior and an exterior, defined by decisions made within the collective regarding what to include and what to exclude. Latour gives careful and detailed consideration to how decisions should be made about what to include and exclude from the common world. His agenda is to democratize the decision-making process. He is particularly concerned that scientists have obtained unfair advantage in discussions about new entities, because they have successfully positioned themselves as speaking for nature through their ability to determine what are the 'facts.' This, combined with the unfettered ability of firms to introduce new products, creates a process by which new alliances of humans and non-humans are admitted to the common world without 'due process.' Similarly, alliances of humans and non-humans are dismissed from the common world without due process. This occurs especially when new alliances conflict directly with old alliances. Examples relevant to this book are the conflicts between dams or forest harvesting and salmon.

This target of Latour, the democratization of consideration of entities, would seem very well adapted to application to processes of environmental assessment. My interest is different, in ways to think about humans and nature without assuming that nature is separate from humans. The Northwest Coast then becomes a 'world' made by alliances of humans and non-humans. The engagement with salmon is a major part of the making of the Northwest Coast. This idea of 'world' is close to the idea of 'social–ecological system' used by those interested in the study of resilience. But the terminology 'social–ecological' continues to embody the society/nature dichotomy, which distorts efforts to understand indigenous systems.

The main idea is that humans, when they live in one place for a long time, learn how that place works and may increase its productivity or usefulness for humans. In the pre-industrial ages, use of energy such as coal, oil, or nuclear power was not available. Therefore humans had to be inventive and insightful in order to make their world more productive.

M. Kat Anderson (2006) argues that the peoples of California increased the productivity of their land through many practices which increased biodiversity as well as increase the harvestable surplus. Her analysis is supplemented by evidence from other sources that human intervention in ecosystems encouraged mid-successional species, keeping many ecosystems from proceeding to the last stages of succession. See Delcourt and Delcourt (2004) for this as a general pattern in the East, complementing Anderson's assertions for California. Similarly, peoples of the Northwest Coast encouraged other entities with whom they liked to cooperate.

Within the collective, one can make many distinctions. One can regard the collective as made up of both material and non-material entities. Umeek (2004) uses this distinction to explain ideas of causality within the Nuu-chah-nulth world. For Umeek, ultimate causality originates in the non-material world. He does not divide the material world into society and nature. The Kwakwaka'wakw believed the world to be made up of beings who ate each other; it was constituted by the flow of material things through a succession of beings. Every person and animal had a soul, and the collective was composed of a fixed number of souls, which circulated through bodies and kept the whole system going. They, too, regarded humans and animals as similar beings, creating no distinction between society and nature (Walens 1981).

Once the idea of nature is dropped, then so also must be the assumption that the best condition for nature is one that occurs without human intervention. If nature does best by itself, then the metric for measuring quality is the amount of influence by humans. The 'pristine' ecosystem becomes the best ecosystem, least modified by humans, and the metropolis is the most modified ecosystem, the one with the least nature and the most society. This continuum needs to be replaced by a consideration of different worlds or 'systems.'

A collection of different systems suggests the need for a different metric for comparing them. If one removes the metric 'amount of influence of humans' from the judgement, what can replace it? Several measures come to mind: total productivity of the system in a biological sense; total productivity of material for humans to utilize; amount of biodiversity measured by numbers and variations of species; total annual net product measured by a system of accounts, such as some of the green accounting systems that have been developed. This work assumes the metric for judging success is resilience and survival for a long period. It may be that such resilience rests upon the other measures, such as preserving biodiversity and enhancing the total biological productivity of the system.

To summarize, my response to the rhetoric of the 'ecologically noble Indian' is as follows. First, my metric for study of the social–ecological system containing the peoples of the Northwest Coast is resilience and sustainability. While many other systems did not persist for more than 2000 years, that of the peoples of the Northwest Coast did. Further, the collapse of their system occurred because of intervention from outside, not because of internal difficulties. Such persistence is a noteworthy characteristic with potential relevance to present-day problems, especially because the primary sources of livelihood on the Northwest Coast were fisheries, a common pool resource.

Second, in investigating the Northwest Coast, great care must be taken to avoid imposing assumptions or definitions taken from non-indigenous knowledge systems. This requirement for care affects all the chapters that explain the key institutions of the Northwest Coast. Chapter 3 examines the ethical systems of the Northwest Coast, with particular attention to the idea of reincarnation as used by them. That they believed in reincarnation of salmon is used by Krech to debunk the idea that the belief systems supported something like conservation. The chapter explains why a different interpretation supports the persistence of the systems for so many millennia.

Chapter 4 deals with another slippery concept, giveaways called the potlatch. The chapter emphasizes the usefulness of the potlatch system for people dependent upon a common pool resource, the salmon fishery. This chapter opens by explaining the difficulties Nisg̲a'a leadership created by using the word 'common' in describing their view of the resources of their river valley.

Chapter 5 deals with they system of territoriality used on the Northwest Coast, and points out ways in which the terminology and ideas associated with the concept of 'property' can mislead in understanding how the Northwest Coast system worked.

Chapter 6 deals with ideas of leadership and the conduct of political processes on the Northwest Coast. This chapter deals with difficult terms such as 'consensus' in decision-making. It addresses issues of power and limitations on power in a political system that, on the surface, appears quite undemocratic.

3 Northwest Coast world views

A book that originated in a conference about *The Ecological Indian* provides many chapters addressing the controversy. In one of them, anthropologist Stephen Langdon (2007) documents that the Tlingit living on the west coast of Prince of Wales Island had developed a long-standing relationship with the salmon that returned to their rivers every year. Langdon and the Tlingit people he consulted explain the relationship by telling the story of Salmon Boy, a mythic charter that prescribed proper behavior toward salmon.

> A young boy is hungry and asks his mother for some food. She directs him to the remaining small amount of dried fish. The piece he selects has mold on it, and he throws it down in disgust. His mother reprimands him for his behavior. He leaves the house, wearing a copper necklace, and goes down to the beach to check his bird snare. He slips and falls into the water but is saved from drowning by the salmon people, who take him to live with them in their village at the bottom of the ocean. There the boy sees that salmon are people, and the salmon chief teaches him many things about how to treat salmon. Finally, the salmon chief tells the salmon people to get in their canoes, as it is time to return to their streams. As they approach the stream, the chief tells Salmon Boy to stand up in the canoe to see where they are. He stands up, but in actuality, because he is a salmon, he jumps out of the water. He notices his parents on the bank at their fish camp. Salmon Boy proceeds up the estuary to where his mother is processing other salmon. She notices the beautiful fish presenting itself to her and tells her husband to come and catch it. So he spears Salmon Boy and hands him to his wife. She begins to cut the head off at the gills but then notices the copper necklace. In amazement, she recalls that this was what her son was wearing when he disappeared, and calls her husband. Then they ask a shaman what they should do. He tells them to lay the salmon on a plank and place it high up in the house overnight. They do this, and the next morning Salmon Boy comes down and greets his parents, who are astonished and overjoyed to see him. They ask what happened to him, and he tells them of his experiences and what he has been taught. He then teaches the other humans how to respect salmon and how to place all the bones in the fire so the salmon can be regenerated. In some versions the

salmon bones are to be returned to the water. Salmon Boy goes on to become a powerful shaman.

(Langdon 2007: 236–37)

Langdon argues that the story provides reasons for a large number of behaviors by Tlingit in regard to salmon. They are instructed how to kill salmon, with a blow to the head. They are told not to waste salmon, and how to dispose of remains. Most of all, they learn that salmon are like people. A Tlingit elder summarizes the lessons as follows: 'In order to understand how we treat salmon, you have to realize that we treat them like we would like to be treated' (Langdon 2007: 238).

Most of Langdon's article reports on his archeological explorations of a location called the Little Salt Lake on the west coast of Prince of Wales Island. This location is a tidal zone fed by two small rivers. Remains of tens of thousands of wooden stakes reveal patterns of fish traps from 2280 to 310 BCE (before the common era, i.e. before 1 AD). (To convert this to years BP, add 2008.) Langdon determines that from approximately 1100 BCE (approximately 3100 before now), a change occurred in the capture strategy in the traps. In the prior period, salmon were captured as they swam in with the incoming tide; in these traps, no salmon could escape. After 1100 BCE, the trap design changes to capture salmon only on the ebb tide. During high tide, some salmon could pass over the traps and into the rivers. Langdon attributes the design of tidal zone traps to allowing salmon to appear to decide whether or not to swim up the stream or be caught by the trap in the tide as it ebbs. The traps were designed to allow escape of some of the salmon. He argues that this design is consistent with a logic of engagement as told by the Salmon Boy story.

He closes his paper by suggesting that the engagement of people and salmon led to actions that increased the number of salmon. His data show an increase in the population of people and in the harvest of salmon at about the same time that the trap designs were changed. Not only did the method of trapping allow significant numbers of salmon to proceed to the streams, the Tlingit also protected the spawning areas of salmon, which meant harvesting ducks and Dolly Varden trout in order to protect the eggs and fry (Langdon, 2007: 264). The Tlingit saw salmon building houses in the streams as they fertilized eggs. His very rich paper is full of details, and he connects the timing of structure construction at the Little Salt Lake to other developments up and down the coast. In particular, the period around 3150 years ago was a time of climatic variability or social unrest. Something may have triggered the shift to tidal pulse fishing, which lasted until contact with Old World explorers and colonists.

In spite of all the evidence that Tlingit actions and beliefs were consistent with one another, and that salmon numbers had increased rather than declined when the current Northwest Coast system had come into existence among the Tlingit, Krech remains unconvinced, because he can point to the belief in reincarnation as a concept that would justify profligate harvest. Commenting on Langdon's chapter in a concluding afterword, Krech argues as follows:

Largely elided are the *implications* for conservation of the idea, widespread among Northwest Coast people, that to guarantee the annual recurrence – the reincarnation – of salmon all one need do is burn their bones or return their carcasses to the water (Gottesfeld 1994). As Michael Alvard suggests, a similar methodological problem plagues the equation of contemporary Huna Tlingit seagull egg procurement behavior to a conscious conservation strategy or its projection to the past (Hunn *et al.* 2003).

(Krech 2007b, 345) [emphasis added]

The above quote is from Krech's concluding chapter to the collection of articles. In the introduction, written for the conference that led to the book, Krech makes the same point slightly differently:

For example, the Northwest coast Gitksans ritually treat each year's first salmon ... with great care. They construct an elaborate cultural context for salmon modeled on human sentience and human social life. Yet all that is required to renew salmon, they say, is to return their bones to the water.

(Krech 2007a: 12, citing Gottesfeld 1994)

Langdon reports that both returning bones to the water and burning them are practices among the Tlingit as well; the Salmon Boy story requires such behavior. Note that Krech refers to an elder of the Gitksan for the assertion is that 'all one need do is burn their bones.' Langdon clearly gives evidence that taking care of the spawning beds is part of the strategy followed by the Klawock and Hinyaa Tlingits; for them, burning bones or returning them to the water was just one of the activities.

Krech is arguing that a belief in reincarnation is not consistent with conservation: treat the remains properly, and the fish will return; nothing else is required. Krech's interpretation of belief in reincarnation is his last line of defense against the evidence provided by Langdon (2007) and Hunn *et al.* (2003) for the Tlingit behavior that conserves salmon in one case and gulls in another. In his book and in his subsequent comments on the book, Krech repeatedly uses beliefs in reincarnation in order to distinguish Indian ideas from the ideas of 'today's conservation biology.' After referring to a number of different examples of belief in reincarnation, he summarizes: 'For all, the indigenous idea of reincarnation is antithetical to Western conservation' (Krech 2007b: 347). In referring to Cree management of beaver: 'senior hunters have gained a detailed and sophisticated understanding (although cultural) of their surroundings and the animals they have pursued during their lives' (Krech 1999: 209). The parenthetical 'although cultural' refers to beliefs such as reincarnation. He argues that rules such as hanging bones in trees or burning remains are rules 'that Western ecologists would argue are unrelated to breeding success and conservation' (Krech 1999: 207). He does not say that conservation biology is limited by any cultural bias; scientific definitions of conservation are his basis for judgement.

If proper treatment of remains is all that is needed for the return of animals, then limitations on harvest are not logically required. Not only is reincarnation not scientifically plausible, it encourages profligate harvest (Krech 1999: 149). While this is a logical conclusion, it is contradicted by other beliefs in Northwest Coast societies which emphasized avoiding waste.

But even in regard to reincarnation itself, Krech's analysis is wrong. He focuses upon the reincarnation of salmon, beaver, and buffalo. He ignores the beliefs that humans also rely on having their remains burned in order to assure reincarnation. Among the Tlingit, such reincarnation occurs in the matrilineally defined clan, usually among the grandchildren of a person who dies. Contrary to Krech's analysis, reincarnation beliefs, when applied to humans, provide an excellent reason to use resources sustainably. If a person will exist in the future, he or she has an excellent, personal reason to conserve. Both the chiefs of the salmon people and the chiefs of the human people want to continue the cycle of life and death followed by life that is embodied in the reincarnation belief.

Krech cites Gottesfeld (1994) as the source of the idea that only returning the bones to the stream is what is required. Gottesfeld does quote an elder on that point (*ibid*.: 453), and summarizes her analysis of Gitskan and Wet'suwet'en cosmology as follows:

> The cosmology of both the Gitksan and Wet'suwet'en contains a strong theme of reincarnation, and respect for the dead. Proper treatment of the remains of animals and people allows or facilitates reincarnation.
>
> (*ibid*.: 447)

Although the elder said that placing the remains in the water was all that was required, Gottesfield also reports 'People also believe that the young fish fry upon emergence obtain their food from the rotted carcasses of their parents in a sort of analogy to human parents feeding their children' (*ibid*.: 453).

Gottesfield says that proper treatment of remains applies to people as well as to mammals and fish. That people are included in the cycles of reincarnation is absolutely crucial to understanding its contribution to sustainability and to conservation as understood by Krech. Krech, and conservation biologists such as Michael Alvard, impose a tight requirement: not only must people behave in ways that conserve, they must do so intentionally. He says:

> Motivation and performance are central to conservation: the conservationist intends to and does prevent waste, depletion, environmental destruction, and extinction.
>
> (Krech 2007a: 13)

Krech and Alvard do not accept that actions can be conservation if the people doing the actions aren't acting so as to conserve. But belief in reincarnation provides motivation to prevent waste and depletion of the world in which one lives. If people believe that they continually exist in their world, even after death, then of course they would act to preserve it.

Krech is quite correct to emphasize the strong belief in reincarnation present on the Northwest Coast. Antonia Mills (1994b) and Ian Stephenson (1994) have found many cases in which both the Gitksan and Tlingit name the specific person who has been reincarnated by young babies. Antonia Mills gives three examples of birthmarks on babies' ears leading people to conclude that they were the rein-carnation of specific people who had pierced ears when they were alive. In the process of documenting the cases, she found that many relatives of the people she was investigating were also believed to be specific reincarnations of dead relatives (Mills 1994b: 234). Mills provides pictures of the congenital birthmarks on ears which lead the Gitksan to conclude that specific reincarnations have taken place. Here is how Antonia Mills summarizes the experience of the family of one of her cases, who she gives the pseudonym 'Eddie':

> Eddie is alone in his matrilineal house in having congenitally pierced-ear marks, but certainly not alone in being considered a case of reincarnation. His elder sister and younger brother are also said to be particular people reborn, as are all of the children of one of his mother's sisters. Indeed this aunt quipped, 'I wonder what is the matter with me, that they don't know who I am.' Note that she said, 'Who I am,' not 'Who I was.'
>
> (*ibid.*: 234)

Mills points out that in using the present tense, the aunt implicitly revealed her view of continuity with herself. 'Who I am' is an individual who existed in the past, and who will exist in the future.

Such reincarnation beliefs are a fundamental part of the cosmology that supports conservation and sustainable use of the world. First, belief in the reincarnation of a person to his or her own clan provides a good reason for an individual not to discount the future and to worry about the condition of the land that belongs to the clan. Put another way, it gives a good reason to value future consumption nearly equal to present-day consumption. Such beliefs remove one of the main obstacles to conservation support in today's world, high rates of discounting the value of the future. Second, placing the unconsumed remains of food back into the system is consistent with the need to recycle nutrients. Bones, in particular, contain minerals that are necessary for animals to grow, and that may be a limiting factor in an eco-system. While the people may not have understood nutrient cycling at the chemical level, the principle that the components of beings cycled certainly is consistent with ecological thinking. Introductory ecology books all emphasize mineral cycles.

To an economist, such widespread belief in reincarnation provides evidence that the decision-makers of the society probably placed great weight on the condition of the land they managed. They believed they would personally be reincarnated within the lineage that used the land. If they preserved the land's productivity, they would directly benefit themselves. Stated in terms of economics, the people would have 'low rates of time preference' or a 'small discount rate.' A low rate of time preference or a low discount rate means that a person does not give extra weight to today's consumption compared with tomorrow's, or that in the far future. People with high discount rates 'discount' the value of future consumption considerably.

Graciela Chichilnisky, in an article that provides a mathematical formulation of 'sustainable preferences' or 'intertemporally equitable preferences', summarizes the problem of discounting as follows:

A well-known problem is that standard cost–benefit analysis discounts the future. It is therefore biased against policies designed to provide benefits in the very long run. A sharp example is the evaluation of projects for the safe disposal of waste from a nuclear power plant. Another is polices designed for the prevention of global warming. The benefits of both may be at least fifty to a hundred years into the future. The costs, however, are here today.

(Chichilnisky 1997: 468)

Chichilnisky goes on to formulate a mathematical criterion for evaluation of projects that can provide equal weight for the present and for the far future.

The properties of Chichilnisky's criterion are relevant here, because the idea of an infinite process of reincarnation of individuals on the land on which they live would seem to be a belief system consistent with it. Of course the Gitksan, Tlingit, and other peoples of the Northwest Coast weren't accustomed to thinking about the future in the way economists do, or in the way that Chichilnisky does; she uses calculus to describe her criterion and to prove that it provides neither 'dictatorship of the present' nor 'dictatorship of the future.' It seems to me that people who believe in reincarnation, however, would find her criterion something that would express their views of the future quite well.

Her criterion is the weighted average of two components. The first component is a standard present net value formula, with the interest rate used allowed to take any reasonable form. The second component is the upper limit of sustainable utility, which can be interpreted as the most valuable combination of average consumption and average stock of resources that is possible.

One might argue that the Northwest Coast belief in reincarnation might support a criterion consisting only of the upper limit of sustainable levels of consumption and the stock of resources, that is, dictatorship of the future. If this were the case, then reincarnation beliefs would be an even stronger support for sustainable decisions than a weighted average of near-term utility and long-run utility. Without more specific information on how Northwest Coast peoples interpret the meaning of reincarnation, it is difficult to determine which alternative would be preferred. One can say that the use of only a net present value formula, which is 'dictatorship of the present,' would not be acceptable, because it gives no weight to generations far in the future. Eddie's aunt would be concerned about this.

Not only does Chichilnisky introduce her intertemporal function, she also uses a utility function that values both consumption of the stock of a renewable natural resource and the stock itself. This part of her formulation is consistent with the Northwest Coast ideas that salmon and other non-humans are similar to humans in having societies and in deserving to have a place in the world. It is also consistent with the idea that humans and salmon are made up of the same substance. To value humans is to value salmon, and vice versa. So the stock of salmon would be valued directly.

Based on this reasoning, I would say that a belief in reincarnation is one way for a group of people to see the world in a way that encourages them make decisions that promote sustainability. They believe that decisions made which impact on the future will in fact impact on themselves. They feel a continuity with the past as well as the future.

A second way in which returning salmon waste to streams or to the ocean can contribute to sustainability is through support for nutrient cycling. That such behavior would be responsible for bringing salmon back in great numbers seems absurd to Krech. Gottesfield, in reporting the beliefs for the Gitksan, however, notes that the cycling of nutrients might be a consequence. But Gottesfeld discounts nutrient cycling as quantitatively significant. For salmon spawning grounds, the nutrients left by the dying parents would be much more important. The injunction to deposit waste in the stream would in fact send many of the nutrients into the ocean, where, again, the quantitative importance might not be great.

In what sense might the disposal of fish remains into the rivers, and eventually the ocean, contribute to bringing salmon back? Since salmon are a top predator in oceans, the issue of nutrient cycling deserves some attention. A portion of the waste sent to the ocean, upon decomposing, would serve as food for small plants and animals, which would be eaten by larger ones, which eventually would lead to their being eaten near the top of the food chain by salmon. (The top of the food chain is whales, which eat salmon, as do humans.) As a metaphor for respect for nutrient cycling, the rule that the waste be sent to the ocean makes sense. Such nutrients would be available (after processing through the food chain) to feed salmon as they grow. But the nutrients would not contribute to the birth of the salmon, which occurs on the spawning grounds. If nutrients are not available in the ocean, however, the salmon would not return in sufficient numbers and sizes to feed humans.

While the recycling of nutrients in the ocean may be at such a large scale that returned salmon remains may not be important, the situation on land is more plausible. The Gitksan and the Wet'suwet'en both believed that the remains of terrestrial animals killed for food had to be burned. Alternatively, bones were to be left hanging in trees (Gottesfeld 1994: 457). Certainly, the burning of the remains would assure that nutrients were recycled quickly.

Another issue is the problem of maintaining balance among the populations that eat each other. The Kwakiutl believed that the system had a fixed number of souls and living positions for those souls to occupy. If the number of humans was fixed, then this would provide a reason to keep population growth in check. When Eurocanadians encountered them, the Kwakiutl were dealing with population loss due to disease. Their problem was underpopulation, not overpopulation. Hence no-one observed or talked about matters that would have related to the control of human numbers.

The idea of a fixed number of positions in the world provides a way for long-run average consumption to hold constant without increasing humanity's demands upon the system. It is also an idea of a steady state. Such ideas would support considerations of sustainability.

I emphasized in Chapter 2 that peoples of the Northwest Coast did not have a concept of 'nature' in which the world is made of two systems: human society and nature. Instead, humans are part of the system, as expressed by the Kwakiutl in the idea that all beings both consume and are consumed, both eat and are eaten.

Many people have explained the ways in which the world view of Northwest Coast peoples contained ideas that would encourage sustainable use of the land and the resources from the land. In his book emphasizing the importance of emotional and religious support for conservation, E. N. Anderson (1994, 1996) elaborates the many ways in which the religious beliefs of the Northwest Coast peoples supported careful use of the land and bounty that was available. The Nisga'a have spelled out their beliefs in textbooks for schools. Dr Richard Atleo, Chief Umeek (2004) of the Nuu-chah-nulth, has written a book, *Tsawalk*. The title means 'all is one.' Enthobotanist Nancy Turner (2005) titled her book *The Earth's Blanket*, using a metaphor taken from the Nlaka'pmx. The 'Earth's blanket' is the covering of plants growing on its surface. Irving Goldman (1975) and Stanley Walens (1981) have each used the enormous collection of Kwakiutl texts created by George Hunt and Franz Boas to examine Kwakiutl religious thought in great depth. Similar works exist for the Tsimshian, Tlingit, Gitksan, and Wet'suwet'en.

All these works emphasize that the peoples of the Northwest Coast, in addition to believing in the reincarnation of themselves and other beings, recognized that they existed in a cycle of life. The Kwakiutl were clear that every being both ate, and was subject to being eaten. Irving Goldman entitled his study *The Mouth of Heaven* to emphasize this emphasis on eating. The sky is the mouth of heaven, and it eats the Sun; but having been eaten, the Sun is disgorged and returns to life. In the famous hamatsa winter dance, the central character has an insatiable appetite, which has to be brought under control. He is a cannibal, eating people and salmon. Upon completion of the dance, the cannibal's appetite has been brought under control as is necessary. No one component of the cycle of eating and disgorging can be allowed to dominate. The serpent *sisiutl* is magical and dangerous because it has only mouths; without an anus, what it eats cannot be disgorged to feed others. Goldman summarizes the imagery as follows:

> In Kwatiutl thought, the sky itself appears as the great mouth of heaven that swallows the sun. At eclipse it asked to disgorge its mouthful with cries of Vomit! Vomit! The imagery of devouring as a phase of cycle that is always dual is most intimately connected with the inevitable observation that one form of life devours other forms of life, but life is always restored. In scientific thought the life cycle is formulated as multiphasic and complex. In Kwakiutl religious thought, the cycle is compressed to absolute fundamentals. The imagery is at once concrete, vividly affective, and in its compression generalized and abstract enough to stand for a cosmic principle. But the principle that devourer is life-giver introduces its own complexity, thus avoiding a simplified and unreal equation of devouring being offset by sexual reproduction. The ideas of interchange, of circulation, of transformation into diverse forms as well as into opposites, imply a general concept of ecological balances, which includes sexual reproduction.
>
> (Goldman 1975: 201–2)

Scholars interpreting the Kwakiutl texts differ in their emphasis on different parts of the religious philosophy; this chapter cannot provide a survey of the interpretations, and probably Kwakwak'wakw scholars will, in their turn, offer other interpretations. The details are not as important as the general message, which is that humans are part of the cycle of life, with special responsibilities and powers.

The relationship of many of these ideas to behavior that preserves the capacity of the land to produce for humans is clear. That people should use what they harvest, and not waste it, clearly supports limiting the impact of humans on their land. That children should not play with salmon in the rivers shows the desire to protect spawning grounds; the consequence of violating the rule could be a volcanic eruption. That goats may send a landslide that buries an entire village if the goats are disrespected is another powerful story.

In spite of all that supports conservation and sensible use of the land, some authors such as Krech have focused attention on apparently nonsensical aspects of the belief systems. Krech, in particular, emphasizes that reincarnation beliefs seem to encourage profligate use of resources if those resources can be recovered simply by disposing of the remains in a respectful manner. In this chapter, I have explained how reincarnation is a belief that supports conservation and decision-making that favors long-term preservation of resources. Chiefs who believe they are people who have lived before on their land are grateful that the land is productive, and also likely to care for the land's productivity because they will benefit themselves. Other people in the system would agree with the chiefs' decisions because they, too, subscribe to reincarnation. Beliefs that there are a fixed number of positions in society and throughout the system seem to suggest that overpopulation would be a bad idea.

By believing in reincarnation, the Northwest Coast people had a motivation to make decisions as if they were applying what Chichilnisky describes as 'sustainable preferences': a system of weighing the present against the future in a way that gives both adequate attention. In particular, the future is given sufficient weight to encourage decisions that would support the land's continued productivity.

One could even argue that, without the long-term view that the reincarnation beliefs provided, the other components of Northwest Coast ideology would lead to decisions that support wise use of the lands might not be as believable. Rather, that reincarnation beliefs gave the people a long-term view adds to the credibility of their cosmology's support for decision-making that would support sustainability. What remains to be done is to study the ways in which the society had additional mechanisms to be sure that the ideas were carried out.

Eugene Anderson insists that for people to behave in ways that conserve the land for future generations, they need to have emotional or religious reasons to motivate them. He also recognizes, however, that the political power of a society has to be in place to enforce these good ideas. Chapters 4–6 elaborate how other rules in Northwest Coast societies provided ways for the people to watch each other and to be sure that the contents of the ideology were carried out.

In summary, the peoples of the Northwest Coast had a belief system that was consistent with the archeological record of sustained existence in their world. They believed themselves responsible for caring for the world, they were opposed to wasting harvested resources, and through their beliefs in reincarnation they had a reason to save resources for future generations.

A belief system, however, is only part of the story. Certainly, E. N. Anderson is correct that people need good reasons for behaving properly, and that these good reasons include motivating humanity's emotional powers in their support. These are two of the reasons given for the ability of religions to assist in organizing groups of people for their mutual benefit. Not only must the ideology support sustainability, the system needs to be organized politically and economically in a way that allows the ideology to be carried out. Chapters 4–6 explain how the organization of the economy and polity supported implementation of the ideas contained in the belief systems.

4 Indian giving creates consumption connections to mirror ecosystem connections

In the late-nineteenth century, the people living in the lower Nass River valley in British Columbia, the Nisga'a, began to deal with the governments of Canada and British Columbia. The British Columbia government did not recognize the territoriality system of the Nisga'a. As is more fully explained in Chapters 5 and 6, head titleholders of each of the houses (*wilps*) of the Nisga'a were responsible for managing the lands of their *wilp*. When the Province attempted to identify reserves in 1881, the Nisga'a rejected its efforts, stating that they owned all of the land in the lower Nass Valley. When surveyors attempted to demarcate the reserves in 1886, the chiefs pulled up the stakes and threw them in the river. The Nisga'a efforts to reject the Province's actions were not successful, although they laid the groundwork for later efforts and for the eventual settlement of the land claims issue. Daniel Raunet (1996) provides a detailed history of the Nisga'a land claims efforts.

I am interested in one part of the rhetoric that the leaders used to defend their land claims. They took to explaining their valley as their 'supper bowl,' (Raunet 1996: 74) or the 'one bowl' or the 'common bowl.' (Nisga'a Tribal Council 1995) The purpose was to explain both that everyone in the valley depended on the resources there, and that all of the land belonged to the Nisga'a. They used this metaphor in spite of the fact that the landscape was divided into territories controlled by elders of each of the houses, the *wilps*. For instance, here is how the Nisga'a ownership statement describes the situation:

> Throughout Nisga'a history, from the beginning of time, one of the most important principles in Nisga'a society has been that of sharing and coexistence. Both concepts are embodied in Nisg'a tribal laws and traditions such as *amnigwootkw*, the *yukw, hagwinyuuwo'oskw* and a Nisg'a edict which declares the sharing of 'common bowl' – *saytk'ilhl wo'osihl Nisga'a*.
>
> (Nisga'a Tribal Council 1995: 18)

The terminology they used, common bowl, had been used also by other indigenous groups in North America to explain to the newcomers their view of the land. Use of the word common somewhat described the situation the Nisga'a had managed for centuries. But to the English ear, and to many people today, the word common makes one think of the 'commons.' To say that one's resources are managed as a commons was actually very dangerous. One of the founding myths of the industrial revolution in England was that enclosure of the commons contributed greatly to the success of the country (MacFarlane 1998: 104–5). This story continues to be told. For instance, Gregory Mankiw retells the story of the 'tragedy of the commons' in his widely used introductory economics textbook.

> In essence, the tragedy of the commons arises become because of an externality. When one family's flock grazes on the common land, it reduces the quality of the land available for other families. Because people neglect this negative externality when deciding how many sheep to own, the result is an excessive number of sheep.
>
> If the tragedy had been foreseen, the town could have solved the problem in various ways. It could have regulated the number of sheep in each family's flock internalizing the externality by taxing sheep, or auctioned off a limited number of sheep-grazing permits. That is, the medieval town could have dealt with the problem of overgrazing in the way that modern society deals with the problem of pollution. In the case of land, however, there is a simpler solution. The town can divide up the land among town families. Each family can enclose its parcel of land with a fence and then protect it from excessive grazing. In this way the land becomes a private good rather than a common resource. This outcome in fact occurred during the enclosure movement in England in the 17th century.
>
> (Mankiw 2007: 231–32)

The idea that the town commons were mismanaged under common ownership had been debated in the seventeenth century. Enclosures of the commons were justified using the argument Mankiw presents. Others argued that the commons had not been mismanaged, and that dispossessing those who used them had been wrong (Peters 1998).

The rest of the story for England is that enclosing the commons and creating private property is said to have generated the right incentives for investment in factories, and thereby to have started the industrial revolution. This interpretation, which remains the basis of an important literature today, was widely believed in the nineteenth century. When the Nisga'a described their ownership of the Nass Valley as a common bowl, they handed the English reader a reason to reject their management.

The English commons debate was re-energized in the twentieth century, when biologist Garrett Hardin used the metaphor of the 'tragedy of the commons' to explain why modern humanity was in danger of using too much of planet Earth's resources (Hardin 1968). He was worried that human population growth was causing overuse of the commons, just as putting too many cattle or sheep on the town commons created overgrazing.

Partly in response to Hardin's article, a substantial literature has grown that demonstrates the ability of many communities to manage their commons well. Hardin conceded later that he should have labeled his article 'the tragedy of the unmanaged commons,' to emphasize that treating a commons as open access, in which no controls are placed on use of the commons, does create overgrazing. Many solutions are possible to prevent overgrazing, however, if a community manages its commons (Ostrom 1990, 2001; Ostrom *et al*. 1994; Feeny *et al*. 1996).

I show in this chapter that the Nisga'a, like other peoples on the Northwest Coast, had solved the problem of the tragedy of their commons. But the settlers did not realize the significance of the solution. I illustrate their solution by using the 'prisoners' dilemma' model of a fishery or commons. It is the most commonly used model to explain the dilemma of managing a commons, and the simple version of the model captures what more complicated versions also show. An easy modification of the model shows how a potlatch system removes the dilemma. This modification also applies to more complicated models of the commons.

Today's prisoners' dilemma metaphor

Game theorist Ken Binmore credits two RAND Corporation scientists with inventing the game, which has truly captured game theory. Binmore uses the prisoners' dilemma game as a model for the 'game of life,' which begins with Adam and Eve. Binmore tells the story of the prisoners' dilemma as occurring in Chicago, not the Garden of Eden:

> 'The story for the Prisoners' dilemma is set in Chicago. The District Attorney knows that Adam and Eve are gangsters who are guilty of a major crime but is unable to convict them without a confession from one or the other. He orders their arrest and separately offers each the following deal: 'If you confess and your accomplice fails to confess, then you go free. If you fail to confess but your accomplice confesses, then you will be convicted and sentenced to the maximum term in jail. If you both confess, then you will both be convicted but the maximum sentence will not be imposed. If neither confesses, then you will be framed on a minor tax evasion charge for which a conviction is certain.'
>
> (Binmore 1994: 102)

The story is sometimes told with both prisoners going free if neither confesses. This tale serves to assist us in remembering that the incentives of the prisoners' dilemma are such that cooperating, which is not confessing in the story, is much more risky than confessing. The two prisoners, if they could somehow cooperate, would not confess. But they are held in separate rooms and have no way of knowing what decision the other has made. In this case, to avoid the maximum term in jail, each confesses.

This story, and similar ones, apply to many situations involving coordination decisions among people who are using resources. The example of grazing land is just one. Fisheries are particularly important examples that have been well studied. To apply to a fishery, the story has to be changed, but the incentive not to cooperate remains. For fishermen, the choice is between investing a great deal in fishing effort and a big expensive boat, or investing less in a small, cheaper boat.

If both purchase a small boat, they can catch all the surplus fish in a fishery and do very well. If one purchases a big boat, and the other a small boat, the person with the big boat catches all or most of the fish, and the person with the small boat catches very little. After paying the expenses of the big boat, that fisherman ends up with net profit that is greater than he could have had should both have purchased a small boat. If both purchase big boats, then they again catch all the fish equally, but because of the expense of the larger boats, their net return after paying expenses is less than if they had both purchased small boats. The logic of the dilemma is that both operate a large boat. (Other aspects of fisheries can also be addressed, such as incentives restricting harvest to support future fishery capacity, or incentives to invest in other activities that would improve the fishery.)

For the fishery story, the equivalent of being locked in separate rooms is an assumption that fishing can be done in secret, and that monitoring effort is difficult. I want to argue that the peoples of the Northwest Coast came up with a way to solve the dilemma. Their approach has the fishermen sharing the benefits of the catch, rather than keeping the catch for themselves. Under the potlatch system, leaders of the groups with access to the fishery were required to give away wealth through feasts. This requirement, applied to the prisoners' dilemma story, is that the fishermen share their catch.

To illustrate the way in which sharing the catch changes the game, I would like to present a numerical example. There are two players, Player 1 and Player 2. Each has a choice of two strategies: cooperate or defect. Their maximum joint payoff occurs when both cooperate. But the payoff structure of the game is set up in such a way that neither player will cooperate unless some condition outside the game provides inducement to do so.

Let:

C = the payoff each receives if both cooperate
D = the payoff each receives if both defect
b = the amount added to C that a defector receives if the other player cooperates
a = the reduction in D received by the cooperator if the other player defects.

In abstract form, the payoff matrix for the prisoners' dilemma can be written as shown:

		Player 2	
		Cooperate	*Defect*
Player 1	*Cooperate*	(C,C)	(D – a,C + b)
	Defect	(C + b,D – a)	(D,D)

The first amount in each parenthetical entry is the return to Player 1; the second is the return to Player 2.

For $C = 10$, $D = 5$, $a = 1$ and $b = 2$, the prisoners' dilemma payoff matrix is as shown:

		Player 2	
		Cooperate	Defect
Player 1	Cooperate	(10,10)	(4,12)
	Defect	(12,4)	(5,5)

Using the numerical example, the source of the dilemma is evident. Each player can be assumed to reason as follows:

> If the other player chooses to cooperate, then my best decision is to defect, because 12 is larger than 10. If the other player chooses to defect, then my best strategy is to defect, because 5 is greater than 4. Thus, no matter what the other player does, my best strategy is to defect.

With defection, then, both players receive less payoff than they could if they both cooperate. This is called the Nash equilibrium, meaning that both players have selected the best response for themselves.

Using the numerical example, one can demonstrate the consequence of imposing a *symmetric generosity rule*. Such a rule could be that each player shares half their catch with the other. If we interpret each of the payoffs as the surplus received by each player from an economic activity, such as harvesting salmon, then imposition of a symmetric generosity rule changes the payoff matrix:

		Player 2	
		Cooperate	Defect
Player 1	Cooperate	(10,10)	(8,8)
	Defect	(8,8)	(5,5)

In this matrix, the incentive to defect has been removed for each player. The reason is that if players have to give half of their catch to the other one, then the payoffs in the (cooperate, defect) and (defect, cooperate) cells are changed. Instead of the defector receiving most of the catch, he has to share his harvest with the cooperator. Together, they net 16 in profit in this example. The defector has to give the cooperator half of his catch, 6, and he receives from the cooperator half of the cooperator's catch, 2. Both have a net return of 8. Since 8 is less than the individual's return when both cooperate, the incentive to defect has been removed.

The symmetric generosity rule has also been called 'pooling' or a 'linear income-sharing rule' (Gaspart and Seki 2003). If all of the harvesters pool their catch at the end of each hunt, and then divide the harvest among them equally, they have pooled their harvest. In the two-person model, the cooperator would add 4 units to the pool; the defector would add 12; the sum would be 16 and each would get half. The Northwest Coast potlatch could be seen as a form of pooling the catch; giving wealth to neighbors was required by the system.

A different way to solve the dilemma is to imagine that each player can offer a 'side payment' to the other player before deciding whether or not to cooperate. While for many decades economists did not believe that binding commitments could be made in these situations, in the 1990s a number of economists began to analyze the prisoners' dilemma as a two-stage game (Varian 1994; Andreoni and Varian 1999; Jackson and Wilkie 2005; Charness *et al.* 2007; Ju and Born 2008). Their work provides other ways to analyze the dilemma.

In the example above, the amount *b* (2 in the numerical example) can be regarded as the amount a player would need to be compensated for not defecting. If each player were to offer the other player a side payment equal to or larger than 2, the incentive to defect would disappear. Suppose that such a side payment is 3 in the numerical example. Then each player would agree to pay the other 3 units if the other player cooperates; the 3 would be subtracted from each player also when the other cooperates, even if the player defects. The new payoff matrix changes in the (*C,D*) and (*D,C*) boxes, as follows:

		Player 2	
		Cooperate	Defect
Player 1	Cooperate	$(10 + 3 - 3, 10 - 3 + 3)$	$(4 + 3, 12 - 3)$
	Defect	$(12 - 3, 4 + 3)$	$(5,5)$

To understand this, examine the cell in which Player 1 cooperates and Player 2 defects. Because Player 1 has cooperated, he receives from Player 2 the 3 units that were agreed to. Player 1 thus receives a total net return of 7; Player 2 has his return reduced to 9 by his payment. The new matrix is as follows:

		Player 2	
		Cooperate	Defect
Player 1	Cooperate	$(10,10)$	$(7,9)$
	Defect	$(9,7)$	$(5,5)$

Now the incentives are set such that the new Nash equilibrium is for both players to cooperate.

There is no need for the prisoners' dilemma to be symmetric, as in the original story. An asymmetric set of payoffs may actually be better at capturing the types of situation that actually occur, as I will explain for the Nass River in a moment. Economists James Andreoni and Hal Varian (1999) created a laboratory experiment with college students using the following payoff matrix:

		Player 2	
		Cooperate	Defect
Player 1	Cooperate	(6,7)	(0,11)
	Defect	(9,0)	(3,4)

Because the payoffs differ for each player, the needed side payments also are different, making the analysis a bit more complicated. Player 2, for instance, needs at least a side payment of 4 to cooperate; a payment of 5 would be sure to make the cooperate value higher than the defect value. So Player 1 would offer 5 units to Player 2 for cooperating. Player 2 does not need to offer Player 1 as much to cooperate (the difference between 9 and 6); to be sure the payoffs are correct, Player 2 needs to offer a payment of 4 to Player 1 for cooperating. Here is a matrix showing the side payments:

		Player 2	
		Cooperate	Defect
Player 1	Cooperate	$(-5 + 4, +5 - 4)$	$(+4, -4)$
	Defect	$(-5, +5)$	$(0,0)$

Adding the side payments to the original payoffs gives the following new matrix:

		Player 2	
		Cooperate	Defect
Player 1	Cooperate	(5,8)	(4,7)
	Defect	(4,5)	(3,4)

Because of the way the numbers are originally, in the game with committed side payments, the payoff for cooperation for Player 1 is reduced by 1 unit and the payment to Player 2 is increased by 1 unit when both cooperate. Compare the original (6,7) with the new (5,8). When Andreoni and Varian had college students play this game with each other on computers, the students seemed to be affected by the increase in the inequality of the payoffs in the situation where both cooperate, and correspondingly reduced what Player 1 offered to Player 2. If this side payment is reduced too much, however, the incentive to cooperate disappears.

Thus, even if the conditions of the fishery in the Nass River are not ones that should be represented by a symmetric prisoners' dilemma game, if the wealth exchanges that occurred in feasts did not exactly match each other, they still could provide incentives to cooperate in managing the fishery. The rapidly growing literature in economics and game theory that is exploring the logic of side payment shows that many complications exist; I comment below on how the Northwest Coast addressed these complications in the total feasting and potlatch system.

That rules mandating the sharing of wealth could be good was far from the view of the English-speaking people who settled North America. Both in Canada and in the United States, government officials and missionaries opposed public distribution of wealth by individuals. Their model for opposition to the idea was based on the agricultural story, that private ownership made farmers make the right decisions. But farmers, using their own land, do not face the dilemmas that fishermen face, unless the farmers have to deal with access to water for irrigation. In that case, farmers have to deal with the dilemmas involved when they invest in irrigation works, because irrigation works are a public good for the farmers.

The potlatch was outlawed in Canada in 1885. Historians Cole and Chaikin (1990) summarize the motivation behind the suppression of the potlatch:

> Condemnation of the potlatch's demoralization of the Indians was much less on ethical grounds than on economic. Far the most frequent and serious arguments against the potlatch were those that touched on the system's incompatibility with settled habits of labor and industry: the loss of time from agriculture, ranching and even fishing, and the potlatch's destructiveness of the accumulation of savings. Work and savings were directed, not towards material progress, but to hoarding and then the extravagant dispersal of money and goods. Even the West Coast agent, Harry Guillod, who found the Nootkan potlatch largely inoffensive, agreed that it was 'much against the habits of saving' and [Indian agent] Lomas, who estimated that his Cowichans had earned over $15,000 in the 1881 Fraser River fishing season, regretted that the greatest portion of this sum would be spent on blankets to be given away. ... Few would have disputed [Indian reserve commission member Gilbert] Sproat's judgment that material progress was impossible while the potlatch existed. 'It produces indigence, thriftlessness, and a habit of roaming about, he wrote, 'which prevents home associations and is inconsistent with progress.'
>
> (Cole and Chaikin 1990: 20)

Further understanding of the meaning of 'progress' is provided by the attitudes of US Senator Dawes regarding the success of the Cherokee Nation. At the same time that the potlatch was outlawed in Canada, Senator Dawes sponsored the General Allotment Act, which divided the land on reservations among the Indians living on them, with the intention of creating a private property system. In Dawes's view, without selfishness, even apparent prosperity is suspect:

> The head chief told us that there was not a family in that whole nation that had a home of its own. There was not a pauper in that Nation, and the Nation did not owe a dollar. It built its own capitol ... and it built its schools and its hospitals. Yet the defect of the system was apparent. They have got as far as they can go, because they own their land in common. It is Henry George's system, and under that there is no enterprise to make your home any better than that of your neighbors. There is no selfishness, which is at the bottom of civilization. Till this people will consent to give up their lands, and divide them among their citizens so that each one can own the land he cultivates, they will not make much more progress.
>
> (Otis 1973: 10–11)

The senator's interpretation is accurate; Henry George advocated that rent from land should belong to the public. When indigenous leaders and men of wealth distribute earnings from land for public purposes, Senator Dawes is saying 'progress' is not possible because 'selfishness' is absent. Without 'selfishness,' there can also be no 'civilization.'

That wealthy members of the community are expected to be selfish remains a key feature of most analysis of economic prosperity. Senator Dawes's description of the Cherokee Nation's success connects selfishness to proper governance and to private property. His reasoning led him to sponsor imposition of private property on Indians by the General Allotment Act, best known as the Dawes Act. Implementation of the allotment policy led to both the taking of land from Indians, and the imposition of a limited private property system on a portion of tribal lands throughout the country (Carlson 1981; McDonnell 1991; Geisler 1995).

The difference between a system based on selfishness, top-down governance, and private property and a system based on generosity, shared governance, and contingent proprietorship is the subject of this and the following two chapters. The system of rules used in the Pacific Northwest departed significantly by having different requirements for the distribution of wealth, different rules regarding the control of land, and different standards for judging good leadership. The outlawing of the potlatch (1885–1951) is perhaps the best symbol of the difficulties the settlers had with public systems of generosity. The potlatch ceremonies unified three characteristics of the Pacific Northwest system: their system of distributing wealth, their territorial system, and their governance practices.

That the combination of changes in wealth distribution, territoriality, and governance could be beneficial is demonstrated by the success Senator Dawes' reported for the Cherokee: 'not a pauper in the Nation.' Chapter 1 of this book has already described the wealth attained by peoples of the Pacific Northwest Coast. Senator Dawes's blindness is just a 100-year-old example of a blindness that has only recently become less afflicting.

Continuing misunderstanding of the potlatch

Because the prisoners' dilemma game captures the essence of many common pool problems, the generality of the results just given is potentially very great: systems of sharing the output of a fishery have the potential to remove the dilemma and assist fishermen in achieving cooperative solutions to their problem.

If this answer is so simple, why did it take 100 years for those doing economic analysis to realize that some form of sharing or side payments would help in solving the dilemma? The articles cited above are all very recent. The answer has not yet been recognized in widely used introductory economics textbooks, as Mankiw's quotation demonstrates. The answer appears to be complex, a combination of assumptions about enforcement, about man's inherent selfish nature, and about differences among people. First, many analysts assumed that an agreement to share the outcomes of a game such as the prisoners' dilemma is not *enforceable*. Even if players were to agree before playing the game to divide the returns, there is assumed to be no enforcement mechanism. In a society such as one that requires give-aways, however, the enforcement mechanism is credible. Recently, people have realized that contracts could be written to enforce side payments.

Second, sharing of output seems inconsistent with the idea that individuals are selfish. They would not want to share with others. This is the argument Dawes presents in his opposition to 'Henry George's system': if individuals have to share some of what they produce with others, they will not have an incentive to work hard. This particular line of argument ignores the problem of the dilemma. Certainly, if there are to external effects, private selfishness will support good decisions. It is the presence of the external effects that creates the need to avoid the consequences of private selfishness. The dilemma is created by the fact that a fishery (or other common pool good) has to be utilized in common; if each individual is left to an independent decision, then the dilemma will be realized.

Third are concerns about the efforts of fishermen if individual skills vary. Pooling the returns from fishing would mean that the better fishermen would contribute more than the less good fishermen. The problem of over-exploiting the fishery would be replaced by another problem, under-exploiting the skills of the fishermen. Of the three objections, this is the most robust. One solution is to give the better fishermen more social status while at the same time requiring sharing of the output (Gaspart and Seki 2003). On the Northwest Coast, those house leaders who gave the largest potlatches had the highest social status.

Solution to the dilemma is possible, some argue, if the game is repeated many times, or indefinitely. The idea that selfish, rational actors would cooperate in the game if it will be repeated is called the 'folk theorem' of game theory, because no one can take credit for it (Fudenberg and Tirole 1991; Binmore 1994). This theorem is usually invoked when people are seen to have acted differently from how the one-play version of the game suggests that they will act. Binmore goes to great lengths to explain why the folk theorem can explain human cooperation generally (Binmore 1994, 1998). He doesn't credit a sharing solution as reasonable. Economist Hal Varian (1994) reports 'It has long been known that the ability to make binding preplay commitments allows for a solution to the prisoner's [*sic*] dilemma.' He provides no references to published literature, however, suggesting that the solution wasn't really thought to apply to real situations.

What needs explanation is the rejection of the simple solution for so many years. Many easily see that an agreement to share the harvest will remove the dilemma. But people don't voluntarily agree to share. Such an agreement is dismissed by many through calling it 'cheap talk': the fishermen may agree beforehand that they will share, but afterwards one of them can not share.

That humanity is at base selfish has become the fundamental metaphor of the modern age. It is under sustained attack at present in the scientific literature. Anthropologist Marshall Sahlins has explained that the view of man as inherently evil, and consequently selfish, originates with Judeo-Christian beliefs, based on the story of Adam (Sahlins 1996). It received strong impetus from Machiavelli's *The Prince*, from Hobbes's *Leviathan*, from Adam Smith, and from all of mainstream economics. Senator Dawes demonstrated no originality in connecting civilization to selfishness. But the general point is that people's thinking is affected by the general model; therefore some effort is needed to point out that the dominant approach is now recognized to have limitations. Historian Peter Turchin (2006), seeking to base his study of the rise and fall of empires on a solid model of human nature, entitles his fifth chapter 'The myth of self-interest: and the science of cooperation.' He reviews much of the very recent literature that is contradicting the assumption of self-interest. Studies such as the experiments conducted by Andreoni and Varian confirm that college students aren't fully selfish. A large team of people visited 15 societies around the world and had them engage in experimental playing of games like the prisoners' dilemma, especially the ultimatum game, and the results showed that none of the people in the societies fulfilled the selfishness assumption (Henrich 2004). They all, to varying degrees, showed concern about others. Economist Samuel Bowles (2003) has proposed modifications to microeconomic theory to take account of these results, as well.

The usual solutions

People analyzing the prisoners' dilemma model of common pool resources have generally presented three types of solution: (1) a government such as that of a nation-state takes control of the fishery and limits the number of fishermen or their fishing effort; (2) the resource is divided up as private property, as in the enclosure of grazing lands; or (3) communities of resource-users be allowed to organize their own rules for governing entry and removal of harvest from the resource. The first two solutions are the ones Mankiw presents in his introductory economics textbook. The management of Northwest Coast fisheries through the potlatch system should be classified as a type of arrangement that a community of resource-users adopts.

Each of the three solutions has potential problems. When governments take control of a fishery, they have difficulty obtaining the information needed to make good decisions. They also can become captured by fishery interest groups, and fail to create the policies needed to protect the fishery. The private property solution ignores the technical problem that the fishery is a common pool good. Usually the private property solution is individual transferable quotas; but the quota has to be set by a government fishery bureaucracy, and is subject to the same information problems that other government programs have. Many have proposed that communities of resource-users have the best chance to set up rules that will manage a fishery well (Ostrom 2001). The growing literature on the use of side payments, which is showing that people can make agreements and then cooperate, supports the third solution (Varian 1995; Andreoni and Varian 1999; Macho-Stadler *et al*. 2007).

Complexities: the Nass and Skeena rivers

The prisoners' dilemma model, whether explained as a simple two-by-two affair or a more complicated model of a fishery, is nonetheless a simple model. Fisheries aren't actually that simple, and certainly the many salmon fisheries of the Northwest Coast involve complications. There are many types of river, and there are five species of salmon.

The rivers are of several types. Coastal rivers that flow directly into the ocean can be controlled by one or a few houses, such as on Haida Gwaii or any of the islands in the Tlingit area, southeast Alaska. Rivers and lakes on Vancouver Island also fall into this category. These rivers, being small, can be fully controlled by a weir or other barrier, and may not have created a large common property problem. The Nass and Skeena rivers in Canada, and three rivers that flow from Canada to the Alaskan panhandle, however, are large and cannot be controlled by weirs; each of their tributaries, however, is more amenable to control. The Nass is small enough that all those fishing in it were from the related cultural groups, the Nisga'a and Gitxsan. The Skeena and its tributaries are larger, and are used by several major cultural groups, speaking similar languages. The Fraser and Columbia rivers are huge; they drain large areas where the people have many different languages and live far apart.

On the smaller rivers, all the fishermen can relatively easily establish systems in which they share with one another through the potlatch and feasting system. When the titleholders of the Nass describe their valley as a 'common bowl,' it is because they know everyone who is using the five salmon species that migrate to the Nass River. The titleholders had different levels of control in the management of the species. The Spring or Chinook salmon, which spawn in the mainstem of the river, would be controlled only by the amount of harvest. Other species, which spawn in the small tributaries, could be controlled both by the amount of harvest and by taking care of the spawning beds and rearing habitat in the rivers and lakes. As each run of fish swims up the Nass, it could be harvested by equipment along the shores of the river, dip nets and fish wheels being the primary techniques. As the runs enter the smaller tributaries, they could be controlled by wood structures barricading the entire river, allowing detailed control of which fish are harvested and which are left to escape to the spawning grounds. Because all the fish are vulnerable to equipment in the main stem of the river, a common property problem exists for the Nass and Skeena rivers. But the rivers are small enough that sharing of the harvest among everyone on the river would seem to be feasible.

I am not claiming that after each run of salmon had passed up the Nass, the house leaders immediately distributed the catch. The wealth of each *wilp* depended upon the success of its fishing effort and upon the productivity of the rest of the *wilp's* lands. People lived off of the fish they caught and dried, and created other goods with their labor. At a feast, many products would be distributed to the guests – items made by people who lived by eating the harvested salmon, the main staple of the valley, along with berries and other products of the land. Dried salmon were enhanced by use of eulachon oil, which was created by processing the large runs of culachon each spring at the mouth of the Nass. The resulting 'grease' was a major trade item on the coast and inland.

The Fraser and Columbia rivers present another issue, because really large-scale coordination and sharing would be difficult. The people with the control over escapement in the small rivers upstream don't necessarily have a governance relationship with the folks downstream. Hence overwhelming the fishing capacity of the downstream fishers helps in assuring that upstream fishers will have some return. There is some oral history that up- and downstream coordination was discussed on the Fraser; I was told this by people living on Stuart Lake, one of the main sources for sockeye on the Fraser. The peoples of both the lower and upper Fraser River have described their ethics as respecting the salmon, and they do not want to harvest more than they need. But with the high population levels that have been reported, certainly over-harvest was a possibility. The peoples up and down the river all practiced a feasting system similar to that on the coast. But because they did not feast each other, that they actually pooled their catch is not a plausible story. Further work is needed on the history of the large rivers to know how the peoples managed not to over-harvest. We know from the data reported for the Columbia River by Butler and Campbell (2004) that fish were not over-harvested, because there was not a decline in the size of the largest fish and a shift to the smaller ones. These peoples also practiced feasting and sharing of wealth.

The above presentation of the prisoners' dilemma examined a very simple model of the fishery. Many institutional details were ignored, in order to stress the underlying plausibility of sharing output as a way to solve the dilemma of a fishery. In order to be more realistic, I need to review the situation in the Nass Valley. Like other groups on the coast, the Nisga'a were organized into houses, or *wilps*, each with a head titleholder. The Nass, called the Lisims by the Nisga'a, is a large, powerful river. In its main stem, fishing occurs along the banks, where migrating salmon swim to avoid the current in the center of the river. As a run of salmon moves up a river to its birth streams or to a lake (as in the case of sockeye), the salmon pass by the harvesting sites of a variety of houses. This illustrates the common pool nature of the fishery: the people at each of the fishing sites can catch as many fish as possible, depending on their investment in catching technology. If one group caught a disproportionate amount, others would have less.

The tributaries to the Nass are not as large as the main river, and for most of them it is possible to place weirs, or barricades, near the mouth of the tributary. Such weirs would allow the fishermen to place traps that would allow them to control all the fish migrating up stream. The control meant that the entire run could be harvested; it also meant that the managers had considerable discretion regarding which fish to allow to escape for spawning.

Successful management of the various runs of salmon depended both on the harvest rates of the salmon runs as they swam up the Nass, and on the management of the escapement of fish to the spawning grounds through the barricades at each of the tributaries.

The unit of economic decision-making among the Nisga'a was the house: all the territory of the Nass river valley was divided into areas, each area held and managed by one house. The territory of a house included fishing sites, streams and hillsides; the lands extended from the valley bottom to the tops of the mountains. The people lived in villages made up of houses. The Nisga'a have four clans (*pdeek*). Each of the villages had houses that are headed by members of one of the clans, meaning that each of the villages also had four of the clans. Individuals were not allowed to marry within their clan, and clan membership was inherited through women.

A titleholder (*sim'oogit*) for one of the houses, therefore, would be married to a woman from a different clan, and the children of the marriage would be members of the wife's clan and house. The titleholder's first choice for successor would be the oldest son of his oldest sister. This son, while young, would be raised by his sister. The sister would also be a person of importance (*sigidimnak'm*). The oldest male and female children of a matriarch would qualify to become traditional leaders themselves. The brother would become the manager of the house territory; the sister would train the next chief. But in order to assume the offices, they would have to be trained in the knowledge, duties, and responsibilities of those offices. As they grew older, they would obtain titles to positions below that of the head titleholders. The titleholder's successor, raised at first by his sister, would later take a title that placed him in succession to his uncle's position.

Each time a person acquired a title, the house holding the title would have a feast. Although several titles could be passed along at a feast, none could be acquired without public recognition. The house designating the new titleholder would be obligated to give items of wealth to all who attended the feast; the size of the wealth transferred would be determined by the importance of the person receiving it. This transfer of wealth is what others have called the potlatch or the 'giving' of wealth. By accepting the goods provided at the feast, those who attend signal their recognition of the legitimate transfer of the title to the new titleholder.

The transfer of one of the top titles, the recognition of a *sim'oogit* or a *sigidimnak'm*, would require a large feast and the distribution of a great deal of wealth. Only by sharing the produce of an *ango'osk* could the head titleholder hold his position.

This distribution of wealth to others who attended feasts was governed by rules about how much would go to each of the other titleholders who attended. In addition, the assembly of the wealth to be distributed would be from people within the house. A feast would have a period in which people contributed to the amounts to be distributed, followed by a period of distribution. In modern feasts, the money contributed is placed in a large bowl, which could be called a 'common bowl,' and then distributed to everyone attending. Each contribution to the bowl, and each distribution from the bowl, was announced publicly.

The rules that determined how much would be distributed to each of the other titleholders at a feast constitute the details of the way in which wealth was pooled among the Nisga'a. Because wealth came primarily from the fishery, which fed everybody, the transfer of feast goods meant that the benefits from the fishery were distributed to everyone. While complicated by details, the overall pattern is clear: each house in a village, and each village in turn (because feasts occurred among villages as well), would benefit from the prosperity of the other houses.

The system of houses, villages, and river basin-wide sharing also contained elements of difference and hierarchy. In each village, one house was seen as the highest rank; it was expected, in light of that rank, to provide more wealth at feasts than houses of lower rank. Those best able to contribute contributed more, and in return achieved higher status than others. Anthropologists have argued about this system: what comes first, the high rank or the ability to distribute much wealth? At any one time, answering this question would be difficult. One would need to see how the system evolved over time. I suspect that the high wealth came first; those houses able to be most productive came to earn the highest status. Once achieved, that status was maintained by continued good production. If the house became less productive, over time its status would fall, and another house would take the high-status position. The Nisga'a, however, seem to view the inherited status of each house as a fixed thing, which indeed it may be today when the economic system has been taken away by the colonial society. The ranks in place when the fishery and land were transferred to settlers dominate the post-conquest society.

This overview of Nisga'a traditional society demonstrates that more is involved in the potlatch system than just dividing the annual salmon harvest. Hereditary leaders are expected to care for the lands under their control. They are also expected to participate in the feast system and seek the approval of other hereditary leaders by demonstrating their ability to provide goods at those feasts. Careful account is taken of what is distributed at feasts, as a way of holding leaders responsible for what they do. If other titleholders object to a titleholder's actions, they will refuse to attend his feasts, and will say why.

Those analysts, such as game theorist Ken Binmore, who doubt the ability of men to change the parameters of the 'game of life' as represented by the prisoners' dilemma are correct to insist that the ability to enforce alternative payoffs be demonstrated. The requirement that titleholders host each other and distribute wealth among the houses is an example of enforcement of the changed payoff rules. Chapter 5 explains in more detail how accountability was carried out by the titleholding system. It also explains how the leadership system facilitated river system-wide discussion of management issues.

The feasting/potlatch system provides answers to each of the three objections posed by those who object to sharing the harvest as a solution to common property problems. First, once in place, the system is enforceable. Titleholders cannot acquire their title without having a feast and distributing wealth. As the system develops, the amount of wealth expected becomes clear. The second objection is that people are not generous. The system does not require that individuals be generous; they have to participate whether or not they personally would rather keep all the wealth. In the process of selection of leaders, however, new chiefs are taught to be generous, and the society in general rewards those who are generous, rather than those who are selfish. This rewarding of the generous with status provides the solution to the third problem, that sharing wealth will discourage the most able from contributing.

This chapter focuses only on the exchange aspect of the Northwest Coast system, in order to emphasize that a people living from a common pool resource can manage that resource well and avoid the tragedy of the commons through establishment of a system of sharing the catch. That the most able obtain status by distributing much wealth could encourage over-harvest as well. This problem is addressed by the fact that those accepting gifts can remove the right of those giving gifts by refusing to accept. If a house takes an excessive share of the fishery, and then distributes it to its neighbors, the neighbors can object by refusing to accept a portion of, or all, that they are given. This additional complication shows that more is needed than just solving the problem of incentives to over-harvest. Such a solution can create additional poor incentives, by allowing excessive attainment of status to result from distributing wealth. Seeking status could become the non-cooperative strategy. But status is awarded in a political and social system. The system can have checks and balances that limit competition for status. The following two chapters discuss those checks and balances, which occur in the territorial and governance systems.

5   Contingent proprietorship provides cooperation

Consideration of the fishermen's prisoners' dilemma in Chapter 4 revealed that the use of generosity or pooling of a catch has only recently been viewed as a credible solution. The chapter showed how the solution would work if the conditions surrounding the fishery would allow it to function. This chapter describes how the system of the Northwest Coast provided a way to make the solution occur. The solution is very simple: if a fisherman, in the form of a titleholder to a house, failed to share the wealth of his house, other titleholders would cease recognizing his authority. In short, in order to remain a fisherman, the fisherman had to share his catch. If he did not, then he lost his right to be a fisherman. Being a titleholder obliged a person also to share the wealth of the land he or she controlled; an economist could say 'side payments were required.'

Most models of the fishery using the prisoners' dilemma leave unstated the conditions governing how the players came to be in their roles. The solution used in the Pacific Northwest requires examination of that question. Titleholders controlled prime fishing sites on the main rivers, and controlled whole tributaries when small enough to allow barricades near the mouth of the river. Their control of the fishing sites consisted of their right to be fishermen in the sense of the prisoners' dilemma model. The conditions of the prisoners' dilemma doom the players of the game eventually to slide into mutual defection. Some addition to the structure of the game is needed for people to solve the dilemma. Making participation contingent on cooperation is the solution used on the Northwest Coast. Although other solutions exist, and have been modeled in experimental sessions and observed in other commons management system, this is the solution used on the Northwest Coast.

Chapter 4 indicates the importance of reciprocity in contributing to resilience. Reciprocity creates linkages among the levels of human consumption in a system, resulting in reasons for humans to pay attention to the linkages in production in the system. Chapter 6 discusses how particular forms of leadership assist in dealing with the governance issues that a reciprocity system creates. These two aspects of the sustainable social ecological systems of the Pacific Northwest were accompanied by characteristics of territorial systems that differ from modern characteristics of property. This chapter explores the special characteristics that need attention. In order to avoid confusion, the term 'territorial system' is used instead of 'property system,' for the reason that 'property' has come to be associated with one particular territorial system, that of 'private property rights.' This chapter lays out the components of a private property rights system and compares them with the Northwest Coast territorial system.

This chapter gives special attention to nuances of territorial systems, arguing that the ideas related to 'proprietorship' are closer to what Northwest Coast systems were than are ideas of 'ownership.' A proprietorship system does not allow for sale of land at the discretion of the holder of the land. A proprietorship system also does not allow for succession of ownership to occur without review and attention by others in the community. Furthermore, a proprietor's continuing power to manage a land area depends on the maintenance of a good reputation and compliance with a community's concept of the duties of a proprietor. A proprietor can exclude other people from access, or impose rules on those to whom he must provide access. Although proprietorship rules overlap with some characteristics associated with private property, such as prohibition of trespass and the right to use land, the system should not be described as a property system.

A proprietorship system shares many characteristics with what is known as a private property or freehold estate system. Proprietors are able to exclude whom they wish; if exclusion is not fully possible, they are able to direct anyone with access to the land regarding their behavior on the land. This power of exclusion is a fundamental component of the concept of private property, in contrast to open access. Proprietors also have great influence over to whom they bequeath their land, even if a set of kinship rules indicates which of their descendants or relatives has the first right to inherit. In the matrilineal systems of the Northwest Coast, in many cases the eldest son of the eldest sister of a titleholder had the first right of inheritance, a matrilineal rule. This differed from the patrilineal systems in which sons inherited from their fathers. I will not argue that the type of lineal descent was key to the territorial systems. Other factors were much more important.

Before turning to a detailed analysis of the territoriality systems used on the Northwest Coast, I need to comment on the use of the word 'property' to describe such systems. Chapter 2 emphasizes that the application of Western concepts to aboriginal societies is full of difficulties. These difficulties also exist in the application of the idea of property.

In Chapter 2, I asserted that to use the idea of 'nature' in discussing the relationship of aboriginal peoples to the world is to impose an assumption that prohibits full understanding of their ideas about the role of humans in relationship to non-human entities. I agreed with Bruno Latour that aboriginal people cannot live in harmony with nature because they have no concept of 'nature.' At issue is building a relationship with non-human entities, and creating a 'common world' that consists of humans and others, both animate and inanimate.

In this chapter, I assert that use of the idea of property is also a great problem. In order to understand the way in which peoples of the Northwest Coast worked out their relationship to salmon and other non-humans, one must carefully avoid making assumptions that come as baggage with the notion of property.

By way of introduction, consider that the concept of property in contemporary Western law, especially law drawn from English sources, fundamentally assumes that people are separate from land. Property is conceived as a relationship between an individual or collection of individuals and a thing. Regarding land, property is a relationship of 'ownership' between an individual and a parcel of land. Legal analyst John Penner begins his definition of property as follows: ownership of property is 'the right to determine the use or disposition of a separable thing (i.e., a thing whose contingent association with any particular person is essentially impersonal and so imports nothing of normative consequence) …' (Penner 1997: 152). I will consider the rest of his definition below. Note that Penner is insisting that the 'separable thing' is absolutely not connected with any particular person. In doing this, he wants to be able to say, for instance, that a person does not 'own' his or her own body, because a person's body is not separable, and obviously a person has a normative connection to his or her own body. If humans and nature are separate, certainly the things of nature have to be unconnected to particular people, so that society can exist anywhere.

In contrast to this view, many aboriginal people don't begin with the assumption of separateness. Consider an elder cited by anthropologist Paul Nadasdy. He explains her view as follows:

> Lena Johnson, A Kluane First Nation elder, likened herself to a tree with roots in the ground. She said that she and her people would stay forever in the place they were born and that her parents and grandparents, too, had been born and buried there. She was not opposed, she said, to sharing the land with white people; for a long time, in fact, they had done so without many problems. But then the government started trying to take over, to push Kluane First Nation People from their lands, and that was not acceptable.
>
> (Nadasdy 2002: 524)

She was commenting on the land claim question in the Yukon Territory in Canada. Here connection to the land is permanent, a concept foreign to Anglo ideas of property as articulated by Penner. In addition to a permanent connection, she was willing to share access to the land; this willingness to share is also not part of the Anglo-American understanding of 'owning' land. Ownership means exclusive use; people who share their land don't have exclusive use. Anthropologist Catharine McClellan, who did Yukon field work in 1948 and 1951, in interpreting the aboriginal words for 'my country,' said:

> I believe that in using these terms the speaker wants to emphasize his sentimental ties to a region. The sentiment arises from the fact that either he or his ancestors once exploited the area and it involves the feeling that he continues to have the right to do so. However, it does not necessarily imply that he 'owns' the land.
>
> (Nadasdy 2002: 482–83, quoting McClellan 1975)

McClellan describes the ties as 'sentimental,' which certainly reduces the meaning of 'having roots like a tree,' a permanent connection. She also says the sentiment arises because the speaker 'once exploited the area.' The word 'exploited' both expresses an exclusively extractive view of the land and carries a connotation of intermittent use.

The Gitksan hereditary chief Delgam Uukw explained his connection to the land as follows:

> My power is carried in my House's histories, songs, dances and crests. It is recreated at the Feast when the histories are told, the songs and dances performed, and the crests displayed. With the wealth that comes from respectful use of the territory, the House feeds the name of the Chief in the Feast Hall. In this way, the law, the Chief, the territory, and the Feast become one. The unity of the Chief's authority and his House's ownership of its territory are witnessed and thus affirmed by the other Chiefs at the Feast.
>
> (Gisday Wa and Delgam Uukw 1992: 7–8)

Delgam Uukw emphasizes the unity of a chief and his territory, based on wealth that comes from the territory. In describing the Gitksan system to others, he uses the term 'his house's ownership.' He tries to explain the meaning of ownership within the Gitksan territoriality system by emphasizing unity between himself, as a chief, and the land. Yet the Anglo-American understanding of ownership denies this permanent connection.

Settlers used, and still use, the fact that the territoriality systems of aboriginal people in North America were not the same as private property systems as a reason to deny aboriginal people their right to retain control of the land. The idea that Indians did not have the correct ideas of ownership has long been part of the ideology that justified taking lands from them. Francis Jennings attributes the first use of the distinction between roaming and cultivating to Samuel Purchas in 1625. In commenting on the settlers' acquisition of land in Virginia, Purchas said that the Indians 'range rather than inhabit' (Jennings 1976: 80). Jennings describes the result as follows:

> Although Purchas's 'range rather than inhabite' phrase was contrary to known fact, it held the magic of a strong incantation and the utility of a magician's smokescreen … and its capacity to smother fact was still so highly valued as late as 1830 that Secretary of War Lewis Cass synonymized it elegantly ('traversed but not occupied') to justify the expropriation of the sedentary and agricultural Cherokees.
>
> (Jennings 1976: 81)

Even though the Cherokee were agricultural, quite possibly their views about sharing the products of the land would have meant their ideas of territoriality were not exactly ownership in the sense of private property. Francis Jennings, like many others who have studied the process of colonization, cites use and utilization of the land as good evidence that the land was held by aboriginal people and that expropriation was not justified. The justification that Indians were not sedentary had continued to be used throughout the nineteenth century, and it remains a key issue up to the present.

The fight over retaining control of the land colors all analysis of the territoriality systems of aboriginal people. Given that the courts of Canada and the United States insisted on using Anglo-American concepts of property as the standard for judgment, naturally Indians and their allies have tried to argue that Indians did hold the land in ways that qualify as ownership. But these attempts have to deal with the existence of none-too-subtle differences in the systems. A sensible solution in the politics of land claims would be to recognize aboriginal law and determine how aboriginal law assigns powers to use land. Canadian legal scholars such as John Borrows (2002) have made this argument. Recently, the Supreme Court of Canada has shown a desire to recognize aboriginal ideas of territoriality as a basis for assertions of aboriginal title. As recently as 2007, the extent to which a hunting and gathering people can assert rights to title has been litigated in the case of *Tsilhqot'in Nation v. British Columbia* (2007, British Columbia Supreme Court, BCSC 1700). When the court ruled in favor of recognizing intermittent annual use of berry grounds or hunting areas, the lead attorney for British Columbia objected by citing all the reasons that the strict standards of private property definitions did not apply (Foy 2008).

The issue of land claims is one area that creates possible bias in examination of aboriginal territoriality systems. Another issue is that of achieving economic efficiency, and of organizing a system to maximize economic growth. In this area, numerous scholars defend the idea that private property rights contribute to aborginal economies (Demsetz 1967; Bailey 1992; Anderson 1997). Economist Martin Bailey has argued that aboriginal territorial systems should be examined because they have survived a test that suggests they would be optimal systems:

> The study of aboriginals can make especially clear the advantages of one type of property right over another because, in most cases, these people lived at the margin of subsistence. ... Unsound rights structures generally implied lower population size and, perhaps, the disappearance of the society. ... One therefore expects the data on aboriginals to provide relative direct evidence on the structure of an optimal system of property rights under various circumstances.
>
> (Bailey 1992: 183–84)

He goes on to examine property rights, allowing for common property as well as individual private property. With regard to the Northwest Coast, he says,

> Private property in land was found much less frequently among people without horticulture. Two notable instances – the Hupa of California and the northwest coast tribes – strongly emphasized private property and were relatively prosperous, as one would expect. They had family property rights in the superior fishing, hunting, and gathering sites and in personal property, which included slaves. The emphasis on family property, ostentation, and social standing probably reduced population pressure: food and artifacts were plentiful.
>
> (*ibid.*: 194)

Bailey asserts without detailed analysis that the territorial systems of the Pacific Northwest included private property. He is not surprised by this, because he recognizes that Northwest Coast societies were 'relatively prosperous,' a condition that should be expected of a society that uses private property in land. His position would have been strengthened if he had known that the Northwest Coast societies did practice horticulture (Deur and Turner 2005).

He also confuses 'family' with 'house.' In other parts of his article, even when he expands the concept of family, it includes only children and grandchildren, or in exceptional cases, brothers and sisters (Bailey 1992: 192). In a matrilineal system, it has to include nephews. Houses usually included many families, understood as a nuclear family of a mother, father, and children. Houses included extended family members, including cousins, aunts and uncles. The concept of 'family' as a substitute for 'individual' in a private property system is incorrect.

His reference also implicitly assumes that there were areas – non-superior sites – that were not private property and hence were not included in the territoriality system. Yet the entire landscape was identified with one or another house. In addition, areas in the ocean were identified as well, as fishing occurred near the shore.

For Bailey, describing the systems as private property promotes a general assertion, 'the structure of rights tends to respond to economic incentives' (*ibid.*: 192). On page 194 he states this a bit more carefully: 'the structure of property rights will usually reflect economic advantage in those cases where the balance of advantage is clear.' Bailey clearly argues that private property rights have an advantage in many situations, including that of the Northwest Coast. Yet as this chapter shows, the territoriality system of the Northwest Coast was not a private property system. One should be careful in even calling it a 'property' system, because it did not use ideas that are tightly connected to 'property.'

Territoriality analysis

In order to avoid biases created either by legal cases considering land claims or concern over proof that private property systems are best, one should take some care in specifying the details of a property system (Hunt and Gilman 1998). That some parts are similar does not mean that the whole system is. A framework is needed that provides a way to compare different systems of territoriality. Within the framework, those systems that are property in the sense inherited from Europe can be specified, and distinctions made with the systems indigenous to North America. In order precisely to describe the Northwest Coast system in relationship to current property law, I draw upon the framework recently created by Elinor Ostrom and Sue Crawford (Crawford and Ostrom 1995; Ostrom 2005). They propose that different institutional situations be described in terms of seven types of rule: position, boundary, choice, aggregation, information, payoff, and scope. Use of their framework assists greatly in showing the differences between property rights and contingent proprietorship.

I will explain each type of rule in the process of contrasting private property systems to systems of contingent proprietorship. As I go through the analysis, the reason for the name of the system will become clear.

Rules or institutional statements

In order to classify rules, it is helpful to state them all in a similar way. Ostrom and Crawford propose that an effort be made to state rules in the following format or syntax:

> ATTRIBUTES of participants who are OBLIGED, FORBIDDEN, OR PER- MITTED to ACT (or AFFECT an outcome) under specified CONDITIONS, OR ELSE.
>
> (Ostrom 2005: 187)

When written in this syntax, a law must have all five components. If there is no consequence for violation of the rule, no 'or else,' then the statement is a norm. If only the first three components, a subject, a specification of the requirements, and a verb are present, then the statement is a shared strategy. With this more precise use of language, a rule is a complete statement. Ostrom calls the set of statements that can be laws, norms, or shared strategies 'institutional statements.' She does not call them merely institutions, because many people think of an institution as an organization of people. Rather than use institutional statements to designate the set of all three types, I follow Ostrom and use the term rules to mean all types of institutional statement. I depart from Ostrom and name the full statements, with an 'or else' clause, to be laws, not rules.

For example, one of the important laws for the Gitxsan and Wet'suwet'en can be stated as follows:

> A Chief must ensure that the animals and fish in his House's territory are given respect, by not being wasted and by being treated properly, or else the animals and fish will disappear.

This is a condensed version of the following more extensive statement:

> As steward, the Chief is responsible for ensuring that the animals and the fish are accorded the respect which Gitksan and Wet'suwet'en law demands. Thus, by ensuring that salmon are not wasted, the Chief maintains his House's relation- ship with the salmon to ensure their annual return to provide for the needs of House members. In accordance with Gitksan and Wet'suwet'en world-view, if something goes wrong with the relationship, it is not considered an accident. In his or her role as representative of the House in animal and spirit world, the Chief is responsible for determining the reason for the breach and for correcting it.
>
> (Gisday Wa and Delgam Uukw 1992: 33)

The longer statement has another rule provided in the last sentence; the 'or else' that enforces that rule is not clear. These examples of laws and rules from the Gitxsan and Wet'suwet'en provide an introduction to the difference between the Northwest Coast contingent proprietorship system and a private property system.

In summary, rules come in three forms: laws, norms, and shared strategies. The rules used in territorial systems can be compared in seven categories. Position rules determine the positions in the system, what roles are available for actors to take. Boundary rules determine who enters and leaves positions. Choice rules describe what people holding positions may or may not do. Aggregation rules describe how decisions are to be made. Information rules describe what information is available to actors in the system. Payoff rules describe how benefits from harvesting or other activities are distributed to participants. Scope rules define other matters that are not handled by the first six types of rule. By applying this systematic classification of rules, one can obtain a clear idea about the differences between a private property system and a contingent proprietorship system.

Positions

The first type of rule defines the positions available to people in the system. In considering systems of territoriality, the fundamental position is the one that describes a relationship between a person or a group of persons and a territory or area of land. Other positions are needed for enforcement of the rules.

Private property

In private property systems of land tenure, the key position is that of 'landowner.' The definition of position only involves the fact that an owner has a connection to a thing, a piece of land. The powers of the position are defined by other types of rule. In addition to owners, private property systems define the role of 'individual': individuals can be land-owners, or they are non-owners. Groups of people are allowed to be classified as individuals if they are organized as a corporation or similar business entity (in Canada, as a society, cooperative, company, or partnership). In the role of non-owners, other types of rule will define actions for them. A private property system also has a state or government role, and that role has officials such as judges and policemen. In addition, private property systems have bankers, who help owners in making purchases. In a private property system, the organizations that are groups treated as one individual, such as a corporation, have major roles such as shareholder, board of directors, and chief operating officer.

Another position is that of 'parcel of land' or 'unit of land that can be owned.' Such parcels of land have boundaries that are easily recognized. In state systems, there is a government office that keeps track of the parcels of land that are owned.

Contingent proprietorship

In Northwest Coast societies, positions in relation to land consisted in the first place of the idea of a house connected to a house territory. House territories were defined by the history of the house, which told what lands the house held. Within the house, a system of titles began at the top with the head titleholder of a house, and all the lesser titles of that house. Each position was well defined with a name. Often the heir to the top position himself would have a named position before moving to the chief's name. Women's positions also were named. The Northwest Coast also had commoners, who held no title, and slaves, who were owned by titleholders.

Persons could be members of houses, but could not themselves hold land. They might control a parcel of land under the general direction of the head titleholder of the house. Houses are a kinship-based membership corporate group.

Comparisons

On the Northwest Coast, houses are the entities with relationships to land. 'Individual' as a position that can hold land is not part of the system. Persons can hold roles in houses, however, and one might accidentally call such persons individuals. Houses have many positions (titles); this is similar to corporations having many positions (jobs). House and territory are connected in a way that is different from the system in which exchange is possible. Parcels of land are defined by deeds and other instruments; on the Northwest Coast, parcels of land are defined by the oral history of the house, which is recognized each time the control of the land changes. In private property systems, this same function is played by government offices and title insurance companies, which can provide a purchaser with a record of the ownership of a parcel of land. The two systems are similar in that the history of a parcel is necessary for 'clear title.' They are different because titles are roles connected to territories in the Northwest Coast system, whereas job descriptions apply to corporations, which are not tied to specific territories.

The word title means different things in each system. In the Northwest Coast system, titles are the names that describe the official positions within a house. In private property systems, a title is the document that describes a parcel of land and is registered with the government.

Boundary rules

Boundary rules govern who enters or exits from positions. Boundary rules describe the process of putting particular persons and groups into the roles available. For instance, to have a position as a member of a house in the Northwest Coast, kinship with the members of the house provides one basis for inclusion.

Private property

The primary method of an individual (person or a corporation) entering the role of 'landowner' for a piece of land is either purchase or inheritance. Being able to pay the purchase price defines the ability to become a landowner. Bankers can assist an individual in purchasing by lending money. Qualifying for a loan means meeting the requirements set by bankers, which involves having adequate income and few other debts. For corporation, ownership is attained by purchasing shares. This is stated in the grammar: 'An individual must pay the price desired by the seller of a parcel of land in order to become the owner of the land.'

Exit consists of accepting the amount to be paid for the land by another individual wishing to be an owner. Non-voluntary exit from the role of landowner would occur if a loan could not be repaid, in which case a banker would engage a court in taking possession of the land from the owner who could not pay the mortgage.

Contingent proprietorship

In the Northwest Coast, a great deal of attention was paid to the process of assigning titles to persons. Sales and purchases were not part of the system. Upon the death of a chief, the head title position would be vacant. A chief and his relatives would have trained a designated successor, who would temporarily take the position after the death. This is stated in the grammar: 'In order to become a titleholder, a person must be eligible by kinship and training.' During a period of time, usually a year, the successor would accumulate the necessary goods to hold a pole-raising feast containing a potlatch or distribution of goods to other titleholders. This would add another condition to being a titleholder: in order to become a titleholder, a person eligible by kinship and training must sponsor a feast and acquire approval of other titleholders. Enough goods had to be collected to impress other titleholders. This made entrance to the role of titleholder depend upon the approval of the house members, through their willingness to work for the candidate and provide the wealth needed in the potlatch feast. By accepting the distributed wealth, the other titleholders would approve of the acquisition of the title by the designated heir. Although the feast provided evidence of the ability to accumulate wealth through the efforts of other members of the house, the designated heir would need to recite correctly, from memory, the history of the house.

Anthropologist Antonia Mills summarizes the rules for entrance and exit to the chief's role as follows:

> Having a chief's name is an honour and a responsibility, requiring the holder to act correctly and with decorum. ... Those who desire to receive feast names know that they have to earn them and maintain them through proper conduct; in the same way, those who are worthy of names must be treated with the respect due to such titles. ... If someone given the honour and responsibility of being a chief does not live up to expectations, the title may be taken away.
> (Mills 1994a: 136)

Exit from a titleholding position by a means other than death was unusual in the Pacific Northwest. The reason for removal would be failure to care for land and to be generous to people of the house and other titleholders. Removing a titleholder required considerable effort on the part of the titleholder's family and house. The Nisga'a claim that they seldom had to remove titleholders, because the training and selection process meant that this was rarely needed. Among the Kwakwaka'wakw and the Nuu-chah-nulth, it was possible to kill titleholders who failed to carry out their duties. Among other groups, titleholders could be allowed to be captured as slaves; a house would avoid reinstating the titleholder by refusing to pay the ransom (Walens 1981; Donald 1997).

Comparisons

The large role played by kinship and approval by other titleholders in structuring entrance into positions is absent in the private property system. Buying and selling land is not present in the Northwest Coast system. Titleholders and chief executive officers of corporations both have to be qualified; but individuals in purchasing land only need to have the money to pay the price. They have to meet qualifications if they borrow funds. But as an individual, a corporation doesn't have to demonstrate knowledge of land that it purchases. Separately, a corporation does have to show that it can produce a profit from all of its holdings. Control of land in the Northwest Coast system requires knowledge of the history of the land as well as knowledge about how to manage it. These knowledge requirements continue after the roles have been assumed.

Choices

Choice rules describe what holders of positions may, may not, or must, do. Choice rules do not involve setting conditions of entry and exit to positions, or choices that deal with the other categories of rules, such as sharing benefits or managing information. Choice rules are primarily those that define the management authority of owners. Both systems allocate much management authority to those who control land.

Private property

Legal analyst J. E. Penner defines the ownership of property as:

> the right to determine the use or disposition of a separable thing (i.e., a thing whose contingent association with any particular person is essentially impersonal and so imports nothing of normative consequence), in so far as that can be achieved or aided by others excluding themselves from it, and includes the rights to abandon it, to share it, to license it to others (either exclusively or not), and to give it to others in its entirety.
>
> (Penner 1997: 152)

This definition focuses on the positions of owner and thing, the boundary rules for exit from the role of owner, and the choices open to the owner. He describes this definition as the result of an 'underlying strategy … to isolate those norms which most closely characterize the practice of dealing with things that we recognize as property.' The 'we' in his statement refers to people who study law, particularly in England. His definition addresses boundary, choice, and payoff rules.

His definition begins by stating that the owner may use his property, and then gives a list of the main things a manager can do. Individuals who are not owners of an item of property must exclude themselves from the property, unless given permission by the owner. The definition also addresses matters such as entrance and exit from the role of owner, by referring to the power to give property to others.

Penner's definition of property is noteworthy in that he does not include the power to sell as part of the definition; instead, he places the power of buying and selling within the area of contract law, not property law. He acknowledges that this distinction is not usual in defining ownership.

Another author, John Christman (1994), maintains that at the core of ownership in his schema is that a holder must have final say over the use of a thing, such as a territory, versus all other people or all other groups of people. He uses the example of a lease: the lessee (the landowner) issues a lease with particular terms. The lessor may have most of the modalities of ownership signed over for a period of time. But the origin of the lease was a decision by the landowner, and at the end of the lease the land reverts to the owner. Also, usually the conditions of a lease impose duties on the lessor, such as not to waste the value of the item leased through poor practices, lack of maintenance, and so forth, which apply to the lessor but do not apply to the owner. Christman, in line with others writing about ownership, includes the power to sell.

In the case of private property, courts enforce the prohibition of trespass; owners have to involve the police and the law enforcement system in order to prevent others from entering the land. The rule is: 'a court must enforce the right of a landowner to exclude whom he pleases.'

Both Penner and Christman are concerned primarily with individuals as owners. In private property systems, governments can own land. Governments have legal jurisdiction over privately owned land, which they do not own; but they can own other land with the same powers as other owners. A rule may exist, however, that prohibits a government from excluding its citizens from its land. The sale of land owned by a government involves the rules for decision-making within the government in question. Similarly, corporations have rules about who in the corporation has the authority to sell assets; often the board of directors must approve large sales and purchases of assets.

Contingent proprietorship

Turning to the Northwest Coast, Penner's list of allowed actions describes fairly well the choices open to a titleholder, except that disposition of the territory and complete discretion about payoffs are not among the powers of the titleholder. He may nominate his successor; but that nomination is subject to ratification after the titleholder's death. Abandoning the territory is also not an option, since others have claims and rights, which are discussed below. A titleholder could abandon his title; but the title is tied to the land and could not be separated from it.

The requirement that others exclude themselves from the land is one of the most emphasized rules describing the Northwest Coast system. A common full version of the law is that 'no-one may enter a territory without permission from the titleholder, or else upon the third violation the titleholder may kill the trespasser.' This rule provided an enforcement mechanism. It was tempered in many cases by another rule, that should a titleholder kill someone for trespassing, a compensatory feast had to be given to the relatives of the deceased person.

These two rules, that anyone who entered the territory of a chief had to follow his instructions, and that he could exclude whom he wanted, are shared with private property powers of owners. One exception is that persons with a kinship claim to enter a house territory could not be excluded unless he or she refused to follow the instructions of the titleholder. Although the mistaken identification of the Northwest Coast system with private property makes some sense, these rights of relatives to enter the house territory demonstrate a difference.

Comparisons

Both systems are similar in that holders of land have great authority over decisions regarding that land. Landowners can exclude anybody. Titleholders can exclude anybody without a kinship claim to membership in the house, or anybody who does not obey the titleholder. Land held by the state may or may not have rules of exclusion. Often the default rule is that anyone who is a citizen of the state may enter lands held by the state. The key for state-owned land is that some land, and associated resources, are potentially open-access. For particularly valuable resources, such as standing timber, the state sets up rules to control access and obtain a share of the value. Also, those on the Northwest Coast have some rules about proper behavior towards fish; titleholders are expected to enforce rules about proper behavior, such as protecting spawning beds or keeping streams clear.

As we examine the other comparisons, however, major differences between private property and the Northwest Coast system will be evident.

Aggregation: who makes choices

Ostrom's fourth category of rules is about the rules for joint decision-making. Rules for making decisions describe how some of the other characteristics of the system are carried out. For instance, in discussion of entrance and exit from the role of titleholder in the Northwest Coast, I mentioned that the decision to allow a person to become a titleholder in a house involved approval from the chiefs of other houses.

Private property

For private property, aggregation focuses on the owner's ability to decide without review by anyone except officers of the state enforcing police powers and protecting other owners from harm. This is the 'sovereignty' model of property, in which landowners are sovereign except for the powers of the greater sovereign, the state. In democracies, the selection of rules to use in applying police powers is done through the election and law-making procedures of the community in question.

Local governments, for instance, can impose restrictions on use through their zoning authority. In the United States, the Fifth Amendment to the Constitution states that governments may not confiscate private property without providing compensation. Courts define the difference between police powers, which do not require compensation, and the requirements of the Fifth Amendment.

When property is owned by an organization such as a corporation, the rules for aggregation are typically determined by the charter of the corporation. Most such charters have a board of directors, elected by shareholders, who are the ultimate authority for the corporation. The board of directors delegate day-to-day management to a chief executive officer.

In a system of private property, disputes about who owns land are settled by courts, based on the sets of rules summarized by Penner and Christman, who utilize legal precedent to define ownership and liability for damages to property.

Contingent proprietorship

In the Northwest Coast system, once a titleholder has office, he has considerable authority over what occurs on the territory he manages; 'sovereignty' may be a good description of the degree of authority, subject to the procedures for possible removal from office. Yet, although the titleholder has great authority over what decisions he makes, the ultimate power of his subjects and other titleholders to remove him from office if certain rules are violated needs to be recognized.

Other issues about title can arise, however. If there is a dispute about who should be managing a territory, the question arises: who determines the outcome of the dispute? The answer is that the head titleholders, together, consult to determine the outcome. Among the Wet'suwet'en, for instance, disputes over succession are resolved in the feast hall (Mills 1994a). The methods used for reaching agreement are the topic of the next chapter; the basic approach is to seek consensus.

Comparisons

Both systems are similar in that chief operating officers (head titleholder or CEO) have considerable authority while in office. They differ on the rules of who can install and remove these officers. A corporation allows the owners' representatives, the board of directors, to make this decision. On the Northwest Coast, a new titleholder must be approved both by members of the house (by assisting in amassing wealth) and by other titleholders (by accepting the wealth transfers). Dispute resolution is different, in that private property systems have courts to enforce the rules, and the Northwest Coast uses agreement among titleholders.

Both systems allow property owners to settle disagreements through direct negotiation. A shared strategy on the Northwest Coast is that dispute resolution begins with an invitation to a meal; the invitation may indicate what is to be discussed. Explicit rules about negotiation are not clear in private property systems, except that all such disputes can eventually be submitted to the state's court system to be settled under the rules of property law and contract law.

Transfer of land from one individual to another is done through sales agreement, based on a willing seller and a willing buyer. The decision to sell is solely at the discretion of the owner, as the decision to purchase is at the discretion of the buyer, subject only to conditions imposed by a lender if the buyer has insufficient cash.

Transfer of land among houses is, in the first instance, not normally part of the system. If something has occurred that means one house needs to compensate another house in order to settle a dispute, then territory can be transferred with the approval of all the titleholders who are in a feasting relationship with the houses making the transfer. Such a transfer is then recorded in the oral histories of the two houses, so that the extent of each house's territory is clear to everyone.

Information

Rules about information describe what people in positions know as they interact with each other in an action situation. They describe what information may be exchanged, must be exchanged, or may not be exchanged. The rules address the frequency of communication and the allowed subjects for communication. Ostrom focuses on information: data about the transactions being addressed. The information category could also refer to levels of knowledge that are required. Such levels of knowledge are often used as a kind of boundary rule: persons must have certain levels of knowledge in order to enter a position.

Private property

In a private property system, knowledge about a territory belongs to the owner of the territory, and he or she is not required to share it with others. Private property systems are accompanied by a strong set of privacy rules, which allow the owner of land to keep to himself or herself the characteristics of that land, and of most of the transactions undertaken. Non-interference in activities on the land extends to non-interference about the qualities of the land and the activities on it. For property owned by corporate entities, the knowledge of managers is expected to be high. Their salaries are justified by their ability to use corporate property for good profit. Qualification to be a manager could be described as a knowledge standard, rather than an information standard.

The privacy rules that accompany private property systems do not require that transactions be public. Sometimes sales of land have to be reported; in other jurisdictions the prices remain secret, a rule that complicates the efforts of appraisers to provide estimates of true market value.

Contingent proprietorship

On the Northwest Coast, Suttles (1987) reports that the titleholders were thought to have special knowledge; that knowledge partly justified their positions of power in the system. Thus titleholders were not required to share all knowledge with commoners. We have seen already that a condition for a titleholder to take control of a territory was that he or she demonstrate knowledge of its history. This knowledge, however, was not secret. Part of it had to be revealed in the feast hall to demonstrate a titleholder's right of succession. A titleholder had to be able to demonstrate knowledge of management through productive use of it.

While knowledge about how to care for land could be secret, information about transactions was not secret. Feasts in many communities had roles for people who were 'counters,' who kept track of what was collected and distributed. All contributions were announced as they occurred. The Nisg̱a'a describe this as a fundamental basis of the accountability of their leaders.

Comparisons

The two systems vary greatly. The Northwest Coast system has much less privacy and secrecy than the private property system. Particularly noteworthy is that all the transactions at feasts are announced publicly. Exchanges and sales in a private property system are generally known only to the parties to an exchange, unless a government with jurisdiction over sales contracts requires that the information by recorded when the new owner of title to land is registered in the government's title office.

Payoff

Another set of rules are those that describe the payoffs of interactions in an action situation. For comparisons of territorial systems of land tenure, payoff rules describe the rights to receive the 'rent' for land: the residual between the costs of production and returns from the sale of products.

Private property

In private property systems, the owner has full rights to rental income. The owner may lease the land, and the lease may include providing shares of the net income as a method of dealing with risk. But the decision to lease land on a share basis is made with the full consent of the owner; he or she is not obligated to sign share leases with owners of capital or labor who wish to lease land. Economists recognize this rule by saying that landowners are the 'residual claimants': if they undertake an activity that involves hiring people, buying goods, and selling what is produced, the owner receives the net value, the difference between revenue and costs. Multiple owners of a parcel of land receive their share of the residual amounts in proportion to their degree of ownership of the land.

Contingent proprietorship

Reciprocity obligations on the Pacific Northwest Coast define the payoff rules. Chapter 4 deals with the rules of reciprocity in the Northwest Coast systems. Proprietors of territories are not able to keep the residual profit or return for themselves. Not only must they share with other titleholders, they are obligated to provide access to land to those who have the proper kinship relations with the land. As long as those who have rights of access follow the policies of the titleholder, access must be given.

But the share given to the titleholder might appear large. Walens describes the metaphor used among the Kwakiutl to apportion gross returns from land – boxes. Harvesters filled boxes, with certain quantities going to the titleholder before going to the laborers. The sizes of the boxes thus define rentals due the house and wage rates for harvesters.

Is the obligation to share that of the titleholder, or is it the obligation of the house? Ultimately, the obligation belongs to the house. The titleholder acts on behalf of the house. As stated in the grammar: 'a house must share a portion of its income with neighboring houses, or else those houses will coordinate action and determine a solution.' The titleholder is responsible for complying with this rule.

Comparison

As explained in Chapter 4, the big difference between the systems is in sharing net returns, which solves the prisoners' dilemma for salmon fishing. The lack of sharing supports the dilemma for private owners, since salmon migrate and can't be owned by people in a territorial system until they are captured. Thus the two systems have a profound difference when the items being harvested are common pool goods. The private property system creates a situation where anything harvested in common becomes the full property of the individual who harvested the fish, or deer, or beaver.

With regard to the production of goods that are not common pool goods, such as berries, the Northwest Coast system also prescribes that some of the net return be shared with others. Some of the others who share are people who have rights to membership in a house. Others who share are the people who receive transfers of goods during a potlatch feast. In a private property system, all the net return goes to the owner, who is the 'residual claimant' as described by economists.

People who are concerned about the inequality of wealth that develops in a private property system have focused upon the ownership claims of the residual claimants of that system. Philosopher John Christman, for instance, opens his book, *The Myth of Property*, with a quotation from Proudhon, who also objected to the returns from land going only to the owner. Christman proceeds to make a case within the European philosophical tradition that owners should not be able to retain all of the residual from their property, thus supporting a more equal distribution of income. He builds his case on the ground that all individuals have a right to autonomously managing their own lives, which does not entail keeping all of the profit from property held by an individual. Henry George also proposed that land rentals not be considered as belonging to landowners. These authors both focus upon changing the payoff rules and do not address changes in other components.

Scope

Scope rules are rules that do not fit easily into the other categories; generally scope rules affect the nature of outcomes. Scope rules are distinguished from choice rules as follows: choice rules describe actions; scope rules describe out-comes. Some of the special characteristics of the Northwest Coast system should be described as scope rules. In particular, what is allowed to be owned or held by a house is a type of scope rule. The requirements that a chief respect animals and fish is another type of scope rule.

Private property

In a private property system, the police powers of the nation state often limit the scope of choices available to landowners. For instance, emissions of toxic chemi-cals may be limited. Such rules could be classified either as 'choice' or as 'scope.' For instance, a power plant may be limited in the quantity of sulfuric acid or mer-cury that it can emit. If this is described as an action (emissions of mercury must be below a specified level of parts per million), then the rule is best classified as a choice rule, according to Ostrom. If the rule specifies an outcome (the level of mercury in a river must remain below a specified amount), then the rule could be classified as a scope rule. If many people are affecting a particular outcome, regulation on actions may be easier to carry out than regulation of outcomes.

In private property systems, establishment of a fiduciary trust represents the application of a scope rule: a fiduciary, while given full control to property, must maintain the value of the property. A fiduciary must protect a property against mon-etary loss. In fact, there are many scope rules applied to judge whether or not a fidu-ciary has carried out his duty to take care of an asset on behalf of the beneficiary.

In western Canada and the United States, landownership is usually based upon surveys conducted by governments, which laid out grids used to locate land. In the United States, the landscape was divided into townships six miles on a side, and sections each one mile on a side. In the eastern states, where the holding of land began before the surveys were laid out, defining parcels is less straightfor-ward. The governments held for themselves lands that did not go into the private property system. When Indians were confined to reserves or reservations, this allocation also excluded some lands from the private property system.

Certain lands were defined as not being subject to alienation through the prop-erty system. In the United States, navigable waters remained under the control of the federal government. Similarly, in Canada, courts and the federal government held that private property could not be granted for fishing sites. One result of this has been that aboriginally recognized control of fishing sites was not recognized, opening the fisheries in British Columbia to everyone (Harris 2001: 29–33). In both countries, the federal government can create rules that govern the general public right to fish; but private rights cannot be granted. In some cases the federal powers to supervise fisheries have been transferred to states in navigable waters.

Contingent proprietorship

In non-ownership systems such as on the Northwest Coast, rules that describe the expected condition of resources that are under a titleholder's control could be classified as scope rules. On the Northwest Coast, titleholders were expected to care for their land. An outcome, then, is that 'land shall not be degraded.' Another, related, scope rule results from beliefs in reincarnation: persons were assumed to exist in many different cycles, so that the condition of the land would affect them in the future, as it had affected them in the past.

In the Pacific Northwest, all of the landscape was under the control of one or another house. This included fishing sites, which were particularly important. Beaches were also owned. This contrasts with the common law doctrine in the private property systems that fishing was a public right in navigable waters.

Comparisons

The scope rules differ in terms of what is required of landowners. They also differ in terms of what land is considered to be within the territoriality system. On the Northwest Coast, all territory (including beaches and near-shore areas of the ocean) had to be held by one or another house. In nation-states, all land is held either by the state or in private property. Some of the land held by the state is viewed as held in common by all citizens, such as public waterways and shorelines below the high-tide mark, with the state not being allowed to move such property to private property.

An interesting difference in scope rules was illustrated by Barbara Lane (1973) in her testimony regarding differences in territoriality systems and their implications for interpretation of the treaties signed by Isaac Stevens in Washington Territory. During the negotiations, a Makah chief asked Stevens who would own a whale that had been killed and washed up on a beach. Stevens wanted to know who had captured and killed the whale, because that would determine who owned the whale. For the Makah, the answer was that the whale belonged to the chief on whose beach it had landed. The Makah rule would not work for Governor Stevens, because the beach could not be owned under the laws of his government.

The Northwest Coast had rules requiring the quality of land being managed to be held constant or improved. That humans have a duty to care for the land, meaning healthy outcomes for the land, is present in the Northwest Coast system but absent in the private property system. An owner of land in a private property system could choose to preserve its productivity; but the owner could also choose to use up the land's productivity, and then abandon the land.

Summary: comparison of territoriality systems

This chapter focuses on the territorial aspects of the Northwest Coast systems that distinguish them from territorial systems in use today. While private property and proprietorship systems are similar in the degrees of control given to the persons occupying the positions of 'owner' and 'titleholder,' they differ greatly in the rules of entry and exit into those positions. In contemporary systems, entry and exit is through purchase and sale. In proprietorship systems, sale is not an option. Entry into chieftainship depends upon compliance with rules that ensure qualification for the role, and maintenance of the role depends upon continuing demonstration of competence. I have called this 'contingent proprietorship.' The contingent part of the name refers to this need to maintain qualification. The proprietorship refers to the absence of the option of sale.

Whether or not the contingent proprietorship system should be described as a 'property' system depends upon what set of rules one implicitly accepts as defining 'property.' Authors such as Penner and Christman emphasize full control over property as a key to ownership. Penner emphasizes the power to exclude others, which intersects with Northwest Coast ideas. While agreeing that ownership does involve full control of income, Christman objects to full rights to income from property; he would find the reciprocity systems defining alternate rights to payoffs to be an interesting feature of the Northwest Coast. He builds an alternative model that limits full rights to income.

But Christman's proposal would not go as far as the system in the Pacific Northwest. Other components of contingency are that titleholders had to:

- comply with requirements to share, both with members of their house and with other titleholders
- maintain the quality of the land
- retain the support of members of their house
- demonstrate knowledge of the history of their land and the land of other houses
- train their successors.

The inability to buy and sell converts the system to proprietorship; the three requirements of sharing income, demonstrating knowledge, and caring for land mean that proprietorship is contingent, not absolute.

I began this chapter with quotations about property from economist Martin Bailey. His statement: 'the structure of rights tends to respond to economic incentives' (Bailey 1992: 192) or 'reflect economic advantage' is unexceptionable if one is open-minded about the meaning of 'economic incentives' or 'economic advantage.' Usually those terms are to be interpreted within the normal economics paradigm, which is not generally one that supports ideas of resilience and sustainability that are advocated in this book.

But Bailey does open the door to the task of this book in his introduction. 'The study of aboriginals,' he says, 'can make especially clear the advantages of one type of property right over another because, in most cases, these people lived at the margin of subsistence. ... Unsound rights structures generally implied lower population size and, perhaps, the disappearance of the society. ... One therefore expects the data on aboriginals to provide relatively direct evidence on the structure of an optimal system of property rights under various circumstances' (*ibid.*: 183–84).

His use of 'optimal' must be interpreted carefully. From an economist, it means 'optimal' in the sense of 'maximizing the present value of human satisfaction from the production of goods and services.' But optimal could mean 'resilient.' Because of his reference to the possibility of the disappearance of society, Bailey could be interpreted as making the same argument that I am making in this book. As I argued in Chapter 3, 'optimal' from an economist means accepting a strong present orientation in the evaluation of human satisfaction by use of the present value formula. That formula does not allow for consideration of long-term survival of a society. Bailey, however, writes as if he is considering long-term survival.

I have argued that the word property contains presuppositions about the separability of land from people, and about the presence of a market in land. If one replaces 'property rights' with 'territorial system,' then one could rewrite Bailey to say, 'One therefore expects the data on aboriginals to provide relatively direct evidence on the structure of a resilient territorial system under various circumstances.' 'Optimal' is replaced by 'resilient' and 'property rights' by 'territorial system' with its own rules.

The territoriality rules of contingent proprietorship provide enforcement mechanisms for other components of a sustainable social ecological system. The territoriality rules are only part of the entire system. A system of ethics, as described in Chapter 3, is one important component. Another is a system of reciprocity, as described in Chapter 4. The present chapter describes the rules governing a territorial system. All these components do not operate automatically; the system needs to be run by someone, as addressed by the 'aggregation' category. The Gitxsan and Wet'suwet'en explained the connection as follows:

> The roles of the Chief are not limited to those relating to the proprietorship or stewardship of the territory. Both within the Feast Hall and outside of it, the hereditary Chiefs mediate and resolve disputes between House members, between Houses, and with neighbouring Indian nations. Sometimes the exercise of this peace-keeping and conflict resolution role is highly visible in the Feast Hall; at other times his authority is exercised informally, operating through consensus and consultation.
>
> (Gisday Wa and Delgam Uukw 1992: 33)

This list of the additional roles of chiefs connects the territoriality system to a general system of governance. The principles of governance are the topic of the next chapter, which deals with questions of governance and the ways in which leaders kept the whole system operating.

6 Chiefs empower generous facilitators to resolve conflicts

In the late 1980s and early 1990s, a conflict developed in British Columbia over clearcutting of the rain forest on Vancouver Island in Clayoquot Sound, on the west coast of the island. The conflict had two bases. One was unresolved land claims of the Nuu-chah-nulth people; this issue led to an injunction stopping logging on Meares Island in 1985. The second grew out of efforts of environmental organizations to stop the clearcutting that had removed so much forest on the rest of Vancouver Island. Several attempts to resolve the conflict dissolved in further dissension. In the summer of 1993, a large act of civil disobedience, a blockade of a key bridge, received worldwide media attention. A public participation process had produced no agreement, and environmentalists disliked a land-use decision that the Province had issued after that process. Although the Nuu-chah-nulth did not engage in that blockade, they were also unhappy with the land-use decision (Berman *et al.* 1994).

In October 1993, the Province appointed a Scientific Panel for Sustainable Forest Practices in Clayoquot Sound (1995). The Panel consisted of 15 scientists and four elders from the Nuu-chah-nulth. The Clayoquot Sound Scientific Panel was co-chaired by Dr Fred Bunnell, a professor of wildlife ecology, and Dr Richard Atleo, a hereditary chief from Ahouset, one of the villages within the Nuu-chah-nulth. Both Dr Bunnell, a Quaker, and Dr Atleo were familiar with methods of achieving consensus in groups. Dr Atleo and the three other First Nations elders urged that the Panel adopt 'the Nuu-chah-nulth inclusive process for discussion and sharing to reach agreement.' In their first report, the Scientific Panel described this protocol as follows:

> The protocol reflects the Nuu-Chah-Nulth approach to group processes whereby all members participate in determining the issues, information, and actions relevant to the Panel's task. It is characterized by a demonstrable and inclusive respect for one another, for different values, and for data founded both in science and 'lived experience.' It calls for each Panel member to exercise patience, flexibility, tolerance, endurance, and faith in a process and task that are surrounded by conflict and turmoil.
>
> (Scientific Panel for Sustainable Forest Practices in Clayoquot Sound 1994a: 5)

The Nuu-chah-nulth had the leverage to insist on this protocol; because of pending land claims, the Province needed to have them participate. That leverage was complemented by Dr Bunnell's receptiveness to an inclusive process. He was familiar with such a process, used by the Religious Society of Friends, the Quakers. A footnote in the third report of the Panel, on First Nations perspectives, identified this connection without linking it directly to Dr Bunnell (Scientific Panel for Sustainable Forest Practices in Clayoquot Sound 1995a: 5).

The Scientific Panel succeeded in creating a report that received widespread support. The report integrates scientific and traditional knowledge, proposing variable retention as a harvest strategy. The Panel had asked for a gradual acceptance and implementation of its over 120 recommendations; the Minister of Forests adopted them all at once. While implementation has been slow, the Panel's recommendations have remained the focus of forest planning in Clayoquot Sound (Mabee and Hoberg 2006).

The Panel's report does not provide details on what actions the Nuu-chah-nulth elders would take when the Panel reached roadblocks in its deliberations. David Lertzman, a business school instructor and brother to one of the Panel members, interviewed Panel members in order to learn more about how the process worked. He provided two quotations from Dr Nancy Turner which provided some insight into what the protocol meant for the members:

> We used the Nuu-Chah-Nulth protocols for working together, we agreed on that right to begin with and part of that protocol was that we all solemnly committed ourselves, not only to listening to what other people told and what other people said and believe, but in trying to understand what other people said, in really trying ... hard to understand ... that's one step further than just listening and listening, in itself, is one step further than many people will go
>   ... there were times when people were ready almost to give up and that we could never really come to any kind of agreement and we always, at that point, would go back to the original protocol, think it through, listen more carefully, talk about it, discuss it and then find a way of getting around whatever problem that was ...
>
> (Lertzman 2006: 14)

David Lertzman described the Nuu-chah-nulth inclusive process as follows: 'In current management jargon, we might refer to this approach as a consensus-based management model using a participatory planning style with inclusive decision-making' (*ibid.*: 15). In other words, it is more than any one of those three.

That each member of the Panel had to listen carefully and with respect to every other member is a powerful principle for aiding communication. That all members of the Panel had to agree with recommendations assisted in the quality of the recommendations.

But consensus decision-making has some problems, as Richard Atleo later described:

During the early 1940s, Keesta's son Ahinchate (George Shamrock), who was by then my grandfather, would take me along to his councils. ... Ahinchat and his councillors would sit in a circle and place each item, or issue, of an agenda into the middle of the circle. These councils were sharply focused on issues and their resolutions, rather than on the sorts of personal agendas that often complicate modern decision making. A major feature of this traditional process was the acknowledgment of every member of a council concerning each issue at hand.

While this decision-making process ensured every council member's input on every issue under discussion, it also required an unusual amount of patience, self-control, tolerance, trust, faith, and respect. Patience was required because of the likelihood that there would be a constant repetition of ideas. Hence, whereas a modern meeting might address an issue in ten minutes, Ahinchat's meetings might have expended thirty or more minutes on the same issue.

(Atleo 2004: 88)

Surely 30 minutes is an underestimate when everyone may speak – why is the increase so small? I suspect that other rules have not been reported. The San Carlos Apache have the same rule that everyone may speak. But they also have another rule, that no-one is worth listening to if they take too long to express their idea. I heard this as advice from an employee of the San Carlos elders' council, when he was advising academics about how to approach the council. He urged them not to be long-winded, because the elders would begin to worry about their intelligence. This rule complements the rule that everyone may speak, by requiring short comments. I have not heard it articulated on the Northwest Coast, but would not be surprised to find it. Perhaps a related rule was that the councils consisted of those holding titles, the named positions. To a modern person, to hear that everyone would speak would indeed lead to fears of very long meetings. Yet Chief Umeek says the time is only tripled.

Among the Nuu-chah-nulth, actions could be taken even if not everyone agreed with the final decision. In order to explain this, Richard Atleo tells the story of a decision in his community about a children's recreational facility:

While most decisions were unanimous, others were not. In the case of a minority disagreement, it was usual for the conflict to be openly admitted. A case in point is a decision made by a traditional chiefs' council during the mid-1950s to build a recreational platform for children. The day following the decision, the community turned out in force to begin bringing in the small logs and lumber. One man was found working just as diligently as the other men of the community even though he continued loudly to disagree with the decision because he thought it was not workable. Now, had the project failed, one can imagine that there would have been a rise in community esteem for this one dissenter. As it turned out, the project was a success, and the dissenter just as loudly proclaimed that, even though he had been against the project at the beginning, he could now see he was mistaken.

(Atleo 2004: 89–90)

This story explains that when one person dissents, the decision can go ahead. The dissenter was recognized, but he pitched in and helped in constructing the facility. He had a chance of being right, but once the consequences of the decision were visible, he had to admit his mistake. The requirement that all agree is not absolute.

The experience of the Clayoquot Sound Scientific Panel suggests that one of the peoples of the Northwest Coast had a system of public discussion of problems which was capable of integrating diverse viewpoints and determining a solution. The previous three chapters have discussed three very distinctive features of the Northwest Coast system: world view, public reciprocity, and territoriality. The world view, particularly the belief in reincarnation, created a system of ethics which encouraged rewarding actions that kept a system in good condition for future generations. The distribution of goods at feasts created incentives that facilitated good fisheries management, by discouraging excessive investment in fishing gear as competing houses sought to harvest fish. The sharing of the wealth from the ocean created by the reciprocity system dealt with the prisoners' dilemma faced by fishermen. The territorial system of houses and titleholders provided additional ways for members of the societies to make their leaders accountable for good stewardship of the lands and waters upon which the people depended. The territorial system gave clear responsibility to titleholders for good stewardship of their house lands and for the runs of salmon that passed through their weirs. If that responsibility was not carried out, ways existed for the leaders to be removed from office. The members of a house could either kill a titleholder or arrange for his abduction. Other titleholders could withhold approval of his leadership by refusing to accept the distribution of wealth at feasts. All of these characteristics are plausibly related to the long-term resilience of the system.

The regional political structure of the system also contributed to the long-term resilience of the Northwest Coast social–ecological system. The feasting system provided a forum in which titleholders and others resolved conflict. It also provided a way for titleholders to deal with crises, whether arising from inside or outside the system. One should expect that a system that persisted for several millennia would have a method of dealing with crises which would have an impact on all the houses.

When the Nuu-chah-nulth elders proposed that the Panel use its principles of dispute resolution and public decision-making, they recommended principles that appear to have been widely shared on the Northwest Coast, although the specific manifestations of the ideas may have differed from area to area. Antonia Mills described the role of the feast hall in governance among the Wet'suwet'en:

> The feast hall ... is a forum in which people can express their different points of view and their grievances, and where they can find either an immediate or a slow resolution to a recognized conflict. While many of the issues to be settled involve territory, other matters are resolved as well. The head chiefs guide the resolution of differences because they have been acknowledged as the correct leaders through their succession to the highest names, all of which have been validated by the feast itself.
>
> (Mills 1994a: 71)

If resolution of a dispute took many meetings, then the chiefs took the time needed in order to find a solution that had consensus support. The Gitxsan also settled such issues by engaging in consensus-building processes (Gisday Wa and Delgam Uukw 1992). During a feast, guests are invited to speak, and any public business that needs attention can be placed before the assembly. Sides take turn speaking, there is no limit placed on the time for any speaker, and any decision is reached by consensus of the chiefs present. If no consensus is reached, the matter will be postponed to another feast. If other villages need to be involved, a feast will be scheduled to invite them to discuss the matter (Mills 1994a: 43–71).

Many sources report that warfare was a common occurrence all along the Northwest Coast. Sometimes it became quite serious. Other times it was moderate and brought under control (Donald 1997; Sterritt *et al.* 1998). The peaceful times may have been created by application of processes such as the Nuu-chah-nulth inclusive process. Johnsen (1986) points out that providing goods to neighboring titleholders was probably a cheaper way to protect proprietorship than was investment in defensive military action.

Because the head titleholders were expected to solve problems, the standards for being a chief included having the needed characteristics. A Nisg̲a'a school district text describes the requirements of a chief as follows:

> Many personality traits were regarded as being necessary for a Chief. He had to be an able leader, and an eloquent speaker. He had to project a proud image to strangers while being generous and congenial toward his own people. He had to be a model of good taste and conduct. He had to be able to command wealth and distribute it to the benefit and renown of his people. He had to rely on the good will and co-operation of his people.
>
> (McKay 1982: 39)

The rulers were also constrained by the need to seek acceptance and approval from other titleholders. A person claiming a title had to demonstrate worthiness by conducting potlatches, in which he gave away wealth to other titleholders. The accumulation of the wealth for a potlatch required support from a claimant's relatives. This requirement provided 'commoners' with influence regarding who of those with claim to a title would receive their support. It appears that in some tribes there was open competition for titles in this way, while in other tribes the rights of the eldest children were more secure.

Michael Harkin describes the situation among the Heiltsuk, who live just north of the Kwakwak'wakw:

> The possession of a chiefly title, which would be inherited in early middle age, implied control of resources and thus the ability, as well as the right, to distribute wealth. Successfully discharging these duties required political skill and moral authority, for although the office of the chief was held in great respect, it was rather lacking in enforcement powers. Chiefs cajoled and

persuaded their kinsmen and clansmen to work toward a potlatch or a feast, which would in turn add to the chief's prestige and authority.

(Harkin 1997: 8–9)

The existence of social stratification would seem to be inconsistent with the inclusiveness stressed by the Nuu-chah-nulth, Nisg̱a'a, Wet'suwet'en, and Gitxsan. Yet, as Harkin reports, the power of these leaders seems to be constrained. The emphasis on the authority of the head titleholder in a house is addressed on the Gitxsan website (www.gitxsan.com). They point out that the issue of a chief becoming dictatorial was a concern; the following quotation describes the situation, referring to the Gitxsan name for a house, wilp, and the Gitxsan word for a house history, *adaawk*:

> The Wilp is a political unit with a considerable degree of autonomy. Each Wilp controls most of its own affairs, yet the chief's power never becomes dictatorial. In fact, dictatorial power is a matter of serious concerns expressed in the adaawk.
>
> One essential reason why the power of a Wilp chief could not become dictatorial is that power within a Wilp is not exclusively held by the chief. Each Wilp has a set of ranked names with power and authority generally corresponding with the rank of the name. There are gradations in rank as well. The Wilp chief is the highest authority and is the spokesperson on behalf of Wilp members. Wilp members with adult names and a seat in the feast hall make up the third gradation in rank within the Wilp. The rest of the Wilp members are actually children or are adults who are children in the feast system.
>
> (Gitxsan Chiefs' Office 2007)

That people born into the chiefs' families were the ones able to obtain chiefly roles does suggest unequal opportunity among the people in these societies. That only some people were eligible for the role of chief is uncomfortable for people from individualistic societies such as England, Canada, and the United States. The general rise of individual rights in the twentieth and twenty-first centuries causes a visceral antipathy toward the hierarchical principles evident on the Northwest Coast.

In explaining Nuu-chah-nulth society, Chief Umeek (Richard Atleo) recognizes these feelings. He tells of arranged marriages in which members of extended families tell young people from each family who they will marry. Such a fundamental decision as selection of a wife or husband seems to violate individual rights. 'Nuu-chah-nulth marriage customs appear to be tyrannical by modern standards,' he writes. After describing ways in which individuals had control over other aspects of their lives, he argues that a balance is needed between group rights and individual rights, in reference to the freedom to select one's spouse:

> However, the price for this kind of freedom appears to be very heavy. There is a significant difference in terms of physical and monetary resources, social

support, availability of experience, and human power between the marriage of two individuals and the marriage of two extended families. An extended family offers more physical resources, more money, the support of more people, more experience as embodied in the grandparents, and greater security from outside threats than does a nuclear family developed by two individuals.

(Umeek 2004: 58)

Chief Umeek makes a defense of the extended family and house system of the Nuu-chah-nulth by emphasizing the advantages to all members of both extended families in having access to the greater resources available to a larger group of individuals. He argues for the advantages of 'corporate' organization, another feature of the Northwest Coast system that is distinctive.

This argument connects to the issue of to what extent individuals in a house would be consulted with regard to decisions in the use of the house's resources. It appears that such decision-making was the prerogative of the chief and his main deputies. Although chiefs who were not generous and kind to their people were ridiculed in stories, such as the one recounted by an elder to Michael Harkin (1998), nonetheless chiefly prerogatives separated them from others in their house.

Berman (2000) observed that among the Heiltsuk, chiefs or youths who were to become chiefs had to lead in a ceremony in which they were themselves eaten by other beings – animals, represented in the dances by other members of the community, including shamans. The experience served to impress on those who held decision-making power over territory that they could be forced to take on humiliating roles.

An aspect of keeping the leaders from becoming too strong may also have been the actions within the ruling class. Not only did commoners remind their chiefs that they had ultimate control; other chiefs similarly kept each other in check. We have seen this aspect already in the area of contingent proprietorship. Why the process of resolving conflicts among titleholders would lead to principles of conflict resolution that empowered all equally is easier to understand: the titleholders, while having some differences among themselves, were fairly equal to one another. To keep peace among themselves, equalitarian participation principles made sense.

That egalitarian ideas dominated is also consistent with the role of chiefs among the Gitxsan, as reported by Daly:

> Since the Gitksan and Wet'suwet'en do not possess institutions that reinforce chiefly exploitation of non-chiefly persons, they have never been at ease with enduring hierarchical leaders. Sectional interests make the political life of leaders a constant factional nightmare if they attempt to form political alliances that go beyond the matrilineal House system … According to the late Jeff Harris Sr., Simoogit Luus, of the Guldo'o Lax Gibuu, the northern Gitksan would make fun of, and look down upon, any chief in their own clan who put on airs, or became preoccupied with his prestige, or issued orders in an imperious manner. They would remind him that he was not, after all,

> Chief Skat'iin – a Lax Gibuu trader chief from the Nass who was known to be somewhat despotic and whose own villagers were said to defer to him in ways that the Gitksan found restrictive and undemocratic.
>
> (Daly 2005: 202)

Although leadership was hereditary, the leaders were not allowed to be despotic. Daly's citation of Simoogit Luus confirms the view expressed by the Gitxsan website: leaders had to consult widely. It appears titleholders did not exercise authority that could be described as fully 'sovereign' in the sense of the sovereign kings of Europe. Their positions were more tenuous, relying on approval by other titleholders and ultimately by the members of their houses in order obtain and maintain their positions.

Chiefs, therefore, had to comply with a list of personal qualities such as that provided by the Nisga'a, and they had to know how to carry out public decision-making processes like those described by both the Nuu-chah-nulth for use by the Scientific Panel, and by the Wet'suwet'en in the public processes in their feasts. Among the Heiltsuk, they had considerable power during the secular season, but during the sacred season they had to submit to considerable ritualistic humiliation.

This respect for other people's views showed up in another recent conflict, the case brought by the titleholders of the Gitxsan and Wet'suwet'en in seeking title and governance powers over their traditional territories. This case came to be known as *Delgamuukw v. the Queen* [Delgamuukw v. British Columbia (1997) 3 SCR 1010]. One of the expert witnesses in the case, Antonia Mills, reports the following:

> Before *Delgamuukw* commenced, the Gitxsan and Witsuwit'en put on an opening feast. Initially, they had intended to invite the lawyers for the opposition as well as Chief Justice McEachern, but they were advised that such an invitation would be considered inappropriate. The Witsuwit'en and the Gitxsan found it hard to accept that the gesture was not proper, that it could be construed as a way to influence the judge and the lawyers for the opposition or make them feel indebted to the people launching the court case. Eventually, however, they were persuaded not to invite their opponents.
>
> (Mills 2005: 39)

Given the existence of a dispute, the aboriginal tradition is to have a feast, invite the parties to the dispute, and proceed to deal with solving the problem. That the feast creates an obligation to negotiate is part of the strategy. This idea is a fundamental contribution to the idea of 'shared decision-making'; it means that one treats one's opponent with respect. When external effects are great, every decision-maker is an agent for every other one, creating a system of interlocking principals and agents. The feast tradition allows these connections to be dealt with.

Within Northwest Coast tradition, by attending the feast, the judge and lawyers would agree to recognize the role and position of the feast givers. I doubt that, had the invitation been extended, the judge and lawyers would have rejected it for that reason. Rather, the judge in particular would have felt that his impartiality would be questioned, just as Mills supposes. The outcome was that the lawyers for the Wet'suwet'en and the Gitxsan successfully discouraged the idea of a feast to start the court case.

The Delgamuukw case remains one of the key cases in aboriginal title law in Canada. The Supreme Court of Canada used the case to make extensive statements about aboriginal title. But the case did not resolve anything for the Gitxsan and Wet'suwet'en; the Supreme Court dismissed the case on a major technicality, and sent it back to lower courts for another trial. Many of the courts in Canada do not decide aboriginal title cases, rather, they want the issues resolved outside the courtroom. Perhaps if some of the dispute resolution procedures used traditionally were applied to these cases, some resolution would be worked out.

Certainly the evidence from Nisga'a, Gitxsan, Wet'suwet'en and Nuu-chah-nulth suggests that the leaders of those societies had to consult widely, both with ranked members of their houses and with other leaders, in making major decisions. As the arguments in the Delgamuukw case proceeded, the Gitxsan and Wet'suwet'en needed to explain to the judge their views about facts. A major issue in the case was the extent to which the court could rely upon the *ada'ox* of each of the houses. Each house has an *ada'ox* that serves to verify the history of the house and the territories held by the house. These oral histories were discussed in Chapter 5; a titleholder had to be able to recount the history of his or her house in order to be recognized as qualified to administer the territories. (The word for house history has been written both as *adaawk* and as *ada'ox;* x is used for a sound that is like a w in English. The two transcriptions are describing the same Gitxsan word.) A major issue in the Delgamuukw case was whether or not the oral histories of the houses would be admitted as evidence. The lawyers for the province argued that the oral histories were 'hearsay,' and therefore not sufficiently documented to be relied upon as evidence. The trial judge agreed, and the case went to the Canadian Supreme Court, where the justices ruled that oral histories had to be considered along with the other evidence available.

The argument presented to the trial court is interesting because it connects to the work of the Scientific Panel in Clayoquot Sound. In presenting the evidence, the lawyers for the Gitxsan and Wet'suwet'en argued as follows:

> Each Chief tells his history in the living context of the knowledge in other's minds. Thus, when a Chief describes the events that took place long ago, events that he or she could not possibly have witnessed, these can be told as established truths by virtue of having been tested and validated at a succession of narrations. These typically occur at the Feast where other Chiefs are responsible for ensuring that all that is told is told as it should be. Elders knows that the important parts of their history, contained within the ada'ox or expressed through the kungax have been told, heard, and acknowledged many, many times. This accumulated validation lies behind the present day Chief's insistence that a particular story is true and is not anything like mere hearsay.
> (Gisday Wa and Delgam Uukw 1992: 39)

Of course, if the plaintiffs could not use their histories of the houses as evidence, they would not be able to establish their control of their territory to the satisfaction of the Canadian judicial system, and therefore would have little chance of establishing aboriginal title to those lands.

The knowledge contained in the house histories (*ada'ox* for Gitxsan and *kungax* for Wet'suwet'en) is just one part of the knowledge that the chiefs have. The issue of what is 'true' is a cross-cultural issue of some importance. The lawyer's brief continues:

> In the course of his commissioned evidence, Fred Johnson, Chief Lelt, several times insisted that things he was saying were true because they had been witnessed and acknowledged. He used the Gitxsan word *nidn't*, which Glen Williams, the translator at the time, rendered in English as 'acknowledged,' 'confirmed,' witnessed.' Translation of this term is difficult precisely because it is used to establish validity of a type that is deeply unfamiliar to Western ideas of truth.
>
> (*ibid.*: 39–40)

When facts have been established by the processes that allow them to be described as *nidn't*, they have been confirmed by chiefs who have been trained to 'police distortions.' Since scientific facts are also confirmed by people who are 'properly qualified experts,' an analogy exists between facts described by experts in the Western tradition and facts affirmed by *nidn't* in Gitxsan tradition. Neither are simply an individual's opinion. The Western tradition includes some facts that have been established through hypothesis testing under controlled conditions, such as experiments. Other facts accepted by scientists have been subjected to peer review, to verify that the techniques used to support the assertions are convincing to scientific peers. One might say that review by chiefs is a kind of peer review. If an assertion in the feast hall survives through many different feasts, and is acknowledged by all the chiefs, it has a stronger support than otherwise.

That information acknowledged at feasts should be given weight underlies the arguments in the book *Tribal Boundaries in the Nass Watershed* (Sterritt *et al.* 1998). This book documents a major dispute between the Nisga'a and Gitxsan about territorial control in the upper Nass River watershed. In the context of their treaty negotiations, the Nisga'a had made claims about the upper Nass watershed that were inconsistent with some records provided in the *adaawk* of the Gitxsan and Gitanyow. In response to some of the content of the Nisga'a Final Agreement, the Gitxsan and Gitanyow needed to state their position on claims in the upper Nass watershed. The details of the dispute do not have to be reviewed here. The point is that the dispute can be addressed in the context of the house histories. If the Canadian government had not exerted its jurisdiction over the land, the dispute would have been settled in the feast halls of the communities who disagreed over who controlled what parts of the watershed.

That rules of dispute resolution turned out to be very helpful for the Scientific Panel should be no surprise. The methods of discussing what is and is not fact are what the feast hall processes were all about. Who can control territory is, of course, very important. A society needs to have a way to verify the records of who has title to land; even with a written record, some method is needed to determine what is 'true,' given contradictory information.

David Lertzman has proposed that scientific knowledge and the oral traditions of indigenous people should both be used in processes of analysis of land-use decisions. The dispute over boundaries in the Nass watershed demonstrates that disagreements can occur among peoples of the Northwest Coast. What matters for analysis of the reasons for resilience of the traditional systems is that the methods of resolving disputes existed and worked. Without such methods, armed conflict would have been more common than it was. The stories told in the *adaawk* about the upper Nass watershed reveal that there was considerable armed conflict. Battles led to the need for peace, and feasts were held to settle which house would hold what territory.

Not only did the dispute-resolution procedures provide ways for peers to solve problems resulting from monitoring and sanctioning each other, the procedures provided ways to examine and legitimate knowledge. Thus when the Scientific Panel, consisting of high-ranking, knowledgeable people from different world views, used the dispute-resolution procedures, they were able to reconcile their differences.

This description of the political processes among titleholders in the settlement of disputes, the determination of accepted facts, and the general management of their territories is not consistent with the usual classification of Northwest Coast societies. Such classifications seem to originate with Franz Boas, who classified the peoples he visited as 'exceptional hunter gatherers' (Deur and Turner 2005). Deur and Turner argue that Boas did not recognize that the people cultivated plants, for several reasons. First, the plants cultivated were not from the set of plants normally associated with agriculture in North America – annuals such as corn, beans, and squash. Most were perennials that were propagated by cuttings rather than with seed. This is especially true of the tubers. Consequently, they were classified as 'Indian potatoes,' since they were similar to potatoes in that method of regeneration.

Once the existence of cultivation was ignored, the level of complexity of the societies then seemed greater than should exist for hunters and gatherers. This complexity was used by Boas to demonstrate the falsity of the deterministic models of cultural evolution promoted by nineteenth century anthropologists such as Lewis Morgan and E. B. Tylcr. These models placed European civilization at the top of the evolutionary scheme. They have been updated in modern times, as in the evolutionary model of Johnson and Earle (2000). They also had a strong dose of environmental assumptions, namely that agriculture was required in order to develop the higher-level civilizations. Part of the evolutionary scheme was to claim that the ownership of land was based on mixing man's labor with the land, as John Locke maintained. If the Northwest Coast societies were complex, yet did not have sophisticated agriculture, the evolutionary models were therefore shown to be false. This simple refutation falls apart when the levels of intervention are high and agriculture is determined either to be present or to be 'incipient.'

Yet finding agriculture on the Northwest Coast does not confirm the evolutionary theories either. Bruce Smith surveys the literature about the difficulties encountered by the evolutionary models when they need to account for societies, such as those on the Northwest Coast, that are neither agriculturalists nor hunter-gatherers. He argues for dropping the ideas that limit or channel investigations. Instead, he argues for recognition of a 'middle ground' as a stable end state:

> Northwest Coast societies can be seen as not being in transition, not anomalous or rare; they are not 'incipient' agriculturists. Rather they are representative in general of a very large, very diverse category of middle-ground societies which, although not abundant today, occupied much of the earth for thousands of years. These diverse, vibrant, and successful human societies developed long-term solutions for deriving sustenance from a wide range of environments that combined low-level reliance on domesticates with continued use and management of wild species. So Northwest Coast societies, like those of the middle ground in general, should not be viewed simply as reference points on the way to agriculture, as roadside markers of progress, but rather as stable and progressive solutions, as end points and destinations worthy of study in and of themselves.
>
> (Smith 2005: 54)

The book containing Smith's chapter provides many examples of the peoples of the Northwest Coast utilizing plants, primarily perennial plants, as part of their living strategy. The idea that the Northwest Coast system was an end point raises the question: why? Many societies with agriculture have proceeded to develop political and economic complexity, modifying their environment as they did so. What inhibited such development on the Northwest Coast? Perhaps the answer is in the system of peer monitoring, sharing of output, and dispute resolution. To explore this possibility, one needs to examine why complex civilizations have collapsed.

The evidence seems to be that complex societies are much less likely to be sustainable, and societies of Smith's middle ground are more likely to be sustainable. Archeologist Joseph Tainter has compared the characteristics of all of the complex societies he could identify, in an effort to determine why so many of them collapsed. All the examples in his study did collapse eventually; by collapse he means the complex political and economic structure disappeared. Usually population declined as well, in both the city and the countryside. Monuments are abandoned, and literacy (if present) declined. It would appear that there is something inherently unsustainable about complex societies (Tainter 1988: 19–21).

The lifespans of these societies varied. Some rose and fell in several hundred years; others lasted a millennium. The Chou dynasty, for instance, lasted from 1122 to 771 BC, a duration of 450 years. It was succeeded by a series of dynasties of about the same duration. The Old Kingdom in Egypt endured from 3100 to 2181 BC, almost 1100 years. The Roman Empire lasted from approximately 200 BC to 395 AD, a total of 600 years.

In the Americas, the oldest, the Olmec, lasted about 800 years. The classic Maya originated about the time of the Olmec, in the first millennium BC, and lasted until about 900 AD, a total of almost 2000 years. Contemporaneously, the Teotihuacan civilization in the Valley of Mexico rose and fell, apparently lasting 600 years until it collapsed in 700 AD. The Chacoan society of present-day Arizona and New Mexico lasted about 500 years, from 500 to 1050 AD. The Hohokam lasted in present-day Arizona from the first to the fifteenth century AD, a total of 1400 years (Tainter 1988: 15; Krech 1999: 48).

Tainter specifically rejects an explanation based on resource depletion, pointing out that in the early periods of a complex society, ecological crisis can be handled. He points out:

> If a society cannot deal with resource depletion (which all societies are to some degree designed to do) then the truly interesting questions revolve around the society, not the resource. What structural, political, ideological, or economic factors in a society prevented an appropriate response?
>
> (Tainter 1988: 50)

This manner of viewing the issue implicitly separates human systems from natural systems, placing the question as an either/or choice: either there are resource explanations (resource depletion, natural catastrophe) or social explanations (invasion, class conflict). Tainter proposes a kind of social explanation that contains natural factors: increasing marginal costs of complexity. While Tainter focuses on social complexity, the whole social–ecological system becomes complex in these societies. When common pool management is involved, the complex systems need to have dealt with them.

The system of public resolution of crises also provided titleholders with a way to avoid the creation of a political structure at a higher scale, which could destabilize the system. Although the geography of the Coast may have also inhibited the emergence of an empire, none of the rivers became under the control of one polity. The runs could have been managed by such a polity, had it emerged. Something restrained such emergence, which had over 2000 years to occur.

When large-scale social–ecological systems have an internal dynamic that leads to increasing complexity, that dynamic leads to their eventual demise: the concentration of power in central governments and increasing complexity lead eventually to costs exceeding benefits for the lower-level productive units. Eventually, the whole system has negative benefits. When the diversion of resources by the central government exceeds the benefits to the local units, eventually those units cease to cooperate and the whole structure falls apart. Tainter (1988), stressing diminishing marginal returns to increases in complexity, presents two different cases of collapse: an isolated state or competing states. An isolated state becomes so complex that reasonable people opt for a less complex situation, which would increase net returns. They revolt or aid the invaders, as in the Roman Empire, and a complex situation becomes less complex. A second example of complexity is a situation of competing polities, as in the Mayan case. In this situation, no one of the competing states can reduce its complexity; to do so would invite invasion and incorporation in one of the other polities. The arms race of increasing complexity proceeds until all the competing polities collapse at once.

Must complex societies go down roads that inevitably lead to collapse? Are there ways in which elites can organize themselves or their society in ways that prevent or postpone collapse? How do the principles of the Nuu-chah-nulth protocol directly prevent the emergence of increasing complexity?

Two parts of the feast system clearly would force movements toward additional complexity to be questioned. First, any leader who wishes to rise above the others would need to be able to host feasts of sufficient size to justify his rise in power. If other leaders did not wish to see him increase in status and power, they could refuse to acknowledge his increased control of resources. If he expands by conquest of his neighbors, he always remains subject to other neighbors agreeing to the changes.

Second, the feast system would reveal the negative returns. In cases in which increasing complexity has negative returns, the ruling groups do not necessarily experience the negative returns as strongly as does the rest of the society; the costs are hidden by hierarchy. In the Pacific Northwest, because the feast system requires that returns be sharing among everyone, the costs would not be hidden. Because of the need to distribute surplus publicly, when complexity begins to experience diminishing returns, the expanding chief or chiefs would be unable to free sufficient surplus to satisfy either his followers or the other chiefs. The feedback process of the feasting system would limit increasing complexity to levels that create negative returns.

7   An alternative history of industrialization of the Northwest Coast

In 1913, one of the first dams built for electricity production in Washington State, on the Elwha River on the Olympic Peninsula, totally blocked salmon runs to the watershed above the dam. In 1890, Thomas Aldwell had purchased land that contained a potential dam site on the Elwha River. This land purchase occurred under the laws of the State of Washington, and did not recognize the prior rights of the Klallam Indians who lived on that river and all who harvested its fish. The land that he purchased from a homesteader included the narrow falls that had caused the spring chinook run to become populated with large fish able to swim through the rapid water to spawn upstream. Given that such rapids would create a key opportunity to catch salmon, his land purchase probably included a fishing site held by one of the traditional titleholders of this coast Salish community. But Mr Aldwell did not look at salmon as a source of wealth. He wanted to build a dam to generate electricity for the nearby town of Port Angeles (Lichatowich 1999: 131–35).

The State of Washington legally prohibited the construction of dams that would block migrating salmon. In order to build his dam, Aldwell needed to find a way around that law. Two successive fish commissioners in the state provided him with permission, by supporting the concept of building fish hatcheries to replace the natural regeneration of salmon. Hatchery operators had been constructing 'racks' that blocked streams and allowed the hatchery to catch all the spawning salmon in a run, in order to harvest the eggs and provide the hatchery with fertilized eggs. By allowing the hydroelectric dam to be classified as such a fish rack, fish commissioner Leslie Darwin augmented a rule set by his predecessor that allowed a dam to be constructed if accompanied by a hatchery.

Leslie Darwin required Aldwell to build a hatchery in place of a fish ladder, which Aldwell had been unable to construct. Aldwell established the Olympic Power and Development Company, which began construction in 1910. After the original structure failed, the dam was completed in 1913 and the fish hatchery started operation in 1915. The hatchery operated for seven years, and was abandoned in 1922. The dam continued to operate, generating electricity and supporting industrial operation in Port Angeles. In 1927, another dam, the Glines Dam, was completed upstream from the original dam. Eventually, new fish hatcheries came into existence below the Lower Elwha Dam; they reared coho, steelhead, and chinook. The federal government controlled much of the land upstream from the dams. The government created a forest reserve in 1897, the Mount Olympus National Monument in 1909, and the Olympic National Park in 1938 (National Park Service 2005: xv).

The Federal Power Act of 1920 required all dams to have a federal license, and the Glines Dam had such a license, with a term of 50 years. In 1977, the license for the Glines Canyon Dam came up for renewal. Under the terms of the National Environmental Policy Act, the Federal Energy Regulatory Commission (FERC) had to complete an environmental impact statement. The initial list of alternatives for relicensing the dam did not include removing the dams. They did include requiring the construction of fish ladders to restore the fisheries to the upper reaches of the Elwha River. Unlike many other rivers blocked by dams, prime salmon-spawning and -rearing habitat existed within the boundaries of Olympic National Park. As a result, fisheries restoration would be possible without dislocating broader development, as on other rivers in the Pacific Northwest.

A series of studies by the applicant for a license, and by those advocating for fisheries restoration, generated a thorough discussion of alternatives. Construction of effective fish ladders proved to be so expensive that elimination of the dams appeared cost-effective. Had the environmental impact public discussion been carried to its conclusion, FERC would have had to decide whether or not to approve the dam removal option. This would have been difficult for an entity that favors electricity production. Because of FERC's bias, The Department of the Interior and others had argued in court that FERC did not have jurisdiction on dams built before 1920.

Passage of Public Law 102-495, the Elwha River Ecosystem and Fisheries Restoration Act (1992), ended the impact discussion and jurisdictional battle. This act authorized the US Government to purchase the dams and pay for their removal, after completion of further environmental impact studies. Those studies were completed and the dams were scheduled for removal beginning in 2009 (Olympic National Park 2008).

The story of the Elwha River shows that at the end of the twentieth century, the salmon fishery was more valuable than two dams with a combined power capacity of 28 megawatts and an average energy production of 172,000 megawatt hours per year. A large study completed after passage of the Elwha Restoration Act demonstrated that the salmon were more valuable than the electricity. An economic analysis of dam removal showed a similar result (Elwha Project Human Effects Team 1995; Loomis 1996; Gowan *et al.* 2006).

A counterfactual

The Elwha River story suggests the possibility that, had Thomas Aldwell and the Olympic Power and Development Company, who built the original dam, been required to compensate those who valued the fish, the dam which blocked the entire watershed might not have been built. What might have occurred if the chiefs of the Klallam Tribe had retained control over the river? Quite possibly, they would not have approved of the dam, even though the benefits from electricity production would have been large. The major issue for the chiefs would have been the relative benefits of the electricity compared with the salmon.

In order to make his proposal, he would have had to convince the appropriate titleholder, who would in turn have had to hold a feast and explain the idea to other titleholders in the local feasting system. At the feast, others in the community would have an opportunity to express their views about the proposal. The feast process, already in existence, would have allowed deliberation about whether or not to allow the dam. If it had been constructed, the potlatching process would have provided the means by which the newly prosperous titleholder would have compensated those no longer able to catch fish in the Elwha River.

I would suppose that the other titleholders would refuse to agree to the dam, given that the dam would block all salmon runs from access to the upper reaches of the Elwha River. In order to achieve approval, the funds distributed at the original feast and all subsequent ones would have to more than compensate for the value of the salmon that would no longer be available, should one use a strictly economic comparison. But blocking the salmon from reaching their 'homes' in the Elwha River would have been regarded as extremely disrespectful, threatening the desire of the salmon to return, as well as their ability to reproduce. A requirement that the dam builder satisfy everyone else who relied on the salmon run would have been the end of the story of the lower Elwha Dam that was built in 1906. Subsequent proposals would have met the same fate.

That the revenue from the dam was insufficient to pay for preservation of the salmon run was demonstrated nearly a century later, during the study required for the relicensing of the dam under the authority of FERC, as explained above.

Another aspect of the creation of the Elwha Dam was the simultaneous construction of a fish hatchery next to the dam. This fish hatchery was a failure, and was closed shortly after it was built. Those proposing to construct a fish hatchery as an alternative to use of the river to create young fish would have had to pass an examination by the titleholders with rights to harvest on the Elwha River. They surely would have required proof that the hatchery would work and that the fish culturists knew what they were doing. Most likely, the examination would have been failed, because neither scientists or fish culturists of the 1900–10 period knew much about salmon biology and ecology (Lichatowich 1999: 126–7).

Dams were only one of the many examples of industrial developments that harmed salmon. The decline of salmon abundance in the Pacific Northwest is a dramatic example of the failure of modern economic systems to deal with common pool goods and with productive systems that have extensive externalities. What would have occurred if the governing system had required that all such externalities be recognized and accounted for?

One way to answer that question is to examine a counter-to-fact story of the development of the industrial economy, based on an assumption that the settlers would have recognized the existing governing and territoriality system of the indigenous people. If such had occurred, the new activities the settlers brought with them would have been introduced within the indigenous system.

Telling a counterfactual about the development of the settlers' economy answers the challenge offered by Elster and Moene (1989: 3) to provide a sketch of how an industrial economy based upon reciprocity could have occurred. In order to construct a counterfactual, one needs to distinguish clearly what would have been changed and what would have remained the same. One needs to tie the counterfactual story down, to avoid going too far afield in constructing it.

In the case of the Elwha River Basin, the fundamental issue is whether or not the two dams were built. With the dams' installed capacity of 28 megawatts, the river was able to produce electricity; salmon production was reduced by 99 per cent. Without the dams, salmon production presumably would have continued, although the salmon runs would have been vulnerable to other problems, such as over-fishing. One can leave in place the creation of the Olympic National Park, given that the park would not have been inconsistent with the maintenance of salmon habitat in the streams. Had the drainage become heavily logged, then the counterfactual story would need to address what changes would have occurred to logging plans if the territorial system of the indigenous people had remained.

In order to support a counterfactual history, one should be able to provide some reasons that the alternative is at all possible. How can one imagine that the indigenous people would not have been pushed aside as they were? In both the United States and Canada, indigenous people were seen as an obstacle to settlement. The obstacle was dealt with by removing them from control of most of the land, by segregating them in their own communities, and by undertaking a policy to assimilate the individual members of the native communities into the general society of the settlers. Although what occurred seems inevitable, an alternative story could be based upon the following: (1) there was a legal precedent within the colonists' system that could have justified a different approach; and (2) indigenous peoples were willing to share the land with the settlers. Both these conditions were clear in the years on the American frontier before the power of England was greatly enhanced by the industrial revolution.

The legal precedent that could provide a basis for settlers negotiating with local people, rather than displacing them, is the Royal Proclamation of 1763. The King of England put forward the proclamation at the end of a war with France, when England gained control of the entire eastern side of North America. Because the French had recognized their governments, the Indians wanted to have similar recognition from the English. Peace required addressing the desires of the indigenous nations, and the proclamation was presented to them at a large meeting at Niagara in 1764. The proclamation and agreement recognized the authority of local indigenous leaders, and stated that transfers of property from Indians to colonists could occur only with agreements ratified at public meetings. Here is one key text of the proclamation:

> It is just and reasonable, and essential to our Interests, and the Security of our Colonies, that the several Nations or Tribes of Indians with whom We are connected, and who live under our Protection, should not be molested or disturbed in the Possession of such Parts of our Dominion and Territories as,

not having been ceded to or purchased by Us, are reserved to them, or any of them, as their Hunting Grounds … .

(quoted by Tennant 1990: 10)

The proclamation goes on to say that it applies to all lands to the west of the current area of settlement. The statement recognizes and asserts the authority of the Crown by claiming 'our Dominion'; but it also recognizes that lands have not been ceded. The process of cession was to be governed by the following process:

If at any Time any of the Said Indians should be inclined to dispose of the said Lands, the same shall be Purchased only by Us, at some public Meeting or Assembly of the said Indians.

(Tennant 1990: 11)

The proclamation goes on to authorize the agents of the King to govern trade with Indians, and generally to assert royal powers. To say that the proclamation authorized indigenous leaders to set up rules and determine the terms under which settlers would utilize indigenous lands is probably a stretch: the intent of the King was to exert control over a process in which Indians sold land to the Crown.

John Borrows argues that the Royal Proclamation needs to be understood in the context of a large gathering of indigenous leaders at Niagara in 1764. The Crown's representative, William Johnson, met with the leaders, read the proclamation, and presented the 'Two Row Wampum' to the assembled chiefs. The Two Row Wampum illustrated the idea that indigenous and settler communities would follow the same river with different boats. While the Crown's desire to exert imperial authority is clear from the content of the proclamation, the meaning of the Two Row Wampum and other exchanges of gifts suggests that indigenous representatives accepted an agreement that allowed them to continue to govern themselves. The two rows represent the simultaneous existence of separate governments. But between the purple beads are three rows of white beads, for which 'The belt contemplates interaction and sharing between First nations and the Crown' (Borrows 2002: 126; see also Borrows 1997). Borrows uses the Two Row Wampum and additional information about the exchange of ideas at the Niagara meeting of July and August 1764 to argue for a new basis for federalism in Canada.

Thus the King was willing to have a cooperative process. A similar desire existed on the indigenous side. During the same century as the declaration of the Royal Proclamation of 1763 and the Treaty of Niagara of 1764, Indians and settlers signed many other treaties. In his book *Linking Arms Together*, legal scholar Robert Williams Jr argues that the metaphors and processes of these treaties complied with the desires of the Indians. He labels the period from 1600 to 1800 as the 'encounter era.' He summarizes as follows:

For Indians of the Encounter era, relationships of trust with different peoples were essential to survival and flourishing in a multicultural world. The language of Indian forest diplomacy reflected this basic understanding in a richly evocative vocabulary describing the paradigms for behavior that Indians believed nurtured trust and reliance in a treaty relationship. In Indian diplomacy, such acts of 'confident example-setting' as granting land settlement rights to stranger groups, agreeing to eat out of a common bowl, linking arms together, clearing the path of peace, and sharing each other's sacred stories and rituals signified the commitment of treaty partners to behave as relatives toward each other. These acts, according to American Indian treaty visions of law and peace, initiated the process by which different groups learned to build justice in a multicultural world.

(Williams 1997: 131)

'Sharing the common bowl' means including the settlers in sharing the products of the land. 'Linking arms together' means finding ways to settle disputes, to 'become of one mind,' another Iroquois image. Sharing stories means understanding each other's world views, without giving up one's own. Williams argues that these principles did not make Indians obstacles to the spread of settlers; by adherence to them, Indians aided the presence of Europeans in the Americas (Williams 1997: 14–28).

The Nisga'a petition to the Privy Council in 1913 provides evidence from the Pacific Northwest that sharing the land was acceptable:

While we claim the right to be compensated for those portions of our territory which we may agree to surrender, we claim as even more important the right to reserve other portions permanently for our own use and benefit, and beyond doubt the portions which we would desire so to reserve would include much of the land which has be sold by the Province. We are not opposed to coming of the white people into our territory, provided this be carried out justly and in accordance with the British principles embodied in the Royal Proclamation. If therefore as we expect the aboriginal rights which we claim should be established by the decision of His Majesty's Privy Council, we would be prepared to take a moderate and reasonable position.

(Raunet 1996: 136)

The Nisga'a petition was ignored, however, because neither the Province of British Columbia nor the Government of Canada assented to having the matter placed before the Privy Council. Later Nisga'a leaders also stated that they were willing to be reasonable.

Few treaties were signed with peoples of the Northwest Coast, and none of them adhered to the principles of the early 'encounter era' identified by Williams. The treaties presented by Governor Isaac Stevens to Indians in Washington Territory in 1854–55 were treaties of land cession, not treaties that embodied principles of sharing. The Indians insisted that their fishing sites remain in their hands; but later developments created a different meaning of fishing in common: not a common bowl, but an open-access commons.

Given the importance of sharing and the absence of the idea of buying and selling land, many Indians probably did not understand that the purpose of treaties from the settler's viewpoint was to remove Indians from the land. Even when a chief seemed to understand the cession intent, he argued that a relationship should continue. Williams argues that the idea of the trust relationship and the fiduciary duty of the settler governments rests ultimately on indigenous insistence that even a cession of land created a relationship of trust with the settlers (Williams 1997: 130–37). Later, the supreme courts of both Canada and the United States reasoned that by assuming a monopoly position in regulating the sale of land, the governments had created an obligation to deal fairly with indigenous peoples. In Canada, this became the doctrine of maintaining the 'Honour of the Crown'; in the United States, it became the 'trust relationship.' Had the settler societies honored the agreements reached at Niagara and in other treaties of the encounter era, then perhaps the history would have been different.

In summary, although the settler nations of the United States and Canada departed from the principles set by the Royal Proclamation of 1763 and the treaties of the encounter period, those principles can be used to motivate the mental exercise of imagining what the history of the Northwest Coast would have been had the settlers needed to negotiate with the indigenous peoples for access to land. The result of the process could have been a different type of society, neither fully indigenous nor fully European.

The indigenous people liked the technology that had become available from Europe: metal tools, new systems of powering productive activities, new techniques for hunting animals, and many other technologies. I want to assume that these techniques were available. Europeans brought many innovations that were not present in the indigenous system: a market for salmon outside the region; new technology that allowed extensive harvest of trees; wheat and new plants; and ways to use land to grow new crops intensively.

By the time the settlers reached the west coast of North America, the industrial revolution was well under way. In 1846, Britain and the United States agreed to the border that would divide the two nations in the process of settling the new region. This agreement allowed both the United States and the settlers of British Columbia to proceed. The United States government followed the principle of having the central government agree to land cessions from the indigenous peoples. The government of British Columbia, after a brief start at writing treaties, abandoned treaty-writing.

I am not trying to construct this alternative story for the purposes of showing the costs of expropriation to the indigenous people. Of course they would not have been impoverished if their territorial rights had been respected. I am more interested in the differences that would have occurred for the arriving settlers. If the settlers had been forced to recognize the impacts of external effects and ecosystem connections, how might they have done things differently?

Of course, to assume that the settlers would join in the territoriality system of the indigenous people requires assuming a great deal about the flexibility of the people on both sides. The existence of the Royal Proclamation of 1763 and the willingness of Indians to share the land does not address these other concerns. Europeans would have had to have been willing to come under the jurisdiction of chiefs whose ways of doing things were quite different. Just the differences in world view would present problems: how could Europeans be assumed to accept the idea that animals were people who had been transformed? Would Europeans be willing to accept subordination to titleholders, when the settlers were probably fleeing control by another type of nobility in Europe? Would the settlers be willing to join in the ceremonies that occurred as part of feasts? Would they be willing to give up the idea that fish belonged to everyone (Newell 1993; Harris 2001)?

Just imagining the conduct of a cross-cultural feast reveals the kinds of issues that are raised in the process of creating a counterfactual story. The feast rules give roles to people based upon their clan membership in relationship to the titleholder conducting the feast. People from each clan sit in particular places, as illustrated by the Wet'suwet'en 'all clans' feast that Antonia Mills describes (Mills 1994a: 44–55). To incorporate outsiders, such seating rules would have to be explained to the settlers.

All the misunderstanding that are evident in the reports of anthropologists would occur as settlers try to understand the logic of the system that they would be joining. For instance, Goldman reports that Boas's early analysis of potlatch exchanges was simply not supported by evidence in the many texts that Hunt collected. Boas interpreted wealth transfers as loans and sought to determine the interest rate (Goldman 1975: 163–68). It would be quite a distraction, perhaps, to work out the details of the Kwakiutl rules for the different types of feast and the different types of rivalry. Goldman's explication of the religious thought of the Kwakiutl makes it clear that understanding the different feasts requires understanding the religious side. He explains elaborate metaphors of eating, vomiting, death, and resurrection; all of which are a system of thought that the early Boas did not understand. Both Goldman and Walens have gone to great lengths to understand and explain Kwakiutl religious thought. And this applies only to the Kwakiutl; the Tsimshian had other beliefs, and so forth with the Haida and the Nuu-chah-nulth. Although the different groups all had feasts and give-aways, their interpretations of the meanings and the details of the ceremonies differed.

In order to tell the counterfactual story, then, I have a problem, because the meaning of exchanges is so caught up in the world views of the people. As many have assumed, these societies were 'total,' in the sense that their cultural, material, and people's structures all fit together as a resilient, reproducing, social–ecological system. I have sought to examine the rules that were pervasive across the region, in order to seek out the characteristics that probably created resilience. Because of this focus, I tell the counterfactual story with attention to the rules laid out in previous chapters.

As I take an ecological economic viewpoint, I am focusing on the intersection of the political, ecological, and economic systems. I have not focused as much on the cultural systems such as religious beliefs. Although I have considered reincarnation, my reason is that reincarnation directly affects a major economic issue. I can't deal with the depth of religious philosophy. I can't deal with the mismatch of kinship systems. The role of the group and the role of the individual is more important, however: in order for the counterfactual to make sense, the strong individualistic ethos of the Europeans has to be assumed to become subordinated to the group-oriented nature of the Northwest Coast. So, in order to put together this counterfactual, I need more carefully to spell out the assumed method of joining such different peoples.

The counterfactual story will be assembled as follows. I will assume that the governance and land tenure systems of the indigenous peoples were not pushed aside. Because introduced diseases had decimated the population, many unfilled positions existed in their system. Land and fishing sites were available for other people to use. These people would introduce technical changes brought by the new industrial economy, but which would be organized within the original system.

In constructing a counterfactual story, I want to focus on the matters I believe are key to understanding the resilience of the Northwest Coast social–ecological systems. As explained in the previous three chapters, the rules held by the settlers and the Indians dealing with exchange, territoriality, and leadership were quite different. Exchange among settlers was organized primarily by exclusive self-interest and voluntarily agreed-to contracts; exchange among the Indians was based on forced generosity. The territorial systems contrasted the difference between exclusive control by an owner and contingent control by a proprietor. Leadership was the difference between the imposition of solutions by external authorities whose powers were not fully derived from the people within the social–ecological system versus joint decision-making among everyone affected by externalities.

Under the territoriality system, the entire landscape was assigned to one or another of the houses. This included the rivers, the ocean beaches, and offshore fishing areas. In order for settlers to create a new economic activity in any of these areas, they would have had to negotiate with the titleholder responsible for each territory. The resulting arrangement would be unfamiliar to settlers from an Anglo-American tradition, because they would not be able to obtain the full control of land that they had been accustomed to. They would need to agree to share a portion of the return on the land with the titleholder. Probably there would be other conditions that would relate to the titleholder's concerns about the long-term quality of the land. I will examine these conditions in dealing with specific economic activities. Once an agreement was reached, the titleholder would have to notify other titleholders, and proceed to recognize their interests in the developments on the particular titleholder's territory. Thus each titleholder would not be able to finalize an arrangement with a cannery or a logger without consulting other affected titleholders.

In addition to accepting the need to seek the continued approval of a titleholder and his peers, new entrants into the Northwest Coast system would need to accept the requirement that they share part of their profit with others in the system. That this would be acceptable to settlers is a major assumption of the counterfactual story; in fact, a major point of the story is to work out the implications of settlers accepting the need to share.

Finally, the Northwest Coast system relied not at all on the existence of a state-level government, with its legal system and centralized authority. The counterfactual story needs to compromise on this; the acceptance of the need to seek a joint working relationship, being based upon the King's policy in the Royal Proclamation of 1763, has to recognize that the settlers would have been under instructions from their government to recognize and join the indigenous system. As explained in Chapter 6, titleholders had procedures for settling disputes among themselves without appeal to higher authorities. The use of national state courts to resolve disputes was not an option. With the presence of national states such as England, Canada, and the United States, the role of courts in settling disputes would matter. I will assume that the courts would have supported local resolution of issues. This would mean that the concept of 'contract' as a fixed document that spells out all of an agreement would be less strong. That is, if a settler made an agreement with titleholders regarding the conduct of a new activity, the state system would need to require that the local dispute-resolution processes be carried out before an appeal to the national system. In addition, the national system would need to be able to deal with the contradictions between a property rights-based system in the rest of the nation and the different system on the Northwest Coast.

Also missing would be the administrative organizations of the settlers' national governments. For example, recognition of titleholders' control of the fishery would leave no room for the Department of Fisheries and Oceans in Canada or the Departments of Fisheries in Alaska or Washington. The US Forest Service would not have created a Tongass National Forest in Alaska, nor all the national forests along the Pacific Coast in the USA.

In order to manage the process of imagining an alternative history, therefore, one needs a clear list of three different categories: (1) matters that will be assumed to be different; (2) matters that will be assumed to be the same; and (3) issues that are set aside and not addressed, even though they would seem relevant.

In category 1, the alternative story assumes that the territoriality system, the rules for sharing output, and the rules for settling disputes will be changed from the processes that were imposed in colonial times.

In category 2, the main matter to assume occurred as it actually did is the introduction of new technologies and new uses for the resources of the Northwest Coast. As a region existing on the periphery of the developing world industrial economy, most innovation was occurring outside the region. The choice of whether or not to incorporate the new technologies then becomes a major issue in the contact between the settlers and the indigenous people.

In category 3 are a great many things not immediately relevant to the economic aspect of a social–ecological system. Differences in kinship systems, for instance, don't seem to matter a great deal. The systems of the Northwest Coast operated with many different types of inheritance. Some systems were matrilineal, others patrilineal. Differences in particulars about the religions also varied across groups. Even greater differences existed between the Christian faiths and the indigenous people, especially regarding spiritual concern and respect for non-humans. Europeans had society and nature, while indigenous people had material and non-material reality. I am not going to consider the difficulties with reconciling the separate fundamental religious beliefs. A justification for this is that the conversion of indigenous communities to Christianity did not signal the end of their identity as separate communities, nor the end of their feasting. One could argue, however, following Durkheim, that religion is extremely important as a method of organizing a society. In this case, changes in the territorial system and exchange system would require that inconsistencies in the different religions be addressed to a greater degree than attempted here.

In order to change the story, treaties such as the Stevens treaties of 1854–55 would have set out procedures more explicitly for settlers to join the indigenous system. Steven's goal of opening up Washington territory to settlers would have been met not by bludgeoning the chiefs into agreement, but by acknowledging their role in structuring a new economy. Instead of assuming that the indigenous systems were an obstacle to settlers, the counterfactual story assumes the settlers would have realized that the system they were joining was productive because of indigenous management.

Based on the feast system, all new entrants to the system would need to define a role in the feasting system. They could either become new titleholders, offering payments to existing titleholders in order to join the system, or become subordinate to an existing titleholder. In either case, they would have become involved in receiving payments and making distributions in order to continue in the system. Let's examine how each of these new entrants might manage to join the existing titleholders. Some may even have showed themselves skilled enough managers to become titleholders.

When the settlers arrived, they brought with them technology for many new activities. Canning allowed salmon to be shipped abroad, primarily to England, where the industrial revolution was proceeding, and workers needed inexpensive protein. Sawmills created lumber to fill the needs of the growing cities of the United States. Agriculture, always a main desire of settlers in both the United States and Canada, needed land. Mining also supplied necessary supplies to the industrial economy. All of these activities required energy, and damming rivers provided such energy, either directly or through the generation of electricity. Damming also allowed irrigation of agriculture. Temporary dams could facilitate the transport of logs to sawmills.

The following deals with how each of these major new activities could have been handled by the aboriginal system, and what differences the aboriginal system might have made in the pattern of development. In doing this, I deal only with the initial period of industrialization, focused on resource extraction, in order to indicate how things might have been different. Once the industrial economy was established in the Pacific Northwest, other industries arrived, such as airplane construction, which were not tightly tied to the available resources of the region. To go further than consideration of the resource-based industries would spin the counterfactual story beyond plausibility.

Canneries

I begin with canneries, not because they were the first historically, but because they had the most direct impact on salmon harvest and are easiest to fit into the

Northwest Coast systems. An entrepreneur seeking to set up a cannery would need to negotiate a site, meaning making an agreement with the titleholder in whose territory the site existed. Probably the new cannery owner would need to join the house of the titleholder. The arrangement with the new cannery owner would require some review by the other titleholders, and they could force that review through the feast system. Upon obtaining an agreement, the new cannery would start operation and begin to process salmon caught near the river mouth by fishermen, most of whom would be indigenous peoples. The fishing sites on land would also be controlled by titleholders, not necessarily the titleholder controlling the site of the cannery. As the cannery produced and shipped packs of salmon, other titleholders on the river system would expect to be invited to a feast at which the cannery builder and his associated titleholder would distribute wealth based on the new activity. The cannery owner would also receive wealth from other titleholders as they held their rounds of ceremonies to recognize marriages, deaths, and the passing on of titles. Other titleholders will also have made agreements with other cannery operators, or will supply fish to the new cannery.

Thus the new cannery owner would discover that some of his net returns would not be his, but he would also discover that some of the returns accruing to other canneries built on the river would be shared with him. The interdependence of profit among the canneries would make the managers realize that each did not have to harvest a huge share of the runs in order to make a good return. This would reduce the short-term problem of efficient harvest of the salmon by solving the prisoners' dilemma incentives.

Selection of the proper level of harvest for long-term sustainability of the fishery would require additional efforts. One of the big problems reported for the canneries was that they encouraged over-harvest and wasted many fish (Lichatowich 1999: 93–94). Lichatowich reports such waste as occurring during the large runs in particular. If the cannery owners had been embedded within a feasting system led by titleholders, such waste would have threatened to create sanctions. Each titleholder would probably have insisted in the agreement with the canneries that the salmon be treated with respect. Thus unused portions of the fish would be returned to the ocean, and the waste of fish would not be allowed. Harvest would be restricted to what could be processed. A cannery owner would need to deal with his particular titleholder if he departed from such requirements. Should a titleholder fail to sanction the cannery owner, other titleholders would have invited the offending titleholder to a feast, with the goal of discussing the waste. If waste had continued, titleholders would have started to refuse to receive their share of the cannery's profits, as a signal that the entire operation was losing legitimacy. Next would be for the people of the titleholder's house to contemplate action, out of fear that the salmon would not return. Thus the titleholder would need to keep the cannery operator complying with proper behavior toward salmon.

The selection of the correct harvest level for each run would be determined by the titleholders together. In setting harvest amounts, they would use their knowledge of each run and the required escapement needed to assure that the salmon would be able to prosper and return in future years. Having protected spawning grounds and rearing areas in the streams and lakes, the titleholders would be able to monitor the reproductive success of each run. They also would detect quickly a failure of the runs to return in expected numbers. Their own positions as titleholders would remain dependent upon successful management of the fishery. There would be little room for action by any fisheries departments run by the national governments of either Canada or the United States.

This analysis refers to the early years of cannery development, when fishing occurred in a non-mechanized fashion, prior to the invention of motors for fishing boats. Prior to the growth of the ocean fishery, fishing would have remained a river-mouth affair, where some distinctions among individual runs would be possible. In large rivers such as the Fraser and Columbia, mixed-stock fisheries might occur under this system; but such mixed-stock fisheries had occurred with traditional methods, as well, when runs arrived together.

Thus, had canneries been built within the aboriginal system, that system would have given the many people utilizing the fishery at the mouth of a river both incentives not to over-fish, and ways for them to punish cannery operators who wasted fish or refused to participate in the system. Participation in the system would have meant compliance with rules set down by titleholders, using the feast system as their method of governance.

I could speculate on whether or not cannery operators would have become titleholders themselves. Given the population losses caused by diseases, the traditional systems up and down the coast would have had surplus named positions and associated crests. A cannery owner or operator would need to learn about the history of the crest and be willing to join in the traditional system in order to actually hold a title. He would need to prove the spiritual powers that titleholders hold. Given such high requirements, titles offered to cannery operators would probably be the subordinate ones, not the head titles of the houses in the aboriginal systems.

But as the system developed, mixed between indigenous people and settlers, there may have been adjustment in some parts of the traditional system. If the settlers came to understand the importance of the indigenous procedures in preserving the quality of the salmon runs, they would be able to apply those lessons to other common pool goods.

Lumber production

At about the same time that canneries were becoming established at the mouths of all the big rivers, timber harvesters were beginning to establish sawmills in the region. The timber harvesting in early years had a number of characteristics that had an impact on the fishery. First, transporting trees was a challenge. Timber harvesters in Wisconsin had used both rivers and railroads to transport logs. In the Pacific Northwest, timber harvesters used rivers to transport logs to mills. They also found it easiest to cut timber on the shores of rivers, because the haul to the transportation network was shortest in that case.

Had titleholders been able to retain their ability to control access to their lands, they each would have had to consider the benefits of allowing trees to be cut and sold to sawmills. While cannery owners and the fishermen they hired were using the resource which was the basis for livelihoods in the Pacific Northwest, timber harvesters were using a resource that had not been as intensively used in the aboriginal system. The Northwest Coast peoples did live in wooden houses and utilized the products of trees for numerous purposes, such as canoes and totem poles. Bark was valuable. Native harvest and management of trees on Vancouver Island was at a level sufficient to allow Douglas fir regeneration near settlements; without human intervention Douglas fir could not have become as large a component of the forest as it was (Hamish Kimmins, personal communication). Although they had used trees, cutting and selling them represented a new activity. Historically, we know that the Tsimshian living at the mouth of the Skeena River did participate in timber harvest in the form of 'hand logging.' The early scale of logging did not prevent indigenous people from becoming loggers.

If the trespass rules of the house system had been successfully applied to timber harvesters, then each logger would have had to negotiate with the titleholder of the house that held the land he wished to harvest. We can imagine that the titleholder would have been concerned about the impact of the logging on all of the subsistence resources used by the members of his house. The returns from logging would provide the house with a source of income to use for participation in the new market economy that the settlers brought with them. Forests are extensive, and we know streams and other resources can be protected during harvesting operations. Some harvesting would help important food plants, if done correctly. Therefore one can imagine that some logging would have been permitted.

But one can similarly imagine that the impact of logging on salmon habitat would not have been allowed to be as great as it was. Particular houses relying on salmon and on logging would have been concerned about the effects on salmon habitat. They would have taken care of streams in their territory in order to assist salmon spawning and rearing. Thus they would have been concerned about protection of the streams, and would have monitored the effects of logging and log transport on salmon habitat. Clogging streams with sawdust would not have been allowed.

We do not know if the returns from forestry were so great that titleholders would have accepted some degradation of habitat and reduction in salmon runs in return for increases in logging above what they used to do. We don't know the answer because, without enforcement of the proprietary rights of the houses, no one ever calculated the nature of the trade-off between logging and salmon production. (This contrasts with the study of the Moran Dam on the Fraser River, discussed below.)

The main impacts of the timber industry on salmon came from the release of sawdust from sawmills into the rivers, from using the rivers to transport logs, from harvesting trees right to the edge of streams and rivers, and from landslides and other events that increased sediment loads in streams. Landslides from poorly constructed roads could completely fill stream channels with gravel and soil from the hillside (Lichatowich 1999).

The feasting system would have provided other titleholders with ways to sanction the behavior of a titleholder who decided to support high rates of harvest, if that harvest and the wastes generated by the sawmill affected other house territories. The titleholders would also expect to obtain a share of the revenue generated by the timber harvest through the wealth transfers required by the feasting system. If the timber generated more wealth than did salmon and other resources, then some harvesting would have been allowed.

Similarly, if an upstream titleholder used the river to transport logs to a downstream sawmill, the effects of such transport on salmon reproduction would have become a subject of discussion in the feast hall. The largest salmon species, chinook, is known to spawn in rivers. If logging activity was associated with reductions in the return of chinook, the impact of log transport on river spawning would have been given attention.

Loggers also used splash dams to assist in transporting logs in streams with insufficient flow for continual log transport. They built temporary dams to collect a pool of water which would be released all at once. Logs placed in the stream bed would be lifted and moved further down the stream, eventually reaching a river that could take them to a mill. Use of a stream for such transport of logs disturbed the gravel and reduced the ability of salmon to spawn. Had this occurred on a stream controlled by a titleholder, compensation would have been required through the feast system. Probably the titleholder would have had enough authority to prevent the destruction of salmon habitat. Timber that could only have been transported by destroying streams would have remained uncut until railroads and logging trucks could provide transport.

Logging had an impact on resources other than salmon. Clearcuts of old growth in a watershed would remove all plants and animals that lived exclusively in such stands of trees. As with salmon, we do not know the numbers that would describe the trade-off between the value of the timber extracted, and the value of the other plants and animals whose populations would fall after logging. Since some useful plants, such as berries, benefit from forest disturbance, logging done properly could have increased the productivity of those resources.

In a river valley such as the Nass, or in any of the valleys of the small rivers in the Alaskan Panhandle, Haida Gwaii, Vancouver Island, and along the other coasts, acknowledgement of the governance and ownership powers of the traditional titleholders would have meant that the impacts of logging on these other resources would have been considered because of the interdependencies that the feasting system created among the titleholders.

Forest management involves the use of a long time horizon and concern about the regeneration of the forest after harvest. Given their concern for future generations, titleholders would have paid considerable attention to the conditions that were left for their descendants. This would be particularly important if revenue from timber harvest had replaced the harvest of food as a source of support for the population.

The long time horizon of titleholders would conflict with a major idea used by private industry and by centralized state bureaucracies, such as the provincial ministry of forests in British Columbia or the US Forest Service in the United States. All industrial systems of harvesting timber operated on the idea of converting

stands of old-growth timber to younger, faster-growing stands of regenerated timber. While the old-growth trees had reached ages of 300 or more years, under
the formulas motivated by maximum sustained yield, growing trees to such ages
would not be acceptable. Usually the rotation ages used for maximum sustained
yield were in the range of 80–100 years. If indigenous opinion had been important
in determining forest policy, what rotation ages would have been selected?

The Menominee Indian Reservation in Wisconsin is a major case in which
indigenous people have chosen rotation ages for a forest under their control. The
forest on the Menominee Reservation consists of dense stands of trees allowed to
grow to ages much older than the youthful ages used in forestry neighboring the
reservation. The forests of Wisconsin outside the reservation are young stands of
red pine and aspen, serving pulp mills. The stands of older trees on the Menominee
Reservation feed a lumber mill built for large trees (Trosper 2007).

Because the Menominee Tribe lives a long way from the Pacific Northwest
Coast, perhaps one should be careful in asserting that their methods of forest
management are the ones that would have been adopted along the coast. The
Menominee emphasize that they want to preserve the forest for future generations,
under the principle that they are borrowing the forest from their grandchildren.
They are proud of the fact that the volume of timber growing in their forest has
increased under their management. One indication that similar ideas exist on the
Northwest Coast is that the Haida have proposed a very long rotation age for cedar
management. They want to grow monumental cedar, which requires 800 or more
years. This contrasts greatly with rotation ages recommended by standard forestry
for maximum sustained yield, less than 100 years. One of the Gitxsan houses has
also proposed a different management approach for its lands (Pinkerton 1998).
When forests are managed for fast growth and maximum short-term economic
return, the standing volume of timber does not increase as it has on the Menominee
Reservation.

Had titleholders retained their control over their house territories, the role of
provincial and federal forest services would have been different. The central governments would not have been able to assert their authority over large tracts of forest. The consequence would have been a very different pattern of development for
such centralized bureaucracies, and for the forestry profession that developed to
staff the bureaucracies. In this counterfactual story, local control of forested lands
would have dominated. One can speculate on the different pattern of development
of forestry and forest science, with an ecosystem perspective developing much
sooner than it did without the central bureaucracies' exclusive focus on timber
production.

To prove this assertion, consider the role of fire in forests. In the United States,
the US Forest Service established its authority over the nation's forested lands,
in part by promising and delivering on the promise of fire exclusion. Because
the wealth of forests was believed to lie exclusively in the timber, protecting the
forest from fire made some short-term sense. Many people pointed out that fre-
quent, small fires would prevent large ones; but that argument was derided as
'Paiute forestry,' meaning forestry that depended on ideas of indigenous peoples

(Pyne 1982). In this counterfactual, indigenous peoples would have had sufficient control over their lands to insist that their practices, which included using fire as a management tool, would have received more respect. In the rain forests of the Northwest Coast, fire was rare; but dry areas existed, such as in the rain shadow of the coast ranges. The Williamette Valley and the interior parts of the Fraser and Skeena river basins had areas dry enough for fire to be important.

In summary, development of the forest sector would have been very different if titleholder authority over their house territories would have been recognized. Markets for lumber would have meant that titleholders would have been willing to cut their large trees for the return available; but the extent and rate of cutting would have been moderated by concerns about the impact of forestry practices on other resources, primarily salmon. With lower cutting rates, the boom-and-bust cycle caused by liquidation of old growth would have been moderated, perhaps to a great degree. Knowledge about the role of fire would have been recognized sooner; other practices would also have had consideration not given them in the actual history. Nation-state bureaucracies managing timber would not have developed; as a consequence the structure of the forestry profession and forestry science would also have been different.

Agriculture

The counterfactual story for agriculture has to begin with the recognition that the peoples of the Northwest Coast had domesticated some plants not generally recognized as important for agriculture. The strict division of peoples into hunter-gatherers on one hand and agriculturalists on another is now recognized as incorrect. It may have had roots in the ideology of conquest of North America, which portrayed the indigenous peoples as not using the land. Such beliefs justified occupation of indigenous farms, as occurred in Gitxsan and Wet'suwet'en territories. Since the peoples were cultivating, tending, and in other ways conducting various types of agriculture, a counterfactual history should focus on the incorporation of new plants and animals into the existing systems. Settlers, too, could become occupants of the lands, under the jurisdiction and control of titleholders. The settlers would have been incorporated into the feasting system. As with forestry, introduction of new practices in the feasting system would mean recognition of external effects when they were important.

Telling the counterfactual story is difficult because little has been written about the existing systems. The recent book edited by Douglas Deur and Nancy Turner (2005) provides some guidance. Northwest Coast agriculture mainly used perennials, not annuals, which changes the look of the fields and the methods of tending plants: sowing seeds is not an annual event with perennials. In addition, the local plants were more adapted to climatic conditions.

The settlers' agriculture often required irrigation. The practice of farmers radically restructuring the hydrological systems in order to support agriculture would have come under the control of titleholders and, as with forestry, new practices would have been judged in the context of their impacts on existing resources, particularly fisheries. Among the practices with the most impact would be irrigation, which required the building of small dams to control local water flow. Such dams affected streams directly, reducing flows in the streams when water was diverted. The diversion structures, if not screened, channeled young salmon returning to the ocean into the irrigated fields. Lichatowich (1999: 71–78) provides reports of salmon observed in the fields. Had irrigators been accountable to titleholders, such a practice would not have survived. Diversion dams would have had fish-passage facilities, and canals would have had screens.

Grazing also had impacts on streams by changing the patterns of runoff, and because of direct damage to stream banks by cattle. As with other external effects of the new activities, the consequences of grazing on other resources, particularly salmon, would have been subject to control.

Although farmers operated independently, many interdependencies exist in agriculture. Irrigation is an obvious case; the joint works need to be built and maintained, and water needs to be allocated on some basis to individual fields. Insects, in their many roles, also stretch across field boundaries. Some insects are pollinators, others feed on valuable plants and are therefore pests. Given the individualistic orientation of the settlers and the central role of agriculture to their identity, perhaps needing to deal with titleholders regarding access to arable land would have been difficult for them. On the other hand, the inherent variability of crops might have made the reciprocity requirements obviously useful, as a system of insurance against bad times for individual farmers.

Mining

Early settlement was driven by gold discoveries. Since the gold deposits were easily accessed in streambeds, gold mining was directly destructive of fisheries. Most of the impact occurred south of the region considered here; California's rivers had salmon, but the titleholder/house/feast system extended southward only into northern California. When the streams were treated as open to all, with no authority to protect them, the result was the wholesale dredging of streams. At issue would be whether or not the value of the gold extracted was large enough to offset all future returns from the use of streams for fish. The longer the time horizon of the people in authority, the stiffer would have been the requirement that gold be valuable.

Large dams

When applied to salmon fisheries and forestry development, the counterfactual story suggests that state-supported bureaucracies such as fisheries and forestry agencies would have been much weaker. From the outset, they would have been accountable to titleholders for their interventions in fisheries and in forestry. Perhaps the centralized bureaucracies would never have developed. Construction of large dams on the big rivers of the Pacific Northwest was the work of such centralized bureaucracies. In the United States, the Columbia River was developed for hydroelectric production. It happened that the Fraser River was not developed in that manner. One main reason seems to be that in 1937, both the United States and Canada agreed to create the International Pacific Salmon Fisheries Commission. The IPSFC was empowered to speak for the salmon of the Fraser River. No similar institution existed for the Columbia (Lichatowich 1999: 178–86).

I would argue that had the titleholders in indigenous communities been able to speak for the salmon upon which their people relied, they would have been able to sponsor a study like the one the IPSFC conducted regarding the construction of the Moran Dam on the Fraser River. When that high dam was proposed in the 1950s for the Fraser, the IPSFC sponsored a study to examine the feasibility of artificial propagation in replacing all the salmon runs above the dam and half the ones below. They recognized that changes in the river below the dam would also affect salmon. Their conclusion is reported as follows: 'the economic costs of the destroyed salmon runs would make the power produced by the Moran Dam too expensive' (Lichatowich 1999: 196).

The IPSFC was in a position to represent the salmon of the Fraser River because it had been created specifically to manage the salmon in that river for both the United States and Canada. Unlike the situation for other rivers, there was a body that could advocate for salmon. In charging the new dam the full cost of the salmon that would be removed, the IPSFC study showed that the dam would not be able to compensate fishermen for the lost fish. This is the kind of comparison that a feast system for the Fraser would also have required.

Lichatowich also argues that the existence of the IPSFC for the Fraser and the absence of a similar body for the Columbia is a key factor in explaining the different outcomes regarding the construction of hydroelectric dams. He also gives weight to the fact that the Canadians had conducted a study to evaluate the effectiveness of hatcheries. Since the study showed that hatcheries could not replace natural regeneration, it removed the option of using hatcheries to compensate for the effect of a high dam on the mainstem of the Fraser River (Lichatowich 1999: 200–201).

Hatcheries

When I was a child, I lived in the small community of Ahsahka on the Clearwater River, opposite the location where the North Fork of the Clearwater joined the mainstem. I watched the river serve as a road for logs going to the mill in Lewiston, 40 miles down the river. After we moved away, the federal government built a high storage dam, Dworshak Dam, at the mouth of the North Fork, with a big hatchery right below it. The image of that dam and its allied hatchery, I now understand, is common. Development of the Columbia River for electricity has occurred, and hatcheries had to be successful because there was no other way to produce salmon. Fish ladders have not been built for the high dams such as Grand Coulee or Dworshak dams. This building of hatcheries to deal with the consequences of dam building reveals a general principle: given that development of the Northwest was eliminating salmon, an answer had to be found. There was no answer other than artificial propagation with hatcheries. If hatcheries would not work, then the salmon were sacrificed for development (Taylor 1999: 220–21).

Two books deal with the use of hatcheries to provide an alternative to allowing salmon to reproduce naturally in streams. Both Jim Lichatowich (1999) and Joseph Taylor (1999) argue that the hatcheries never proved themselves to be successful at replacing natural runs. But the government agencies that built and maintained hatcheries became dependent on them as a source of funding. Rigorous scientific testing of the impact of hatcheries was rare. The major study that showed hatcheries not to be effective took place on the Fraser River. It influenced Canadian policy, but did not affect policy in the United States.

Hatchery operators needed salmon to provide them with fertilized eggs. Because of their belief that hatcheries were better than natural propagation, hatchery operators often barricaded streams and took all of the spawning salmon, allowing none through. Eliminating all natural reproduction for an unproved alternative demonstrates amazing self-confidence in the ability of the fish culturists to improve on reproduction in streams. These fish racks probably harmed salmon runs more than they benefitted them, because the salmon were usually released from the hatcheries at a time, and in a manner, that made them vulnerable to predation.

Jim Lichatowich uses the example of a hatchery on the Alsea River in Oregon. During the period in which the hatchery's rack took the entire salmon run, 1916–26, the catch of salmon in Alsea Bay averaged 158,000 pounds. Before the rack, the average had been 391,000 pounds, and after the rack was dynamited by upstream residents, the catch rose to an average of 340,000 pounds. The hatchery actually reduced the size of the runs while it was in place, because it restricted natural spawning and did not adequately replace the fish it took (Lichatowich 1999: 144).

Had the hatchery operators been required to participate in a local feasting system, and to show the efficacy of their operation by its ability to generate fish so that the hatchery operators could host feasts and distribute returns to other people on the same river, they would not have been able to ruin salmon runs as they did. In addition, the common pool nature of the fishery meant that the titleholders would have been concerned if they were unable to catch the fish that they expected.

Perhaps the federal financing of the hatcheries would have allowed hatchery operators to demonstrate their ability to share with others. But they would also have had to justify the fish racks and weirs that they used to take all of the spawners in a run. Much like the upstream residents of the Alsea River, the titleholders would have objected to such an extreme policy.

Fisheries scientists did not come to recognize the existence of separate stocks or runs of salmon until the 1930s, although the idea was proposed in 1914 (Lichatowich 1999: 161–65). Because titleholders believed salmon were organized into houses, much like humans were organized into houses, the aboriginal people of the Northwest Coast recognized the separate runs. They knew that spring run chinook, for instance, were from a different house than fall run chinook. They would have inquired of the fish culturists, those who ran the hatcheries, to what extent they were accommodating the need for salmon houses to stay together. This question, had it been asked and answered in the nineteenth century, might have led to a better understanding of salmon biology than the operators of fish hatcheries demonstrated.

One of the main difficulties with the operators of fish hatcheries was that the federally funded operation was not accountable. Fisheries scientists and hatchery operators debated the issue of how long the salmon should be held in the hatchery before release. The usual practice was to release the salmon soon after hatching, while the fry still had sacs attached. In the wild, the sac fry could stay in the gravel while the yolk was absorbed. When released directly into the stream, they were vulnerable to predators.

Lichatowich tells the story of a fight between R. D. Hume, a cannery operator who advocated keeping salmon in a hatchery until they were five to six inches in length, and Henry Van Dusen, Oregon's master fish warden, who advocated early release. Hume fought Van Dusen in the political arena. Although he succeeded in having Van Dusen fired, he did not succeed in changing the policy of releasing young fry. The Oregon state hatcheries continued as they had (Lichatowich 1999: 145–46). Funding for government agencies depended on successful use of the budgetary process, not on proved success in increasing salmon runs. Had the state hatchery system been accountable to Hume, who would himself have been active within a feasting system, their practices may have improved.

The ocean fishery

The proposed alternative story above suggests that, had the characteristics of the aboriginal system remained in place, many of the decisions that created the decline of salmon runs in the Pacific Northwest would have been different. New entrants would have had to participate in a system that made fishermen share in each other's success, that required protection for spawning grounds, that treated all resources as having a proprietor who needed to recognize interdependencies with other resources. People who abused a resource or caused damage to others' interests would have been accountable for their actions.

But is this at all plausible when the modern world has also produced a fishery on the high seas? Once gasoline-powered boats allowed the troll fishery to develop at the turn of the twentieth century, control of river mouths no longer provided control of a river's salmon fishery. Purse seiners also could intercept fish on the high seas. While management of the fishery as an open access resource was a choice made by the settlers – they could have used the indigenous system with its controls on entry – control of the high seas is another matter: open access results from high monitoring costs.

Yet, if externalities were being recognized through implementation of the processes used by the Northwest Coast titleholders, perhaps an innovation could have been developed to handle the high seas. Nation-states were the only ones able to organize enforcement mechanisms on the high seas, through the use of their naval power. If they learned lessons about the pooling of returns from common pool fisheries, the existence of separate stocks that could be threatened with mixed-stock fisheries, and ways to reach agreements through the feasting system, perhaps even nation-states would have been able to solve the open-access dilemmas created by the high-seas fisheries.

Summary of counterfactual

What kind of social–ecological system would exist on the Northwest Coast if the principles used by the aboriginal system would have guided development of the industrial economy? Since part of the problem was treatment of fisheries and forests as open access, is this story driven simply by recognition of proprietorship of those resources by aboriginal houses? Certainly, such recognition is an important part of the story. If titleholders are recognized to have the right to manage the lands and fisheries, as well as the right to be compensated if their property is damaged, many of the open-access issues are indeed addressed. When the settlers refused to recognize the proprietorship rights of the aboriginal people, they converted many of the resources into non-owned and therefore non-cared-for resources.

Some might identify the control held by titleholders as demonstrating the benefits of private property. The counterfactual story also contains elements that would not be present if all the resources had been converted to private property. In a private property system, all rents from resources belong to the owner of the resource. For fisheries, owners hold fishing sites, not the resource, creating the common pool dilemmas that lead to over-harvest.

In the Northwest Coast system, rents are shared among all the corporate groups that operate the economy. The traditional system had shares defined by the hierarchies that had grown over the years. Without more specific data, we can't judge the extent to which the payments due at feasts were balanced in such a way as to create incentives to recognize interdependencies as a best solution to the common pool problem.

If this system of sharing rents had existed in the industrial economy, each of the corporate entities managing new activities would have had to join in the existing rent-sharing system. They would have had to negotiate their positions. The easiest system to imagine is that new industrial activities would have to contract with the relevant titleholders, namely the titleholders upon whose house lands the new activities occurred. The titleholders would then deal with the problem of sharing the resulting rents within their governance system. Those titleholders fortunate enough to hold valuable resources, such as dense stands of old growth, would earn the highest income by allowing the stands to be cut. But they would have to share the resulting revenue with other titleholders, receiving higher status in return. The traditional status hierarchies would probably have had to shift as the industrial economy advantaged one or another house.

Titleholders would also be able to recognize and require compensation for damage caused by activities on other lands. Should one titleholder allow timber activities to have an impact on the salmon resource, other titleholders had ways to affect the offending titleholder. In the first place, the titleholders harmed by external effects would have less wealth to share with other titleholders; this is a direct impact of the externality. But the offending titleholder should have more wealth to share, which might compensate for the losses. If the compensation was insufficient, affected titleholders could start processes that let the offending title-holder know he or she was in trouble. Titleholders could refuse to accept the high payments that resulted from the timber harvest, thus threatening the offending titleholder's right to control his house lands. They would be invoking the sanctions of contingent proprietorship, placing pressures on the offending titleholder.

Another important feature of the aboriginal system is accountability. The story of fish hatcheries as substitutes for natural propagation of salmon highlights the importance of accountability. Titleholders were held responsible for the return of salmon; a failed run was potential disaster for them. Those proposing that hatcher-ies could substitute for spawning in the natural system would have had to actually prove their success. Without proof that hatcheries worked, the use of hatcheries to substitute for destroyed habitat would not have been acceptable.

Another important contribution of recognizing the powers of the aboriginal titleholders would have been that their knowledge of the ecosystem connections would not have been ignored. They knew the components of the salmon life cycle, including the importance of food in the ocean that was brought back to land for the benefit of people and every other entity that relied on salmon, such as bears. They understood that every being both ate and was eaten, meaning that those relationships had to be maintained in order to keep the system operating. Many discoveries by fisheries biologists would have been learned earlier by consulting with titleholders.

Structure of the resulting economy

In general terms, the resulting economy in the Northwest would be one with the characteristics resulting from the incentives described above. Common pool resources such as salmon would still be important. Wealth earned from timber harvest would not have been as great, although clearly the value of the standing stock of trees means that significant harvest would have occurred. Agriculture also would not have been as able to dam rivers and develop irrigation. Grazing would not have been able to destroy grasslands and ruin streams. Mining also would have had fewer side effects. Highly interventionist practices would have been structured to balance the various sources of food from the land.

The resulting economy would have been more resilient. Stocks of resources, especially fish and timber, would have been higher than in the actual history. Agriculture would have been more diverse, with less complete displacement of important indigenous plants.

Currently, the province of British Columbia is suffering from years of timber over-harvest; they cut the standing timber at such a rate that now they need to wait quite a while for the second growth to provide a supply of timber. They have expe-rienced a boom-and-bust cycle. Salmon stocks are extremely low. They have an ample supply of hydroelectric power, based on their share of generation from the Columbia River. Had aboriginal people been able to control the cut on their lands, they would have had more concern for the future (which is now), and today's standing timber would have been more voluminous. Boom-and-bust cycles would have been reduced in forestry, fisheries, and other areas.

Of course, the wealthy people in the system would be the titleholders and their descendants and families. Having managed the shift from a ecosystem-bound economy to one utilizing energy to create additional production, they would have remained in control. Many settlers would have found employment in the industries developed. Quite possibly, the big cities of Vancouver, Seattle, and Portland would not have been able to have such a large share of economic development. The people in the rural areas, led by the titleholders, would have more of the economic activity held at home, particularly with salmon. Now rural British Columbia is facing crisis, with timber scarce and much of what remains being killed by the mountain pine beetle. Perhaps as those rural areas attempt to find resilience, they could use some of the ideas that were so important in structuring relationships among people in the aboriginal social–ecological system.

The result would have been a more diverse landscape in which pre-existing ways of managing the land would have been balanced against the new activities. Of particular importance, the open-access treatment of grass, timber, fish, and gold would not have been allowed. External effects would have been recognized; the interests of neighboring titleholders would have had to be recognized, through the rules of the feast system. When external effects are accounted for, the resulting economy has a greater mix of activities. The result is greater diversity and greater resilience.

8   How contingent proprietorship alone aids resilience: Kerr Dam relicensing

Chapter 7 presented a counterfactual story to explain how adoption of Northwest Coast institutions might have led to a different structure for the coastal economy. Since that story did not occur, it actually proves very little about the potential contribution of those institutions to the resilience of actual economies. This chapter presents a case study demonstrating that the presence of one part of the Northwest Coast system, by itself, can contribute to moving toward resilience

Because humans are so important in ecosystems containing them, understanding resilience requires analysis of human institutions. To be resilient, an ecosystem requires mechanisms, institutions or processes that bring the system back to normal conditions when it strays far from those conditions. In response to an extreme shock or a series of small decisions that create problems, more resilient ecosystems are able to absorb larger perturbations without changing primary structures and processes. In a dynamic system with an adaptive cycle, a resilient system perpetuates the current cycle.

This chapter focuses upon an institution, contingent proprietorship, one of the rules used by indigenous societies in the Pacific Northwest of North America in dealing with problems. A proprietor controls a parcel of land or a key harvesting site, may exclude others, may assign the land or site to another person, but may not sell. If he misuses the property, a contingent proprietor may have his proprietorship removed or he may be punished. Misuse of the property can be defined as actions that harm and ecosystem or the land itself.

The purpose of this chapter is to examine an example that shows how a rule like one of those used by Northwest Coast peoples has been used in contemporary conditions to improve some people's relationship to their environment. In particular, Section 4(e) of the Federal Power Act (1920) allows the Secretary of the Interior to modify hydroelectric licenses:

> *Provided*, that licenses shall be issued within any reservation only after a finding by the Commission that the license will not interfere or be inconsistent with the purpose for which such reservation was created or acquired, and shall be subject to and contain such conditions as the Secretary of the department under whose supervision such reservation falls shall deem necessary for the adequate protection and utilization of such reservation.

[16 U.S.C.A.§ 797 (e)]

Because of this law, operation rules for Kerr Dam were changed and the operator of the dam was required to engage in mitigation measures in order to protect river and lake ecosystems on the Flathead Indian Reservation in western Montana. When the original license for Kerr Dam was issued in 1930, this provision was not enforced; but when the Montana Power Company (MPC) applied for a new license in 1980, after the 50-year term of the original license, the *contingency* of this provision was applied. MPC's proprietorship of Kerr Dam was a case of *contingent proprietorship*. Unlike the example of the two dams on the Elwha River, removal was not considered as an option. Further, decisions were made regarding Kerr Dam without having Congress pass a specific new law, as occurred with the Elwha dams.

The Federal Power Act's 4(e) conditions place the Secretary of the Interior in a position similar to that of a Guide Chief of the Upper Kutenai, some of whom now live on the Flathead Indian Reservation. Kerr Dam occupies a major fishing site used by the Kutenai. An anthropologist reported the following rules for use of fishing sites:

> An Upper Kutenai could build a fish trap only after obtaining permission from the chief. No one could build more than one. The fisher was given a definite franchise for a specific stream, in return for which he entered into a contractual relation with the band in the person of its chief. The chief guaranteed him exclusive right to the site, but the owner had to share the product of the weir with some eight or nine families. Since he got the lion's share of the trout *per diem* in the right season, this sharing worked no hardship on the fisher. ... But they [the fishermen] did not own the stream. This was the property of the people at large under the direction of their principal socio-economic functionary, the Guide Chief. The stream could not be abused or the fishermen were punished. As a rental, so to speak, of the resources on the public domain, they had to provide for the public.
>
> (Turney-High 1941: 47, 52)

This quotation contains reference to many of the elements of fishery management that contributed to the success of Indians in the Pacific Northwest: contingent proprietorship; the contingency depended upon a concept of not abusing a stream; exclusive use of sites when granted by a chief; and a requirement to share the catch with other members of the community. Although the quotation does not describe the public accountability or other characteristics required of chiefs, it does describe the role of chiefs in knitting together the system of ecosystem caretaking.

Kerr Dam: a modern case of contingent tenure?

We now turn to consideration of the effectiveness of implementation of only parts of this system, through contingent proprietorship. As shown by the following account of the events regarding the granting of a new license for Kerr Dam, the principle of contingent proprietorship applied. In addition, some improvement in environmental conditions will probably result. After reviewing the story of Kerr Dam relicensing, this chapter considers the extent to which the management of the Flathead Lake and River system also involves any of the other five Northwest Coast principles.

Original license

After a brief period of public controversy about what share of the returns would go to the Confederated Salish and Kootenai Tribes, the Federal Power Commission awarded hydroelectric license #5 to a subsidiary of MPC in 1930. Delayed by the onset of the Depression, construction began late in the 1930s, and Kerr Dam began operation in 1938. It contributed one-third of the power for the company. A third generating unit was added in the early 1950s. During the 50 years of the license, the role of Kerr changed. By the end of the license term, Kerr had become less important as a source of power and more important as a 'peaking' and 'load-following' facility. A peaking facility assists a utility in meeting peak demands, both foreseen and unforeseen. A load-following facility provides the difference between supply and demand on an instantaneous basis, preserving the quality of electricity supplied by keeping 60 cycles per minute of alternating current exactly on target. Load-following also assists in adjusting load to hourly purchases and sales of energy to other generators and other electricity systems.

The original license had no environmental provisions as they are known today. The annual rental paid to the Confederated Tribes was to be adjusted after the first 20 years of the license and if a new unit were added. Enforcement of the provision to change the rental paid the Tribes proved difficult. The Tribes had to appeal to the Federal Power Commission and the federal courts to have the annual rental for the Tribes' lands increased as provided in the license, which followed provisions in the Federal Power Act. [*Montana Power Company v. Federal Power Commission* 298 F2d 335 (1962) and *Montana Power Company v. Federal Power Commission* 459 F2d 863 (1972), cert denied 408 US 930.] As record P-5 of the Federal Energy Regulatory Commission (FERC), Kerr Dam is now listed as the oldest of the licenses in the data base.

Kerr Dam occupies a major fishing site for the Confederated Tribes. It severed the connection between Flathead Lake and the lower Flathead River, thus changing migration routes for fish in both bodies of water. Prior to construction of the dam, Flathead Lake filled each spring behind the natural constriction of the mouth of the lake, and then drained in early summer. Flows in the river were high in the spring, and low in the late summer, fall and winter. Once in place, the dam held the lake at full pool throughout the summer and well into winter. Flows in the river fell during the summer as they had before, but were high during the winter as Kerr generated power. The top ten feet of Flathead Lake serve as the reservoir for Kerr Dam.

Flows in the river also varied on an hourly basis as a result of peaking and load-following by Kerr. The populations of insects and other food sources for fish that normally would exist on the sides of the river's flow were severely reduced. For this and other reasons not the fault of the dam (a major irrigation project affected tributaries to the river), the native fish of the river declined dramatically. Fisheries that had been important food sources for the Confederated Tribes declined. Introduced fish, brown trout and northern pike, also did not reach population numbers that would have been typical of a river such as the Flathead below Kerr Dam. Because Kerr Dam is located just downstream from the natural outlet/dam that created Flathead Lake, water from the lake still flows from the top into the Flathead River. Consequently, no significant change in temperature regime occurred as a result of the dam.

As the end of the 50-year term of the license neared in 1980, both MPC and the Confederated Salish and Kootenai Tribes applied for the subsequent license. While the Tribes' motivation originally was a desire to obtain a higher rental, as FERC issued a series of one-year licenses, the tribal leadership became more interested in actually obtaining the license. Part of the reason was recognition of the economic value of the dam; but the value of controlling dam operation was also recognized. The Tribes had started formal studies of the river, and evidence that the dam had severe environmental consequences began to accumulate. A major tribal rally in support of the new license occurred on an old summer camping site on the river, and another occurred on the bluff above Kerr Dam. A consequence of the rally was that the Tribes became interested in operating the dam in order to deal with the environmental consequences

Emergence of 4(e) with teeth

The 4(e) conditions of the Federal Power Act, quoted at the beginning of this chapter, state quite clearly that the Secretary of the Interior had the power to impose conditions on licenses. In 1984, the Supreme Court affirmed that section 4(e) did indeed give the Secretary of the Interior the right to impose conditions on hydroelectric projects that affected Indian reservations. After reviewing the language and legislative history of the Federal Power Act, the Supreme Court concluded as follows in *Escondido Mutual Water Company v. LaJolla Band of Mission Indians:*

> If the Secretary concludes that the conditions are necessary to protect the reservation, the Commission is required to adopt them as its own, and the court is obligated to sustain them if they are reasonably related to that goal, otherwise consistent with the FPA, and supported by substantial evidence. The fact that in reality it is the Secretary's, and not the Commission's judgment to which the court is giving deference is not surprising since the statute directs the Secretary, and not the Commission, to decide what conditions are necessary for the adequate protection of the reservation. There is nothing in the statute or the review scheme to indicate that Congress wanted the Commission to second-guess the Secretary on this matter.

[466 US 767 (1984), at 778–79]

In a footnote to the above quotation, the Supreme Court indicates that the issue of 4(e) conditions had not been tested much before this case. Previously, the Federal Power Commission and its successor, FERC, had either accepted the conditions without disagreement, or few conditions had been imposed that the Commission did not approve as well. The emergence of the issue regarding Indian lands coincides with increasing self-determination efforts by tribes; in fact the La Jolla, Rincon and San Pasqual Bands in this case had applied for a non-power license to operate the same facilities that were awarded to the Escondido Mutual Water Company. The Secretary of the Interior had also asked for federal takeover of the project.

Second license provisions

The *Escondido* decision occurred as both the Confederated Tribes and the Company faced risks in their competition for the new license. The Confederated Tribes were having difficulty satisfying a FERC administrative judge that they were competent to be licensees. At the same time, MPC faced the chance that the annual charge would be placed at approximately one-half of the net value of Kerr generation, which was worth $50,000,000 per year in the mid-1980s.

FERC's administrative law judge urged the parties to reach a settlement. The company, the Tribes, and the Department of the Interior negotiated in late 1984, after the *Escondido* decision in May of that year. The company and the Tribes agreed to become co-licensees; the Tribes' annual rental would start at only $9,000,000 per year; but the Tribes would have the option to become the operator of the dam for the last 20 years of the license, from 2015–35. To become operator of the dam, the Tribes could purchase the dam at original cost less accumulated depreciation (book value, not replacement cost). The Tribes insisted that articles of the new license recognize the Secretary's 4(e) environmental responsibilities. Article 45 addressed fish, and article 46 addressed wildlife.

Somewhat mirroring the two parts of section 4(e), each article contained a first clause requiring a plan to be submitted for Commission approval that would 'protect and enhance' fish or wildlife resources. The plans were to be based on studies currently under way with Bonneville Power Administration support, or to be conducted under other funding before the deadline of October 1, 1989 for plan submission. Each article contained a second clause, which referred to the Secretary of the Interior's 4(e) powers. All parties agreed to waive any claim that the secretary's action would be untimely (since it would occur after the new license was issued). A selection of the language of the section is as follows:

> (b) Notwithstanding the adoption of conservation measures pursuant to the preceding provision of this article, and without resolving the question of whether Section 4(e) of the Act applies to this proceeding, the Secretary shall be allowed, within a reasonable time upon completion of the studies described in Articles 45(a), 46 (a) and 47, to impose such reasonable license conditions with respect to fish and related environmental concerns as the Secretary

would be empowered under Section 4(e) to require with respect to an initial license.

The language in Section 4(e) states that such conditions would be necessary 'for the adequate protection and utilization of such reservation.'

The standards and the enforcer differed for the two parts of each article. In part (a), the standards were to 'protect and enhance' specific resources, and they would be enforced by the Federal Energy Commission through approval of a management plan. In part (b), they were for 'protection and utilization' of the Flathead Indian Reservation, and would be conditions placed in the license as determined by the Secretary of the Interior without review by the Commission. The license added provisions that the conditions be timely and reasonable. The Tribes wanted quick action, and the company feared unreasonable conditions.

That the environmental issues were not settled before issuance of the new license was unusual. Normally, FERC and the parties have to comply with the requirements of the National Environmental Protection Act. In this case, the Tribes were anxious to receive the new rental, which was much larger than the previous rental of $2.6 million per year. The company was anxious to have its right to operate the dam assured, and realized that delays in complying with the new license provisions would delay the expenses that would be incurred in such compliance.

Environmental mitigation discussion under the license

For 15 years, the parties negotiated, litigated, and mediated enforcement of the environmental provisions of the new license. The final result was a substantial mitigation package, which will be described below. The company almost met its deadline in the license to provide a mitigation plan; it submitted a plan in 1990. The Secretary of the Interior, through the Bureau of Indian Affairs (BIA), studied the plan and provided proposed conditions in 1994. The Secretary's proposal reflected the desires of the Confederated Tribes. The company strongly objected to the proposed conditions, which eliminated both peaking and load following from the operation of the dam, in addition to requiring annual payments into a fund for further fisheries mitigation in both the lake and the lower river. In addition, the proposed conditions required purchase of substantial amounts of land to provide replacement wildlife habitat. The Secretary also proposed that the company pay for mitigation that had not occurred between 1985 and imposition of the 4(e) conditions.

FERC prepared an environmental impact statement using three alternatives for analysis: the current operation of the dam; Montana Power's 1990 proposed plan; and the Department of the Interior's proposed conditions. After reviewing comments on the environmental impact statement, FERC amended the license on June 25, 1997, adopting the conditions of the Secretary of the Interior that carried out his 4(e) powers. On October 8, 1998, FERC modified its previous ruling slightly, including an article allowing FERC to continue to deal with the consequences of the listing of bull trout under the Endangered Species Act. FERC refused to review the reasonableness of the Department's conditions, since the Supreme Court had delegated that authority to the courts, not to the Commission.

After final determination by FERC, MPC appealed to the Court of Appeals in Washington, DC, in late 1998. The dam ceased peaking and load following FERC's 1997 order. Once the Court of Appeals took up the case, it appointed a mediator to assist the parties in reaching an agreement without having to present the case to the Court.

On February 11, 1999, under the 1997 deregulation actions of the State of Montana, MPC sought to sell all its generating plants, including Kerr (Montana Power Company 1999). The purchaser of Kerr, PP&L Montana, a subsidiary of Pennsylvania Power and Light, became involved in the negotiations. PP&L Montana needed to know the cost of the environmental conditions prior to purchasing Kerr Dam; this need pressed upon Montana Power to settle the litigation quickly. On April 20, 2000, all parties agreed to settle the outstanding issues and asked FERC to amend the license to enforce the agreement.

The final deal and license

The purpose of this section is to describe the outcome of the settlement, and to determine whether exercise of 4(e) powers was to move the Flathead River and Lake ecosystem toward better ecological conditions.

Provisions

In the final agreement, the parties agreed to the following provisions. Most of them were the conditions imposed by the Secretary of the Interior, modified by the parties so that MPC would withdraw its appeal of FERC's decision that incorporated the Secretary's original 4(e) conditions.

- The project would operate as a baseload facility; no peaking or load-following would be allowed.
- According to Article 63, the Confederated Salish and Kootenai Tribes would be responsible for conducting a Fish and Wildlife Implementation Strategy (FWIS). The operator of the dam pays an annual amount to support the FWIS activities. The annual payment was set at $1.3 million in 1997 dollars, to be adjusted annually with the consumer price index.
- Montana Power and PP&L Montana contributed initial funds for establishment of a fishery supplementation program to replace the fisheries damaged by the dam. Total contribution to this effort was approximately $7 million.
- The two companies paid the Confederated Tribes for acquisition of habitat to replace that damaged along the lake and river by the operations of the dam. A total of 3089 acres would be purchased at an estimated total cost of $17.3 million. Lands already owned on the river by MPC, 669 acres, were included.
- Funds were provided for restoration of the habitat acquired, a total of $10,875,000.

- Total expenditure by MPC, $32 million, could be recovered from its rate-payers through the activities of Montana's Public Service Commission. Any funds that were recovered in that way would not later be added to the original cost of the license if the Confederated Tribes decided to become the dam operator in 2015.
- Because the bull trout had been listed as an endangered species, the final license recognized the role of the US Fish and Wildlife Service (USFWS) in reviewing measures proposed under the FWIS, to prevent excessive take of bull trout. FERC insisted that the operator of the dam, not the Confederated Tribes, be responsible for compliance with the Endangered Species Act, because FERC had no authority over the Tribes until they were to become operator of the dam.

Contribution to ecosystem improvement

The amended license placed the Confederated Salish and Kootenai Tribes in charge of management of the mitigation measures that had been agreed to. The Secretary of the Interior's 4(e) conditions gave the Tribes the responsibility to carry out the other 4(e) conditions. The Tribes assigned management responsibility to their Division of Fish, Wildlife, Recreation and Conservation. In the introduction to the FY2001 4(e)-Condition Submittals, the implementation of the provisions were placed within the overall goals of the Division:

> … the central purpose of this document is to describe an integrated process that provides for the adequate protection and utilization of fish and wildlife resources and attendant habitat of the Flathead Indian Reservation. That purpose is consistent with the overall mission of the Tribes' Division of Fish, Wildlife, Recreation, and Conservation, which is to protect and enhance the fish, wildlife, and wildland recreation resources of the Confederated Salish and Kootenai Tribes for the continued use of future generations. The goals of the individual programs within the division are tiered to this overall mission. These goals are listed below and will guide each program's implementation of the FWIS.
>
> The Tribes' traditional use of resources is closely tied to their culture and language. Work will be done with the Tribal Preservation Office to benefit from this traditional knowledge in the restoration of our native habitats. In addition, the Tribes consider the education of the public and the enforcement of laws and regulations to be an integral part of fish and wildlife management. The Information and Education, Conservation, and Wildland Recreation programs are included here to increase the effectiveness of the mitigation program and to further guarantee the adequate protection and utilization of fish and wildlife resources and attendant habitat of the Flathead Indian Reservation.
>
> (Confederated Salish and Kootenai Tribes 2000: 12)

The program follows this general statement with specifics for each program. A sample of the specifics is the following mission statement for the Wildlife Management Program:

To protect, restore, enhance, and manage terrestrial wildlife species and habitats to provide for viable populations of all wildlife species on the Flathead Indian Reservation for use by the generations of today and tomorrow.

(ibid.: 13)

Within the program supported by Kerr Dam, the Wildlife Management Program has the following specific goals statement for the lands that are to be purchased:

The goal for enhancement of acquired habitat is to restore habitat quality and functions to a state similar to that lost. The ultimate goal is to restore native plant communities and maximize the habitat and wildlife productivity of each parcel to the greatest extent possible within the limits of what is economically feasible.

(ibid.: 19)

The settlement agreement for Kerr Dam, by empowering and financing the activities of the Confederated Tribes, will support restoration activities on the Flathead Indian Reservation, both along Flathead River and in uplands near the river which can serve as replacement habitat for riparian lands along the river that cannot be restored because periodic large floods have been removed both by Kerr Dam and by Hungry Horse above Kerr. In addition, purchase of lands on the reservation can create corridors that allow wildlife to use broader areas than they would without corridors.

Article 63, paragraph (8) explicitly refers to adaptive management; the entire article reads as if written with the idea of adaptive management as a motivation: much monitoring and evaluation of program results are required. The Strategy is to be designed in consultation with other entities involved, such as the Montana Department of Fish, Wildlife and Parks, and the USFWS. The Secretary of the Interior reviews the plan and each annual workplan and report.

When FERC accepted the amended articles, market prices for electricity were low in terms of recent price history– around $20–25 per megawatt hour. In late 2000 and early 2001, the energy crisis in California accompanied an increase in the price of electric power back to the level of $50 per megawatt hour, which had been in place in the 1980s when the license was originally negotiated. Because Kerr produces about a million megawatt hours a year, the value of Kerr at $50 per megawatt hour is $50 million. In comparison with these numbers, the cost of Kerr Dam mitigation is modest, in terms of both the one-time cost to purchase lands and the loss in value from moving to baseload operation. The total cost of land purchase and rehabilitation was about $34 million; the annual costs of the FWIS is about $1.5 million, and the annual cost of baseload operation is somewhere between $3 and $6 million from the foregone values of peaking and load-following. When FERC agreed to the compromise, these figures seemed large in proportion to the annual value of the dam; with the increase in prices due to the California crisis, the numbers do not seem so large. The annual charge paid to the Confederated Tribes reached $13 million in 1997.

But in comparison with the levels of mitigation in the prior license term, the provisions under the 4(e) conditions imposed by the Secretary of the Interior are a significant move toward improvement in ecosystem functioning. They empower the Confederated Salish and Kootenai Tribes to improve ecosystem management, which the Tribes wish to do. Annual FWIS reports, which began in 2000, will provide data on the improvements if and when they occur.

The Kerr Dam Settlement and Northwest Coast principles

With the final form of the Kerr License, the Secretary of the Interior played part of the role of the Guide Chief, punishing MPC and its ratepayers for damaging Flathead Lake and River and requiring a change in behavior. This shows the presence of contingent tenure; were others of the principles present? The answer is that proprietorship, environmental ethics, and public information join with contingent proprietorship as key features. Examples of reciprocity and of chiefs acting as facilitators are not present to any significant degree. This section of the chapter examines the story of relicensing in light of all six of the observed characteristics in the Pacific Northwest, beginning with the most important one, contingent proprietorship.

Contingent proprietorship

The authors of the Federal Power Act intended to keep control of the nation's rivers in the hands of the federal government: no license for a hydroelectric dam could exceed 50 years. These authors probably did not foresee that the Commission in charge of enforcing the act would come to favor electricity production over other concerns. Consistent with the experience of other such regulatory bodies, FERC did come to be captured by its constituency. It also became quasi-judicial in character (Echeverria *et al.* 1989).

Because the enforcing Commission of the federal government came to have a pro-electric power bias, the contingency of the 50-year license had to have other agencies enforce other interests. Several such powers developed in federal law, chief among them being the National Environmental Policy Act. But that Act is a purely procedural one; it requires agencies to provide thorough review of alternatives; it does not provide standards for selection of an alternative. Although the Federal Power Act states that FERC is to consider the public interest broadly, a pro-power bias can exist within those rules. Amendments changing the matters FERC is to consider, such as those in the Electric Consumers Protection Act (100 Stat. 1244), still leaves considerable discretion to FERC regarding its interpretation of the law.

Section 4(e) of the Federal Power Act, however, after the *Escondido* decision, gives authority to Secretaries of Agriculture, Interior, and Defense to impose conditions that FERC must accept. In the case of an Indian reservation, the Secretary of the Interior becomes capable of 'punishing' a licensee if he has damaged a river by imposing conditions to reverse or at least mitigate that damage. Past experience had shown that peaking and load-following operations damaged the fishery in the Lower Flathead River.

Evidence also existed that holding the reservoir at full pool throughout the summer damaged wildlife on the lake, and operation of the reservoir during the winter damaged salmon reproduction. But both these assertions are clouded by other influences. Residential development around the lake also would have affected wildlife. Introduced species also changed the lake's food web.

One might assume, however, that a Guide Chief would have been able to punish a weir owner on an annual basis. The power of the Secretary of the Interior exists only upon issuance of an original license (when the damage must be predicted) or upon relicensing, when some damage can be documented but additional damage must also be predicted. Thus the power of the Secretary of the Interior (or Agriculture or Defense) is not as great as the Kutenai Guide Chief used to have. Further, once the license is issued, FERC, not Interior, is responsible for enforcement, although the license specifies that the BIA reviews FWIS plans.

An effort to weaken section 4(e) in President Bush's new energy policy did not succeed. Congress mandated only a study of the effects of 4(e). Thus 4(e) conditions have enough bite in them to worry energy firms, and to create support for continuing to have the Secretary of the Interior be able to impose them (Energy Policy Act of 2005, Pub.L. 109-58).

Proprietorship

The ecosystem affected by Kerr Dam involves a considerable amount of proprietorship, and in that way contrasts with situations where land is held by owners. A proprietor holds a piece of property with the power to exclude, manage, and give to another. An owner holds a piece of property as does a proprietor, with the additional power of selling it to whomever the owner wishes. A hydroelectric licensee is a proprietor, because any sales of the license require the approval of FERC. FERC reviews sales to require that the purchaser is a qualified operator; a sale requires a FERC order to be valid.

In addition, the licensee of Kerr Dam does not have exclusive control over operation of the dam. Even without the license 4(e) requirements, the Corps of Engineers prescribes lake levels for flood control each spring; the basin-wide rules for salmon recovery affect timing of flows through their effect on Hungry Horse, the large upstream reservoir.

Because tribes cannot sell trust land, the Salish and Kootenai Tribes are proprietors of the river, the dam site, and all land that they own. Lands designated for wildlife mitigation become the property of the Tribes with a conservation easement in perpetuity, further limiting land-use choices for the Tribes. The Tribes do not object; in fact they are in favor of the conservation easement.

Environmental ethics

To what extent did decisions regarding relicensing Kerr Dam show evidence of the unity of man and nature, the importance of restricting consumption, and concern for the future? A pro-ecosystem ethic was involved in the Secretary's determination of the appropriate conditions to impose on the licensee. In its presentation of the 4(e) conditions, the Department simply claimed that the provisions were necessary to protect the Reservation – using the language of the Federal Power Act. When challenged in comments, however, the Department responded with more detailed justification for its actions. In justifying baseload operation, the Department criticized peaking as 'highly damaging to tribal resources, held in trust by the Department, on the lower Flathead River' (Department of the Interior, 1995: 7). Referring to studies commissioned by the Department to evaluate Montana Power's proposed operation rules, the Department stated:

> As indicated in Stetson (1994) and Garcia *et al.* (1994), a substantial body of scientific data attributes the loss of productive capacity and currently impaired resources within the lower Flathead River primarily to peaking and load following operations. If the Department were to accept the proposed changes from commentators [MPC] in the operational flow condition, unacceptable impacts would continue to occur to the resources on the Flathead Indian Reservation.
>
> (Department of the Interior 1995: 17–18)

As quoted above, the Tribes' FY 2001 4(e) Condition Submittals on the overall fish and wildlife goals of the Confederated Salish and Kootenai Tribes departments show a desire to establish conditions that were present prior to the construction of the dam.

In fact, the license itself, as revised, has statements that show concern for the environment. A portion of Article 64, for example, reads as follows:

> Methods for achieving avoidance, minimization, restoration, and/or replacement should be designed to protect, enhance and restore native fish stocks, including fish species listed pursuant to the Endangered Species Act, through appropriate fishery management actions, which should address control of non-native species and/or supplementation of desired species populations, and which may include, but are not limited to, restoration of native fish species spawning habitat and enhancement of native fish species' rearing habitat in Flathead Lake, and the lower Flathead River and its tributaries.
>
> (93 FERC 62:198)

Although pro-environment, none of these statements clearly places man and animals in the unity of relationship represented by the Northwest Coast idea that man and salmon are the same; the concern is for the functioning of the ecosystem. The idea of restraint in consumption is consistent with baseload operation, a sacrifice of maximum economic value for other benefits. The idea that reservation resources are 'trust' resources involves an ambiguous reference to the future. One can say that some environmental ethics were present in the statements of the Department of the Interior; but the strength of the statements do not match those of the Northwest Coast beliefs.

An environmental ethic is stronger in the actions of the Confederated Salish and Kootenai Tribes. The deal struck between MPC and the Tribes shows a significant difference between them in valuing the future. The Tribal Council gave up an annual rental of $25 million/year for a rental of $9 million/year in return for the opportunity to purchase the entire dam 30 years after the start of the license. The Company (whose cost of capital at the time was about 11 per cent per year) was quite happy to make such a trade. The Tribes could anticipate a return of $50 million per year after transfer of the license in 2015: with its low implicit discount rate, the Tribal Council was also willing to make the trade.

The best alternative to not agreeing for both parties was most likely awarding the operation to MPC with a rental of $25 million per year for 50 years. For the Tribes, the alternative agreed to was $9 million rental for 30 years followed by purchase of the dam for $2.5 million in 1985 dollars at year 30, and a return of $50 million per year for 20 years. Ignoring the cost of purchasing the dam (which involves uncertainty about inflation rates – assumed to be 5 per cent per year at the time), compared with the alternative, the company had a return of $16 million for 30 years followed by a loss of $50 million for 20 years, and the Tribes had the reverse. For the company at its cost of capital, 11 per cent nominal interest, the present value of the deal was positive ($122 million). For the Tribes, the deal was positive at any real discount rate *below* 2.91 per cent, which is the discount rate at which the present value of the deal is exactly zero. (At a discount rate of 2.5 per cent, for instance, the net present value was $37 million.) For the company, the deal was positive for any real discount rate above 2.91 per cent. The deal was possible because the Tribes valued the future at a higher rate than did the company.

In its plans for use of the mitigation funds, the Tribes show recognition of the unity of man and nature in the mission and methods of the Natural Resource Department, which include management and education of humans as well as investment in the lands purchased for mitigation purposes. The willingness to accept baseload operation indicates acceptance of reduced consumption from the monetary value of the dam.

Reciprocity

The prominent role of potlatching in the Pacific Northwest Coast suggests that a system of reciprocal exchange of the net returns from an ecosystem is a key feature of their incentives that supported sustainability and resilience. To what extent did the final license provisions create a system of reciprocity (side payments, in current economics lingo) among the entities charged with key decision-making powers regarding Kerr Dam and the associated ecosystem? The answer is that no reciprocity system is present. Rules designate payments to be made among the parties involved; but these payments and the conditions governing operation of the dam are fixed solidly in the license and do not depend on operational decisions. The operator of Kerr Dam is required to pay a fixed annual charge to the Tribes, and thus shares a portion of the net return – but not a proportion of the net return. When the value of electricity fell to around $22 per megawatt hour, the possibility arose that the annual rental, tied to the consumer price index, might rise above the net value of the dam on an annual basis. No clause addressed this contingency; the increase in electricity prices in 2001 in the West has reduced its likelihood.

The possibility of one party throwing a large feast with the purpose of opening a discussion about changes in the management of the dam is not credible; changes in the terms of the license would involve a judicial process in front of FERC.

The license provides that the operator of the dam will pay for some rehabilitation of the ecosystem affected by the dam. There is no reverse payment planned; if the rehabilitation is especially successful, and those using the river's resources benefit as a result (through increased fish harvest, for instance), the operator of the dam will not benefit in any automatic way.

Prior to deregulation, MPC received a payment on its invested capital and the remainder of the net value of power generation was transferred to MPC's customers. After deregulation, the customer's share should decrease, since the generation capacity has been sold and now MPC, as a power distribution firm, will purchase the power on the wholesale market at whatever prices are set by competition on that market. During a transition period, Montana Power will purchase power at low rates on long-term contracts from PP&L; eventually, however, those contracts will expire and new market conditions will change the price of power purchased by Montana Power from the wholesale market. In the case of pre-existing hydro-electric power dams, deregulation involves a transfer of net value from consumers to producers, mediated by the rules that govern transition between systems. The national policy goal was to achieve efficiency in electricity distribution by eliminating the low prices received by some power consumers in places such as Montana. The result in the case of Kerr Dam will be to reduce 'sharing' with the consumers of Montana Power's electricity. Neither of the two situations, however, is a system of reciprocity. When MPC's customers benefitted, they simply benefitted. When the current operator earns profit on the dam, it benefits.

Accountability through public information

Since a reciprocity system is not in place, openness about exchanges is less of an issue; public accountability in a reciprocity situation is necessary to prevent cheating. Public regulation of utilities involves public information on the costs of electricity generation, often in considerable detail. Until deregulation removed a degree of oversight by public service commissions, much in electricity generation was public. MPC asked that its ratepayers compensate the company for the costs of environmental mitigation for Kerr Dam at the same time that it was pressing for the Confederated Tribes to agree to pay for that mitigation if the Tribes were to exercise their option to purchase the dam in 2015. The public record of the Montana Public Service Commission allowed the Tribes to catch this effort to obtain payment twice, in spite of MPC's attempts to hide its maneuver. As a result, the final agreement provided that the company would be paid only once.

Deregulation has reduced the transparency of electricity markets. The companies that own generation facilities reveal their general profits to their stockholders through regulations of the stock exchanges. When FERC deregulated wholesale power, they cancelled the requirement of annual filing of FERC Form 1, which would reveal the particulars of profit on Kerr Dam.

The FWIS process will also be quite public because of the regulatory powers of FERC. All reports need to be submitted to FERC, and those reports were available for a while on the internet; a recent check of the FERC website did not reveal that the reports are online any longer.

Facilitating leadership

The leadership mode for regulating the use of hydroelectric dams is not one in which leaders facilitate joint decisions; rather it is a system of state regulation of private behavior. At issue is whether or not a 'chief' has been delegated the authority to impose a rule, and whether or not the chief uses that authority to impose the rule. Examination of the leadership system thus involves identifying the powers of each entity, rather than the reciprocal responsibilities of each to the others.

In this case, three entities had power to punish those that harmed the Flathead River and Lake: FERC, the Secretary of the Interior, and the USFWS. Each exercises different standards for defining harm. FERC's standards are defined by the Federal Power Act as amended; FERC's standards used to be biased toward maximizing the market value of electricity generated. But the Electric Consumers Protection Act of 1986 (ECPA) requires FERC to examine environmental costs on an equal basis with the benefits of river development. As a result, FERC has considerable authority to protect the environment, but little desire to use that authority.

The Secretary of the Interior has a vague standard, protecting reservations from harm; but the Secretary also has a nearly absolute power to enforce actions it deems necessary to enforce the standard. The USFWS may protect threatened and endangered species. In this case, the Service listed the bull trout (*Salvelinus confluentus*) on June 10, 1998. The USFWS has the considerable power of other federal agencies, but the scope of that power is limited to protecting listed species.

By becoming co-licensee, the Confederated Salish and Kootenai Tribes obtained a place at the table in all proceedings having to do with the environmental issues affecting Kerr Dam. No provision of the license or of law gives the Tribes authority commensurate with that of the three federal entities. The Secretary's 4(e) powers, however, provided a way for the Tribes to intervene. If the Tribes could convince their trustee that certain measures were required for the 'protection and utilization' of the Flathead Indian Reservation, then the Secretary could impose 4(e) conditions.

As shown in the telling of the story above, the Tribes successfully persuaded the Secretary to impose stringent 4(e) conditions (stringent as measured by the opposition presented by MPC). By this method, the Tribes became a kind of Guide Chief in the process. Strictly speaking, however, as co-licensees, MPC, its successor PP&L, and the Confederated Salish and Kootenai Tribes are 'weir owners.' They are the entities that have been given the right to operate Kerr. In the opinion of FERC, however, there can be only one operating licensee at a time. Until 2015, that licensee is PP&L Montana.

Two entities affect the distribution of the electricity benefits from Kerr: FERC and Montana's Public Service Commission. FERC's influence is determining the annual rental that is due to the Confederated Tribes. FERC also sets national policy for the wholesale electric market, including transmission rules. The Public Service Commission's role is setting rates for the consumers of Montana, based on wholesale costs. During the first license period, Montana Power's ratepayers benefitted from the standard rate-of-return rules of rate-setting, which guaranteed to MPC a fixed rate of return on its invested capital equal to its cost of capital. If the opportunity cost of electricity is defined by the next least costly method of generation, then the benefit to ratepayers from rate-of-return regulation was substantial. During the last year of the old license system, 1984, the subsidy was about $47 million per year. Immediately after the new license began, that benefit was approximately $40 million per year. When the market value of electricity fell to half its previous value and the rental to the Tribes increased, the subsidy fell to the range of $7–12 million per year.

The 1985 license increased the annual charge paid the Confederated Tribes. Rate-of-return regulation continued in Montana until the Legislature enacted its version of deregulation in 1997. The eventual result of deregulation, unless modified again, will be to allow PP&L Montana to charge the long-term wholesale price of power. If this occurs, then the benefit to Montana's ratepayers from rate-of-return regulation of Kerr Dam will disappear. In the near future, however, PP&L agreed to sell power back to Montana Power at the 1999 long-term rate of $22.5 per megawatt hour until 2008.

The Public Service Commission also allowed MPC to charge the cost of mitigation expenses against its rates. Thus, in effect, the consumers of MPC's electricity will pay the costs of mitigation.

Although the Confederated Tribes were not among the entities formally able to change the operation of Kerr Dam, the Tribes operated behind the scenes to encourage the Department of the Interior to impose significant operational and financial requirements on the dam operators in order to reduce the harm the dam causes to the Flathead River and lake system. The Tribes also became major actors in carrying out the mitigation plans. Regarding mitigation in Flathead Lake, the Tribes operate in cooperation with Montana's Department of Fish and Wildlife. With regard to the lower Flathead River, the Tribes are the primary administrators of the adaptive management plans that are called for in the license. In both cases, the operator of the license is responsible for providing reports to FERC that it is complying with the license terms.

When the Department of the Interior provided articles to the license under its 4(e) authority, the Department imposed requirements upon the Tribes. In commenting on those articles, FERC said the following:

> The Commission incorporated Interior's conditions as Articles 55 through 79 of the license. Many of the adopted articles, included articles 63 through 66, allocate specific responsibilities to the Tribes and Montana Power. Because

we determined that the conditions were to be treated as Section 4(e) conditions, we had no discretion to exclude them from the licenses. However, ... the Commission has no authority under the license to require the Tribes to satisfy any license requirements until the Tribes become the licensee upon conveyance of the project.

(94 FERC 61,129 at 61,134)

When the USFWS recommended an additional article so that FERC would comply with the requirements of the Endangered Species Act through making requirements of the licensees, FERC declined to accept the concept of two licensees. The Commission wrote:

... we will not add to the incongruity created by our mandatory acceptance of the Interior's previous conditions by adding yet another license requirement that we cannot enforce. We will, however, modify the reference in Article 82 from 'licensees' to 'licensee.'

(94 FERC 61,129 at 61,135)

FERC, which did not propose the stringent conditions in 4(e) – and which probably opposed them – objected that it had no authority to force the Tribes to comply with the conditions which the Tribes desired to have.

The aboriginal standards were that the Guide Chief be knowledgeable, follow the ethics of the tribe, and enforce ethics of sharing. Guide Chiefs served as chosen by the band. The Guide Chief managed the harvest from Kutenai Lands, and as that manager was empowered to punish those that harmed streams. The chief's role has been divided up into many different ones, and some roles are not present. Multiple chiefs are part of the Northwest system – peer monitoring. But each chief had multiple responsibilities with respect to his proprietorship, rather than separate interests. Are these modern 'chiefs' judged on their ability to be rich and to take care of the poor, or to manage resources according to an environmental ethic? Only the Tribal Council of the Confederated Salish and Kootenai Tribes has to deal with this basis of judgment. Others follow their bureaucratic missions.

Further, when a dispute arises among these organizations, courts are the final arbiters. The Court of Appeals utilized a mediator to avoid having to go through a full hearing and trial process, with success.

Summary

Although the property, governance, and distribution rules used by Northwest Coast tribes probably contributed to their record of sustainability, one can legitimately question the appropriateness of using those rules in today's social and economic conditions. This chapter set out to explore a situation that seems to embody one of the rules used: the idea that control of a productive fishing site should be contingent upon not damaging the stream on which the proprietors of the site would place a fishing weir.

This idea of contingent proprietorship was embedded in a system that included ethics of respect for the environment, a property-rights system that gave clear authority to owners of sites, a system of reciprocity that, by requiring sharing of the salmon catch, also discouraged excessive harvest, public accountability, and standards for chiefs that required enforcement of the other five components. Would the idea of contingent proprietorship have similar impacts in a different institutional set-up?

The Kerr dam relicensing story shows that it can. In the presence of a property-rights system that recognizes exclusion rights similar to the Indian system, in the absence of reciprocity and in the absence of generous chiefs, still it was possible for leverage based on a desire to have environmental improvements to have an impact. The powers of the Secretary of the Interior and the Secretary of Agriculture under the 4(e) provision of the Federal Power Act have been used to protect environmental concerns in other cases in recent years. See Blumm and Nadol (2001) for approval of this trend, and Sensiba (1999) for disapproval of it.

The impact was to change the operation rules of the dam and to provide financial support for non-operational mitigation. The new license prohibited peaking and load-following; steady flows of water under baseload operation should improve fish habitat in the Flathead River below Kerr Dam. Non-operational mitigation primarily involved purchase of land to replace land lost because of operation of Flathead Lake as a reservoir throughout the year, and the loss of riparian habitat due to the elimination of large floods. In addition, fish are to be provided in order to restore the fisheries. Adaptive management under the FWIS provides an annual review of results to monitor the success of both fish supplementation and management of the replacement habitat.

To what extent do the new license requirements represent resilience in the Flathead River ecosystem? The intent of these provisions is to restore the operation of the lower Flathead River to a more productive state for fisheries. Because of changes in the species in the river, a return to exactly the pre-dam fishery is not possible. Flathead Lake has been even more disturbed by the introduction of exotic species, particularly lake trout and mysis shrimp, and the operation of the dam will not change the annual management of the top ten feet of Flathead Lake as a reservoir for electricity generation.

The impact of the change in operation is probably modest: an improvement of ecosystem functioning in the river through better conditions for fish, and an improvement in wildlife on the Reservation through the restoration of riparian lands (and associated uplands). The provisions also provide funding to the Confederated Tribes, which desire to improve ecosystem integrity on the reservation. Empowerment of the Tribes is a move toward resiliency on the reservation, given the Tribes' desires to improve ecosystem functioning. Requirements of public accountability to other organizations, such as the BIA, FERC, USFWS, Montana's Department of Natural Resources, and the operator of the dam assures that others will review the actions of the Confederated Tribes.

One cannot claim that ecosystem integrity for Flathead Lake and the lower Flathead River has been, or will be, fully restored. But such a stringent test is not necessary to establish the argument of this chapter. All that needs to be shown is a direct connection between contingent proprietorship and improvements in ecosystem operation. Clearly, the Confederated Tribes and the Secretary of the Interior used the 4(e) provisions of the Federal Power Act to force changes in the use of Kerr Dam for power generation. In addition, a portion of the value of power generated by the dam was directed to mitigation of the effects of the dam.

The plan under the Kerr Dam license, however, is quite rigid. License Article 64 prescribes stocking a particular number of pounds of fish; that number occurs because it is what could be proved to have been removed by the operation of the dam during a particular, short time period. The roles of each of the parties remain narrowly defined. No system of reciprocity creates joint responsibility for ecosystem functioning, and therefore adoption of some other features of aboriginal Northwest Coast institutions might provide further resiliency.

9　Nisg̱a'a Nation and Treaty

If the Northwest Coast systems are resilient, then they should be able to respond to challenges of many types. Certainly the colonial efforts of the European settlers were a great disturbance to the indigenous systems. With the expropriation of the fisheries, the setters struck at the core resource of the Northwest Coast social–ecological systems. By outlawing the potlatch, the settlers made illegal the central governing institution. Were these systems strong enough to withstand shocks of such magnitudes? If the argument of this book has merit, then some of the societies on the Northwest Coast should have been able to respond to such challenges to their social–ecological systems and find new configurations that would be satisfactory to them. The Nisg̱a'a have succeeded in making such a response to the challenges that they faced. Their response ties directly to the features of their system; the leadership and accountability of their chiefs contributed directly to their success in responding to challenges.

Before describing how the Nisg̱a'a coped with the colonial system, a description of their success in fisheries shows how resilient they were. In 1992, as they worked negotiating a modern treaty, the Nisg̱a'a Tribal Council established a fisheries program. They found outside funding and cooperation from the governments with whom they were nearing an agreement. This meant that, after more than a century of trying to obtain recognition for their importance in the Nass valley, the Nisg̱a'a had obtained a foothold in formal management of the fishery that they had used for millennia. Early work in the fisheries program quickly showed that the Nisg̱a'a intended to contribute to understanding the resource itself, beginning with accurate measurement of the numbers of fish returning to spawn.

The Nation installed fish wheels on the Nass River, with the goal of providing an accurate assessment of the size of the returning stock. By placing two fish wheels in the river, some distance apart, they could mark and count sockeye at the lower fishwheel, then establish the proportion of marked fish in the second fishwheel, upstream. Dividing the number counted at the upstream fishwheel by the proportion of those fish that were marked gives an immediate estimate of the size of the run. As a run of sockeye swam up the river, this marking and counting program provided a quick and accurate estimate of the number of fish that had escaped the ocean fishery and were available to spawn.

The Nisg̱a'a demonstrated that the fish wheels were far superior to a test gill net fishery in assessment of the size of the returning stock. Prior to the fish wheels, the

Department of Fisheries and Oceans (DFO) had conducted a gill net fishery near the mouth of the Nass. This fishery caught a smaller percentage of the total stock, could be overwhelmed by numbers in years with large runs. In every year, the gill net test fishery could not obtain accurate estimates of the size of the run, because it had no reliable way to measure the proportion of fish caught. Use of pairs of fishwheels in the main stem of the Nass River was far more accurate. Fishwheels were also able to handle larger volumes of fish. (Link and English 2000)

In 1995, the Minister of Fisheries awarded the program a commendation for the quality of its work. Because the primary goal of the program is to improve the resource (although defining the Nisga'a share of the resource has also been part of it), and because the Nisga'a have insisted on the best science, the program has achieved a high degree of credibility. They have hired consulting fisheries scientists of the highest quality. These scientists have an excellent publishing record, including an article in a major book on sustainable fisheries management of the entire salmon area (Link and English 2000).

By establishing their fisheries program before they signed the final agreement, the Nisga'a demonstrated the priority they gave to obtaining an important role in the management of fish on their river. They had been fishermen for generations, and when the DFO agreed to Nisga'a participation in monitoring and evaluating sockeye runs in real time, as the fish arrived, they finally allowed the Nisga'a to return to the role of fishery managers from which they had been excluded during the height of colonial expansion into their territory. Although the final agreement allocated a small proportion (13.5 per cent) of the sockeye fishery of the Nass to the Nisga'a, the fact that the Nisga'a had any role at all in the management of the fishery illustrates the tenacity with which they had pursued their desire to protect the fish from over-harvest and to assure the continued availability of salmon in the Nass Valley.

When the Nisga'a Final Agreement was signed, the parties created the Joint Fisheries Management Committee to oversee fish monitoring on the Nass River. The activities would be funded by the Lisims Fisheries Conservation Trust, created as part of the final agreement. The accompanying financing agreement provided that the DFO would assure annual funding for the fisheries activities of $1 million of the first five years. The funding was for stock assessment of sockeye, chinook, and coho salmon. Additional provisions of the fisheries chapter provided for support for an increase in Nisga'a Nation participation in the commercial fishery.

In setting up their new fisheries program, the Nisga'a joined one of the organizational forms for fisheries that has a positive stock of the fish. I argue in Chapter 10 that there are at least three separate 'regimes' in fisheries: The fished-out open-access regime; the healthy harvest pooling regime under a potlatch system; and the bureaucratic control regime, where a state fisheries agency, with the cooperation of fishermen in monitoring, issues licenses or supervises an allocation of the annual harvest (possibly through individual transferable quotas in order to reduce over-investment).

Bureaucratic management of a fishery by itself does not lead to survival of the fishery, because the top-down system of control limits the amount of feedback available to those in control of policy (Holling and Meffe 1996). In addition, the politics of the modern nation-state can allow a bureaucracy to become captured by one or another of the fishery interests, which then weakens the ability of the bureaucratic managers to avoid the tragedies caused by open access. The focus on the distribution of the fishery among fishermen distracts attention from management of the total number of fish. Some have argued that for a bureaucratic system to succeed, successful understanding and control can be achieved through a co-management relationship with the fishermen. The Nisga'a fish wheels show how such co-management can help. With the fish wheels, monitoring data accurately represent fish stock structure. On the Nass, people living close to the spawning area and utilizing the fishery have a significant and important role in fishery management. Although the Nisga'a have not been able to recreate the pooling regime, they have been able to modify the bureaucratic regime in a direction that could mean the fishery resource will survive. Their first contribution was to establish an accurate monitoring system, which is needed for feedback to judge the value of management decisions.

That the Nisga'a were able to obtain a role in the management of the salmon that return to the Nass River every year is an example of the resilience of the Nisga'a society. The establishment of the arrangement with the DFO represents the Nisga'a obtaining a role in the co-management of the fishery, something that means one of the components of the previously resilient system had been re-established: the role of Nisga'a leadership in making decisions about the management of the salmon fishery.

The restoration of Nisga'a participation in the Nass fishery is one of many examples of the resilience of the Nisga'a in general. The approval of the Nisga'a Final Agreement, which came into effect on May 11, 2000, suggests that the Nisga'a, while not resilient enough to preserve the system as it had existed, were able to respond to the challenges and transform the system.

As I began the research that led to this book, many advised me that the peoples living on the Nass and Skeena Rivers in British Columbia were the ones to visit if I wanted to learn about the traditional systems of the Pacific Northwest. Because one of her daughters was studying forestry at the University of British Columbia, I met the President of the Nisga'a College, Deana Nyce. She invited me to visit and I was more than happy to accept the invitation. Indeed when I traveled to the Nass, I found that the Nisga'a could tell me a great deal about their traditional system. They had collected documentation available from early explorers and anthropologists, making those publications available to students. They had written textbooks for their school, in order to teach their children the system that had existed, and the parts of the system that remained. They invited me to a feast, knowing that actually seeing the modern version of the old potlatch system would be very informative.

The first time I visited, the Nisga'a Tribal Council was holding an annual meeting. The primary topic of discussion was final approval by the Nisga'a of the agreement that had been negotiated with the Canadian Government and the Province of British Columbia. All the famous people involved in the struggle the Nisga'a had undertaken were present: Frank Calder spoke, and received great applause. Copies of the agreement were available.

There were occasions when visitors such as myself were asked to leave; only Nisga'a tribal members could stay in the room to hear the leaders explain certain parts of the agreement. I suspected, without any evidence, that the leaders were explaining what they thought some of the long-term consequences would be, and what their strategy was in making one choice and not another.

Critics of the final agreement have noted just how much authority and sovereignty the Nisga'a had to concede in order to obtain a settlement (Rynard 2000). Nonetheless, the agreement achieves a new beginning for the Nisga'a; they have managed to make progress within a tight set of political constraints.

Nisga'a traditional system

Because I have relied heavily on Nisga'a descriptions of their traditional rules, one should not be surprised that their traditional system fits well within the generalizations presented in Chapters 3–6. Their environmental ethics are as strong as any on the Northwest Coast; these values were the basis of petitions submitted by Nisga'a leadership opposing excessive harvest rates of salmon as early as 1881 (Raunet 1996: 113–14). The section will briefly review some of the stories that illustrate Nisga'a ethics, particularly their insistence that a devastating volcanic eruption was caused by children who failed to show respect for salmon. Chief Rod Robinson told me the story of the volcanic eruption caused by young children playing with salmon in a stream. In the 1700s, a volcano on Nisga'a lands destroyed two villages. Rod Robinson attributes the eruption of the volcano to the fact that young children were allowed to play with salmon in a stream, rather than showing respect.

Chapter 4 began with a description of the Nisga'a concept of a 'common bowl.' The Nass River fishery was like others on the coast. Much of the fishery was a terminal fishery, managed at the mouths of tributaries to the Nass River. But part of the salmon fishery occurred in the river itself, meaning that the aboriginal system did have to deal with a common-property system. The important eulachon fishery also occurred in common. Thus the society had to deal with restricting harvest in the interest of the resource. Not only did their value system stress restraint in harvest, their feast system emphasized sharing the harvest and their chiefs were expected to enforce the value system.

The Nisga'a territorial system was based on the division of the valley among the houses, which Nisga'a call *wilp*. Territories were very well defined, and as with others in the region, trespass was a capital offense. Titleholders were responsible for good management of the territories. Inheritance of titles was and is matrilineal. Thus the oldest sister of a titleholder would train her son for the position held by her brother. To become a titleholder, the son would proceed through a succession of lesser titles, showing his capability. Upon the death of his uncle, other titleholders would eventually approve and recognize the succession.

House chiefs and matriarchs had considerable authority over management decisions, supported by subchiefs. Because of extensive training and preparation of the chiefs, no case of the supporters having to remove a chief was remembered by elders in the Nation. In recent years, the strict rules of succession of chiefs have been varied. I was told of a case in which an eligible man was known to be unable to fulfill his obligations; a brother of his was assigned the title instead. This shows that the process of preparation ensures that only well prepared leaders are allowed into the top management positions. This was a pattern historically as well, according to the Nisga'a description of their appointments.

Nisga'a standards for chiefly behavior strongly illustrate the view that generous facilitators should be in charge. Chiefs are trained to be generous, to speak well, to facilitate discussions, to comply with community standards, to train and encourage youth, to groom their successor, to be compassionate, to be self-disciplined, and to mediate. Chiefs managed the feast system, which implemented reciprocity. Exchange of goods, property and money in a feast is entirely public.

Colonial history

When the first explorers contacted the Nisga'a, they had 16 villages. Population estimates range between 10,000 and 30,000 people. As the coastal traders and the Hudson's Bay Company started to trade with them, the Nisga'a suffered a series of epidemics that greatly reduced their numbers. They were still contending with the epidemics when British Columbia joined the Canadian confederation in 1870. The consequences of the establishment of British Columbia reached the Nass River in the 1880s, as settlers began to harvest eulachon in the spring and salmon during the summer. In 1881, the first of many canneries was built on the Nass, and the Canadian Government placed limits on Indian fishing by outlawing fishing with nets without a license. The Nisga'a could not obtain licenses in the early period.

In 1881, the Provincial Land Commissioner explained to the titleholders what lands they would be allowed to hold. In 1885, the titleholders sent a delegation to Ottawa to object to the land-grab policy. In 1886, Chief Sgat'iin refused to let surveyors establish the limits of his village, Gitlakdamiks. British Columbia had to send military force to complete the survey (Rose 2000: 71–73).

The titleholders established the Nisga'a Land Committee; Alex Rose (2000: 75) published a picture of the Land Committee, probably taken in 1883. The committee sent many delegations to governments from 1883 to 1927. None of the petitions they submitted were received well. The Nisga'a continually cited the Royal Proclamation of 1763 in their efforts to secure a treaty that would recognize their existing control of the land. British Columbia refused to recognize that they had rights to the land, and refused to consent to be sued in the courts of higher jurisdictions, either Canada or the Commonwealth. In spite of not having permission to sue, the Nisga'a went to the Privy Council in London in 1913, hiring a legal firm to present their case. The Privy Council insisted that the Government of Canada approve the petition, which did not occur, and by 1918 the Nisga'a knew that appeal to London would not work (Raunet 1996: 130–42).

The government of British Columbia adopted the doctrine of *terra nulius*, the idea that even if indigenous people were present, the land was to be treated from a legal viewpoint as empty, available for settlers to claim. British Columbia went further in its discrimination against the local people, because it refused to allow the indigenous people to claim their own land. Thus individual Nisga'a, such as for instance the hereditary titleholders, could not obtain title to their traditional house territories.

The Nisga'a Land Committee continued to work on their problem. But in 1927, Canada made assisting Indians in their land claims efforts into a criminal offense. The law was written broadly, and would apply to anyone hosting a meeting:

> Every person who, without the consent of the Superintendent General expressed in writing, receives, obtains, solicits or requests from any Indian any payment or contribution or promise of any payment or contribution for the purpose of raising a fund or providing money for the prosecution of any claim which the tribe or band of Indians to which such Indian belongs, or of which he is a member, has or is represented to have for the recovery of any claim or money for the benefit of said tribe or band, shall be guilty of an offence and liable upon summary conviction for each such offence to a penalty not exceeding two hundred dollars and not less than fifty dollars or to imprisonment for any term not exceeding two months.
>
> (Quoted by Tennant 1990: 111–12)

Political scientist Paul Tennant argues that this law may well have been adopted because the Judicial Committee of Privy Council, which had earlier refused to listen to the Nisga'a without Canada's permission, had upheld the land claims of indigenous people in Nigeria (Tennant 1990: 101,110). Canada could not afford to have a land claims case from British Columbia reach the Judicial Committee, given the policy of totally ignoring aboriginal land occupation.

The broad wording of the new law meant that the Nisga'a Land Committee had to meet in secret, and could not engage in public activities to pursue their land claims. These dark days lasted until 1951, when Canada changed the Indian Act to make potlatch ceremonies legal and to allow Indians to organize for land claims issues.

The Nisga'a had a strong tradition of training their leaders. The selection and training began with Frank Calder, during this period of absolute resistance from the various British Crowns. Because his heir had died, Arthur Calder selected another nephew to take his place. The story of his training begins like this, as told by Frank Calder himself:

> In 1919, I was four years old. Arthur Calder took me to Kincolith into Walter Haldane's house, where all the leadeing chiefs were gonna talk land claims. There weren't claims in those day, the land question, that's the name. … Jeffrey Benson, who died not too long ago, got married the same year, 1919. And he and his wife were secretaries. He was there, he was the young man who was doing secretarial work at the meeting. And the story that is well known in Kincolith, because that's where it happened, is Arthur Calder picked me up and stood me on the table and said to the gathering: and this is the boy I am

going to send to a white area, and Im gonna make him speak like a white man. I'm gonna make him eat like a white man. Everything that that guy does, this little boy is gonna do. We don't need no interpreters. By the time he is ready, he is the boy that's gonna be using our language, his language, and he is the one that's going to bring this case to the highest court in the land.

(Raunet 1996: 145)

Calder reports that as a young boy he attended many meetings of the Land Committee and learned what they were doing. He went to residential school and learned English, as planned. He enrolled at the University of British Columbia, then graduated from the Anglican Theological College (Rose 2000: 82–83). When Canada repealed the law that criminalized pursuit of the land question, Frank Calder was an adult and ready to lead the effort to start the land claims process again.

He and others organized the Nisga'a Tribal Council as a body to represent their interests. The Tribal Council was more broadly based than the previous land committee, which had consisted exclusively of *simo'ogit*, the hereditary leaders. The new Tribal Council gave every member a vote (Tennant 1990: 123). But not until 1967 did the Nisga'a Tribal Council take legal action in order to have their interests recognized. They sued the Province to have aboriginal title recognized. They lost, both at the trial court level and on appeal. But the Supreme Court of Canada, in 1973, gave the Nisga'a some leverage. In deciding what became called the Calder case, all judges agreed that aboriginal title existed – three holding that it had been extinguished, three holding that it still existed, and the tie-breaking judge dismissed the case on a technicality (that British Columbia had not consented to be sued). Although the tie instated the lower court decision, the Nisga'a won much. The Supreme Court signaled that aboriginal title existed in British Columbia. Subsequent decisions recognized that title. Further improvement in the bargaining position of the Nisga'a occurred in 1982, when Section 35(a) in the new Canadian Constitution recognized pre-existing aboriginal rights.

The Nisga'a leadership pressed for a negotiated treaty. Although their leverage was small, the Nisga'a elders insisted that they use no blockades or other actions that would take them down a non-peaceful road (Chief Joseph Gosnell told me this when I interviewed him in the summer of 1999). Things developed slowly. First, the Federal Government was willing to negotiate. In 1990, the province agreed to join the negotiations, and in 1996, the parties signed an agreement in principle. In 1998, the parties initialed a final agreement, which was ratified by British Columbia in 1999 and by Canada in 2000. The Final Agreement came into effect on March 11, 2000.

This brief summary of the process from 1887 to 2000 does not convey the amount of struggle that was involved. Even at the very end, the Nisga'a had to contend with serious opposition to the final agreement in both the legislature of British Columbia and the House of Commons and Senate of Canada. Before taking the agreement to those bodies, the leaders of the Nisga'a Tribal Council had to obtain approval from the Nisga'a themselves. Turning the legal victory of the Calder case into a modern treaty was no easy task.

The final agreement moved the Nisga'a from a condition in which they were confined to reserves and had no rights in their traditional territory, to a situation in which their right to self-government was recognized and they had obtained firm ownership of about 2000 square kilometers in their traditional territory. Although whether or not the lands and resources obtained will prove sufficient to support the Nisga'a population is unclear, gaining the ability to govern themselves and to set up enterprises is a big improvement on their prior conditions.

What factors contributed to this partial success? Is the establishment of a new government and control of lands and fisheries to be regarded as a successful transformation of a bad situation? Is it evidence of the resilience of the Nisga'a? If so, did this success result from characteristics of their traditional system?

To answer this question, one must identify what has been resilient. The fundamental Nisga'a social structure of houses (*wilp*), clans and villages has persisted. They have restored their self-government, although the new governmental form is not the same as the one they used to have. Their leadership is now elected. If the holders of the highest names, the *simo'ogit* and *sidimiak*, want to have a position in the government, they need to run for election. Only such leaders can run for the traditional council; although it is an elected body, members must qualify in order to stand for election.

The process of reaching the Final Agreement showed the strength of Nisga'a leadership. The intransigent position of British Columbia and Canada on many key issues meant that the tribal public would want much more than their leadership could possibly obtain through negotiations. As a consequence, the Nisga'a leaders had to keep their public informed. They found that they kept their own public more informed than British Columbia did. Third parties interested in the negotiations, such as timber companies, found they could obtain more information about the status of the negotiations from the Nisga'a than from the British Columbia government. This placed Nisga'a leadership in a difficult position: British Columbia and Canada wanted confidentiality; but the Nisga'a could not provide it while fulfilling their accountability to the Nisga'a people (Joseph Gosnell interview).

The agreements recognize the importance of environmental ethics and caring for the land. Although the Nisga'a Nation obtained fee simple title to Nisga'a Lands, the Nation itself imposed significant barriers to sale of the land; their legislation implements detailed leasing procedures. The Nisga'a Constitution provides its people a right to information, and public accountability was a predominant feature of the aboriginal side of the negotiations. Although leadership selection has departed from hereditary principles through democratic elections, one of the bodies in the new government is an elected council of elders; only traditional chiefs and matriarchs are eligible candidates. Checks and balances present in the traditional system are modified through use of an 11-member 'executive council', which directs the implementation of measures selected by a larger legislature. The Nation is free to recognize and utilize traditional values in many aspects of their lives.

Having read the land-use plan from 2002, which ignores the traditional territories, I think that the use of *ango'osk* (Nisga'a house territories) along with the use of sharing of the income from those lands has also disappeared, at least from the official management planning process. So the lands are indeed owned in common, and the common income will be pooled in a different way. I don't know to what extent they will keep the connection to the house territories alive; many houses don't have their territories in the official Nisga'a lands at present. The principle of contingent proprietorship is not strongly embedded; the fee simple land is held by the Nisga'a Lisims Government and the four village governments, to allocate through their governmental processes. The old territorial system is only potentially accessible.

No obstacles are present to utilization of reciprocity for internal Nisga'a exchanges; but use of reciprocity in relationships with outsiders is not a prominent feature. Three major resource conflicts dominated the negotiations: fish, forests, and intergovernmental fiscal relations. In the first two of these, third parties in the negotiation process wished to retain their access to resources claimed by the Nisga'a. The result was dividing up access to the resource, with no ways in which interconnections between resources or among common users of a common property resource such as fish would share net returns from the resources. Regarding fish, the Minister of Fisheries retained final say on all conservation decisions; the Nisga'a, however, would be able to participate in data gathering, harvest, and restoration of the quality of the runs. (Nisga'a Side Agreement on Fisheries)

Intergovernmental fiscal relations are not based on reciprocity. The governments of Canada and British Columbia agreed to support the costs of government and provision of services in the Nisga'a Nation at the start of the relationship. As the fiscal capacity of the Nisga'a grows, however, the contribution from outside will fall; as this occurs, the ability of the governments of Canada and British Columbia to tax within the Nisga'a Nation will also grow. Although the Nisga'a conceded considerable resources to the dominant society through not retaining control of their traditional land base, no provisions of the agreement provide for the dominant society to make its payments to the Nisga'a dependent upon the benefits of the ceded lands. British Columbia does have to pay for timber removed from Nisga'a Lands during the transition period, but not for timber removed from the larger surrounding land base.

Sharing of responsibility for environmental concerns on each other's lands is accomplished through environmental impact studies and environmental regulations, not through interdependencies or sharing of benefits and costs from using the lands. This approach will encourage disputes. The Treaty has extensive and detailed provisions to encourage negotiation and mediation rather than adjudication and litigation. These provisions are partly based on traditional methods of dispute resolution, but also include the latest in such processes as agreed to in the larger society. (Chapter 19 and Appendices M-1 to M-6 of the Nisga'a Final Agreement; see www.ainc-inac.gc.ca/pr/agr/nsga/nisdex12_e.pdf)

Given the historical hostility from Canadian society regarding the potlatch, which was outlawed from 1887 to 1953, it is not surprising that the final agreement is weak in the area of reciprocity. Its strengths in other areas, however, will probably lead to an improvement in the environmental conditions of the Nass area, an improvement in the size of salmon runs, and greater self-reliance on the part of the Nisga'a people. Reinstatement of a potlatch system was probably blocked by the existence of the individualism and selfishness ethic of Canadian society generally – a link to the logic of the capitalist system in the world, in fact.

In terms of resilience theory, what have the Nisga'a shown? They are capable both of adaptation and transformation. They show resilience of the Nisga'a people as a people (or Nation) in response to colonial policies. A great deal of the explanation for their success can be attributed to their principles of leadership.

10 Northwest Coast contributions to analysis of resilience in social–ecological systems

The previous chapter tells the story of the resilience of the Nisga'a Nation. While their language, culture, and identity have survived, their social–ecological system is not the same one that existed in the Nass Valley before Canada asserted sovereignty in 1846. The structure of their government has changed, from the previous leadership by the heads of houses to the current democratically elected government with its executive, legislature, and traditional council. The territory controlled by the Nisga'a Lisims Government is much smaller than the territory controlled by the houses. In addition, planning documents such as the 2002 Land Use Plan (Nisga'a Lisims Government 2002) make little reference to the system of *ango'osk/ankw'ihlwil* – the house territories. If the process of making the plan involved all of the *simo'ogit* and *sidimiak*, who each spoke for his or her territories, the plan does not say so. The plan, however, was adopted by the Executive of the Nisga'a Lisims Government, not by the council of the chiefs and matriarchs.

The economy of the Nisga'a has also changed. Many no longer live in the Nass Valley; they now participate in the Nisga'a Nation through urban representative bodies. The people don't organize the year according to the yearly round reported by McNeary (1994).

In short, the Nisga'a have adapted to the new conditions, not returned to a previous system that is no longer available. They have followed a course that fits within the general models being proposed by the Resilience Network group of scholars who are studying the sources of resilience in contemporary society. Since the previous configuration is not possible any more, they have adapted and attempted to find a new favorable organization of their social–ecological system.

Resilience

This book began as a search for possible reasons why the peoples of the Northwest Coast had a social and ecological system that had survived for over 2000 years with little change in its basic structure, as revealed both by archeological evidence and by the evidence of oral histories. The oral histories themselves were part of the answer, because histories of territorial control are part of the system of territory management. In order to last, such a system had to be resilient. It had to be able to withstand large shocks. Over a period of several centuries, changes in ocean conditions would have changed the return of salmon, creating regional crises. The oral histories tell of periods of warfare in which the feasting system did not preserve peaceful relations.

Recently, a diverse group of scholars have come together in a series of meetings and books to study issues of resilience. The original interest was the resilience of ecological systems; but a great deal of the attention came to be a focus on social–ecological systems. They have formed an association, The Resilience Alliance, and published many books. They discuss their ideas in a peer-reviewed journal, *Ecology and Society*, and have a useful website that includes links to many sources. The website (www.resalliance.org/1.php) has a manual for scientists and a manual for practitioners to guide work in promoting the resilience of social–ecological systems.

Their research program involves examination of contemporary systems. Their recent Special Feature in Ecology and Society, introduced by Walker *et al*. (2006a), seeks to derive generalization from comparisons among 15 examples. The examples demonstrate varying degrees of resilience. The generalizations from the Special Feature then inform the two workbooks (Resilience Alliance 2008b).

This book is about the similarities among a number of social–ecological systems, all of which were resilient. Given that each of the cultural groups spoke different languages, and occasionally raided each other, I could say that I am examining several similar systems, not one. But because they all relied on salmon as the main source of food, the many systems are variations on solving a common problem. My goal has been to establish what was similar among these societies/social–ecological systems, with the hope of discovering some useful institutions for dealing with dependence on a common pool resource. Most of the cases studied by the Resilience Alliance involve common pool resources and external effects of many kinds. Often the greatest concern is with slow variables that increase in their impact until they cause a system to flip from one state to another. This concern with slow variables is a concern with common pool goods and public goods, which have widespread impacts.

Because my project and that of the Resilience Alliance are similar, I propose to close the book by examining overlaps and gaps between their proposed generalizations and mine. I will organize this comparison by focusing on the generalizations offered in this book, beginning with ones that are overlaps, and ending with ones that are not.

Definition of social–ecological system resilience

The Resilience Alliance is interested in the ability of a social–ecological system to maintain itself in the presence of large shocks. These disturbances, if great enough, can move a system outside of its current operating regime. A resilient system is able to re-organize and re-establish its regime. For example, in the Pacific Northwest, if a period of warfare disrupted the feasting system, and led to lack of control over the fish harvest, the people knew that the house system can provide stability. They could agree to re-establish such a system, and the feasting process has ways for new house leaders to recognize each other and agree to the exchange of wealth. In a summary article, members of the Resilience Alliance define resilience as follows:

> Resilience is the capacity of a system to experience shocks while retaining essentially the same function, structure, feedbacks, and therefore identity … . Social–ecological systems exhibit thresholds that, when exceeded, result in changed system feedbacks that lead to changes in function and structure. … The more resilient a system, the larger the disturbance it can absorb without shifting into an alternate regime. In general, the state of a system at any one time can be defined by the values of the variables that constitute the system. For example, if a rangeland system is defined by the amounts of grass, shrubs, and livestock it contains, then the state space is the three-dimensional space of all possible combinations of the amounts of these three variables. The dynamics of the system are reflected as its movement through this space. In complex ecological and social–ecological systems, the term 'alternate states' is a misnomer. Configurations of states in which the system has the same controls on function, i.e., the same feedbacks, and essentially the same structure represent different states within the same system regime. Configurations in which the kinds or strengths of feedbacks differ and in which there are different internal controls on function represent alternate system regimes with thresholds between them. These alternate regimes can have significantly different implications for society and so, from a purely human point of view, may be considered desirable or undesirable.
>
> (Walker *et al.* 2006b)

One can illustrate the changing of feedbacks on the Pacific Northwest Coast by examining the role of chiefs as responsible for the quality of runs. First, if a chief abused a run, it produced less, and one of two things could happen: other chiefs could sanction his behavior at a feast, or the followers of the chief could change him for another. In the new system, after the chiefs' powers were removed, failure of a run did not lead to sanctions as extreme as job losses for fishery managers.

Second, another change in function occurred when new fishermen were not part of the reciprocity system. The exchange of wealth, based on the fishery, established the interdependence of fishermen on each other's harvests. When this was eliminated, the prisoners' dilemma appeared and the regime shifted to a different one. When the fishery managers were no longer accountable and the fishermen were in a race for fish, salmon abundance disappeared.

Often, regimes are summarized by the characteristic of the 'attractor' – the configuration of variables which is resilient (Carpenter *et al.* 2001). In salmon-based fisheries, three different attractor situations can be described, based on the biomass of fish, the number of fishermen, and the wealth of the fishermen. In the open-access regime the fishery is over-exploited, fish numbers are low, and harvest is low. Many fishermen exist, and each is poor. In the traditional Northwest Coast system, salmon are abundant, harvest levels are high, and fishermen are abundant and wealthy. In a fishery managed by a state bureaucracy, several attractors are available depending on the policies of the bureaucracy. Successful avoidance of the open-access equilibrium can be achieved by good controls on entry and high-quality monitoring of the overall health of the fishery. The fishery management agency sets a quota and allocates it among a few fishermen. Individual transferable quota systems administered by a state fishery authority are supposed to be able to achieve a successful attractor. Quota becomes concentrated among a few fishermen, each of whom is wealthy. Use of co-management between local authorities and the state authority, as in the case of the Nass River, can also achieve a 'state property co-management equilibrium.' In this case, feedback from fishery conditions to the governing system is retained.

The Resilience Alliance has characterized resilience in a slightly different way, which embodies hypotheses about what causes resilience. In a paper authored by many people in 2002, they offered this further elaboration:

> The Resilience Alliance (www.resalliance.org) defines resilience as applied to integrated systems of people and nature as (a) the amount of disturbance a system can absorb and still remain within the same state or domain of attraction (b) the degree to which the system is capable of self-organization (versus lack of organization, or organization forced by external factors) and (c) the degree to which the system can build and increase the capacity for learning and adaptation.
>
> (Folke *et al.* 2002)

This description adds two additional components to resilience. The ability to self-organize as a quality of resilience directs attention to factors that contribute to organization, such as functional diversity among components of a system. The ability to remember previous ways of coping with change is also part of self-organization. The third component, the ability to learn and adapt, directs attention to the characteristics of humans: their knowledge systems and their internal organization. These two components contribute to achieving the basic definition, which is the ability to remain within one domain of attraction.

Two major areas of overlap

In searching for characteristics of resilient social–ecological systems, the Resilience Alliance has developed two areas which overlap significantly with Northwest Coast characteristics: world view and governance. In the area of world view, the scholars have rejected analysis of ecosystems and societies as separate, and have adopted a complex systems view of the interaction of humans and nature. In the area of governance and leadership, the scholars are emphasizing the importance of local participation in governance, and governance styles that are responsive to the people in the social–ecological system. The two areas of insight are complementary, because if people are part of the system, then their participation in it has to be taken seriously and dealt with.

Overlap area 1: assumptions about knowledge of systems

The Resilience Alliance urges its members and those in social–ecological systems to recognize that humans are part of each system, and that managing resilience involves managing humans.

> Throughout history humanity has shaped nature and nature has shaped the development of human society. For example, the North American landscape at the time of Columbian contact in late 1400 had already been transformed through land clearing, hunting, farming and fire management practices. Indeed, the tropical rainforests of the Americas reached their current form under the selective pressures of human groups. Hence, these are neither natural or pristine systems, nor are there social systems without nature. Instead humanity and nature have been co-evolving, for good or ill, in a dynamic fashion and will continue to do so. Human actions are a major structuring factor in the dynamics of ecological systems.
>
> (Folke *et al.* 2002) [citations omitted]

In the process of elaborating this view, they have also pointed to other aspects of world view that are similar to those in the Pacific Northwest. In particular, they emphasize that systems encounter surprises, and the nature of the resulting change has to be investigated. The Trickster has returned. They also emphasize the importance of the 'long view.' They recognize that combining analysis of ecosystems with analysis of social systems inevitably leads to recognition of complexity and the need to deal with complex interactions within any social–ecological system.

Regarding world view, are the scholars describing their own knowledge, or the knowledge of the people in a social–ecological system? In the first place, they are describing their own view. The name of their journal, *Ecology and Society*, emphasizes the need to mix ecological and social analysis. They are advocating that the people in a system adopt a similar view. In their case studies, whether or not those actors do in fact adopt a human-in-nature perspective is sometimes not clearly spelled out. But as advocates of advancing knowledge, the Resilience Alliance has embarked on an education program to convince people that such a complex systems perspective is needed. They themselves often provide advice to the actors in a system, in the interest of creating this prerequisite or co-requisite for achieving resilience. For instance, their studies of the lakes in northern Wisconsin led them to define four scenarios that could help clarify the people's understanding of the driving forces and the possibilities of their system (Walker *et al.* 2004; Gunderson *et al.* 2006). With this complex understanding of the possibilities, people could then find ways to make their system move in directions that they desired. As members of these social–ecological systems, then, the scholars are assisting in bringing the complexity world view into the thinking of those in the system with leverage to make changes.

An article with the title 'Shooting the rapids: navigating transitions to adaptive governance of social–ecological systems', however, focuses on the role of ideas and the discovery of new ideas (Olsson *et al.* 2006). Shadow networks are advocated as ways to have new ideas develop; sometimes a new agency stops new ideas, as in a case from Australia. In another article, they remark that the agricultural and environmental interests in the Everglades aren't interesting in learning (Gunderson *et al.* 2006). The main point is that being open to new ideas and encouraging learning is a consistent recommendation.

The idea that 'transformation' not 'adaptation' is sometimes necessary would seem to me to be an idea that isn't clearly present in Northwest Coast systems, which returned to the house system when disrupted. The Nisga'a, however, have adapted and created a new system. Yet social learning is evident.

The Resilience Alliance members often draw diagrams that have 'nature' and 'society' in separate boxes or circles, and indicate the connections between the two with lines showing interactions (for instance Folke 2006: 261, Figure 2). They have not gone as far as Bruno Latour, who advocates abandoning the idea of 'nature,' because the idea itself creates some unintended consequences. One of these consequences is that scientists become 'experts' with special access to the knowledge of nature; this special access gives them rights to speak for nature. Few of the articles, however, take on the tone of 'high science;' most offer tentative conclusions and appear to be written with a general audience in mind.

Some aspects of the Northwest Coast world view are omitted. Although the Alliance recommends people have a long-term view, they don't promote belief in reincarnation of people in their lineage as a way to obtain such a view. They like the consequences of beliefs in spirits when such beliefs protect sacred forest groves, because such groves provide diversity as well as memory to a system. Although ecologists are aware of nutrient cycling as a key function in ecosystems, the scientists probably wouldn't believe that cycling should be understood in terms of souls being reborn. They probably also would not subscribe to the idea that salmon could detect when they were being treated with a lack of respect, leading to retaliation, as in the explanation of the cause of the volcanic eruption in the Nass Valley.

Another of their views was explicitly present in the Northwest Coast systems: nurturing many sources of ideas, for instance, in terms of combining science and tradition. The Nuu-chah-nulth advice to the Scientific Panel showed a desire to respect all viewpoints, even those held by only one person, indicating an openness to many sources of thought. The readiness to accept Christianity and combine it with their feasting system also shows such flexibility. Hence, use of science is seen as reasonable. But prior to contact with Europeans, the peoples of the Northwest Coast would not have had a concept of science as such. The Gitxsan idea of *nidnl*, knowledge recognized and accepted in public meetings by the leadership, was a version of peer review.

Respect for indigenous knowledge probably follows from the overlap between what the scholars are learning and the knowledge of many traditional systems. The scholars set out to study characteristics of management approaches that seem to enable a system to be resilient; when they discovered that many indigenous approaches were similar, they began to recognize and appreciate the indigenous approaches. They also recognize the importance of all sources of ideas for a system, and advocate development of 'shadow networks' as a way to encourage sharing of ideas and the development of new knowledge.

I don't have space here to explore fully the different treatment of knowledge in both the Northwest Coast and the Resilience Alliance. My main point is that the Resilience Alliance has proposed ideas that are consistent with, but not fully coincident with, the world view of the Northwest Coast. Having discovered the joy of dropping the assumption that man and nature are separate, the Alliance is moving quickly to develop the implications.

Overlap area 2: governance

A recent article by Lebel *et al.* (2006) has provided an excellent summary of the role of governance in affecting resilience and vulnerability. They open their article by rejecting a common paradigm for managing regional economic change. Without labeling it, they describe the paradigm as follows:

> A paradigm based on planning for efficiency, standardizing for easier social control, and reducing variability has come to pervade bureaucratic practices. Environmental problems are framed as technical and administrative challenges devoid of politics. People need to be informed and persuaded about the right and wrong uses of ecosystems, and penalized if they do not follow the right practice.
>
> (*ibid.*)

By assuming politics does not matter, this paradigm leads to errors when implemented; people do not cooperate with decisions that they do not understand and have not participated in making. Implicitly, the paradigm assumes a bureaucracy has the power to make people agree, through the ability to penalize those who do not go along. While a resource management agency does have some power, few are as powerful as the paradigm assumes. The paradigm is linked to the rule by nation states; Scott (1998) has explained the attitude as 'Seeing like a State' in his book of that name. Often scientists collaborate with the state and adopt the top-down, technical approach described above. Since nation-states adopt the paradigm, which seldom works, also states have seldom been especially successful at managing for resilience (Holling and Meffe 1996).

If the top-down approach fails, then what kind of approach makes sense, especially in modern conditions? The proposals from Lebel *et al.* overlap significantly with the political structure used by the Northwest Coast. They divide their six characteristics into three groups of two: (1) participation and deliberation; (2) polycentric and multilayered; (3) accountable and just authorities.

Participation and deliberation

Lebel *et al.* (1996) describe participation and deliberation as follows:

> Participation builds the trust, and deliberation the shared understanding, needed to mobilize and self-organize. ... Public participation allows differences in interests

and interactions with other issues to be brought forward for public scrutiny. Deliberation allows the differences in interests, perceptions, and explanations to be explored without forcing consensus. Trust and shared understanding are built up through repeated interactions of stakeholders and enable social learning … These form the foundation for mobilizing around new issues such as looming thresholds and self-organizing around innovative solutions or after crises.

On the Northwest Coast, both of these principles operated. Chiefs were expected to consult with the members of their house, although final decisions remained with them. Probably participation by members of houses was structured by the rankings of nobles and commoners, with the noble class participating to a great extent.

Deliberation was more carefully practiced among the leadership, although with a requirement of consensus for final decisions. Sometimes deliberation had to proceed for several feasts in order for agreement to be reached, as Antonio Mills reports for the Wet'suwet'en (Mills 1994a: 43–71).

Polycentric and multilayered

The second group of recommendations is that governing institutions be polycentric and multilayered:

> Polycentric and multilayered institutions improve the fit between knowledge, action, and socio-ecological contexts in ways that allow societies to respond more adaptively at appropriate levels. … An organizational structure with multiple, relatively independent centers creates opportunities for locally appropriate institutions to evolve by tightening monitoring and feedback loops and by enhancing associated institutional incentives (Berkes and Folke 1998). In this situation, local governance arrangements can develop to better match the varied social and ecological contexts and dynamics of different locations. Local monitoring may provide effective early warning systems, and monitoring of interventions allows safe-to-fail experimentation. Local knowledge can inform local actions in ways that a single centralized system cannot. Multilayered institutions, in addition, allow the possibility for level-dependent management interventions as well as explicit mechanisms to address cross-level interactions … without undermining the capacity to self-organize at any particular level.
>
> (Lebel *et al.* 2006)

The house system was polycentric: each of the houses managed its own land, relatively independently and with considerable possibility for difference. Each house had its own history, its own set of crests, and other distinguishing characteristics such as songs. The chiefs were responsible for monitoring in the house territories. Probably the system developed as it did because the house territories were able to innovate and learn separately, while they managed relations with their neighbors through the feasting system. Successful management meant adequate wealth to distribute to other titleholders, as well as adequate wealth to support members of the house. Because of intermarriage, knowledge of successful management techniques would spread among houses.

In spite of the smaller size of the Northwest Coast system, it was also multilayered. The layers were at least three: houses at the first level, villages of houses at the second level, and associations of villages at the third level. Governance at the levels above house were managed through the feast system. As explained in Chapter 5, the feast system placed obstacles in the way of the emergence of a kingdom or other level above that of an association of villages where decisions were made by consensus among chiefs rather than by one main chief.

For this reason, the house system as an example of a polycentric governance structure might be looked at as most appropriate for local-level organization if the ideas are used in today's setting, which inevitably will involve central governments.

Accountable and Just Authorities

The third of the recommendations from Lebel *et al.* (2006) is that authorities be accountable for their actions and that they pursue just distributions of benefits and risks. This third recommendation very closely fits some of the principles of the Northwest Coast. They summarize their analysis as follows:

> Accountable authorities who also pursue just distributions of benefits and involuntary risks enhance the adaptive capacity of vulnerable groups and society as a whole. … Authorities who are obliged to explain and inform, and who can be sanctioned when they perform poorly, can be challenged by groups that unjustly bear large involuntary risks or receive less than their fair share of benefits. The pursuit of social justice by actively protecting the rights and interests of or empowering socially vulnerable groups is a worthy one without additional justification. At the same time, however, socially vulnerable groups are often dependent on, and contribute to, the maintenance of, aspects of ecological and social diversity overlooked or undervalued by the mainstream or dominant culture. Often, efforts to improve the just distribution of benefits and involuntary risks from the management of ecosystems and their services also help to maintain diversity and enhance the adaptive capacity of these vulnerable groups. These enhancements, in turn, help reduce the vulnerability of the social–ecological system as a whole by reducing destabilizing conflicts and strengthening weak links.
>
> (*ibid.*)

While this assertion is quite reasonable, the authors were not able to provide many positive examples of how such accountability would assist in having leaders make the right decisions. In each of their examples, a system that is supposed to be accountable in fact fails to provide the needed accountability. This does not necessarily show the assertion to be false; it just establishes that the correctness of the assertion is based upon intuition. The case of the Northwest Coast provides additional evidence.

On the Northwest Coast, chiefs were accountable both to the members of their house, and to leaders of other houses. The accountability occurred through the transparency of the transactions at all feasts, which revealed to everyone what was occurring, and through the ability of people in the system, particularly from the titleholding class, to express their dissatisfaction.

The requirement that leaders prove their worth by being generous directly addressed the issues of justice, because wealth was shared. The system had inequality, however. The titleholding class and the top titleholders had more power than the common people, and they kept control of that power.

Although the titleholders had to be generous with wealth, as a group they kept control of the system, approving each other's actions. The redistribution that occurred meant that people could make a living, not that the society was a fully egalitarian one. It was an example of leaders being kept under a degree of control by the community, without displacing the leaders from their positions. All this was explained in Chapter 5.

Left out: reciprocity and contingent proprietorship

In the areas of world view and governance, the Resilience Alliance is making recommendations that overlap significantly with the rules used on the Northwest Coast. Humans are part of the ecosystem in both world views. Governing structures should include wide participation and deliberation, have multiple centers and layers, and be accountable and just. These six characteristics apply to the Northwest Coast.

The three governance generalizations all reproduce aspects of the governance systems of the Northwest Coast. The third one, by addressing accountability and justice, provides a good transition to the next two topics – elements of the Northwest Coast systems that aren't explored very much in the writings of the Resilience Alliance. If local authorities are to be accountable, how is that to be arranged? The text describing accountable local authorities mostly explains ways in which even elected local authorities come to depend more on authorities at a higher level in the governance scale. Their examples are examples of lack of accountability, and the assertions thus aren't supported in a positive way.

This study of the Northwest Coast suggests that the hypotheses of the Resilience Alliance should be expanded to include examination of reciprocity and contingent proprietorship. When added to governance by chiefs, the use of gifts and contingency involves additional rules that provide positive incentives to generate all three components of resilience: buffering small-scale disturbance, providing reorganization after large-scale disturbance, and encouraging social learning. To prove this assertion, I will apply the seven types of rule of the Northwest Coast territoriality system as explained in Chapter 6, although not in the order presented there.

Payoff and boundary rules

I begin with the payoff rules, and the presence of 'side payments' in the Northwest Coast system. While side payments might be voluntarily agreed to by agents in a market system, clearly the payments were required as part of the system and are not voluntary in the sense of contribution freely agreed to. The requirement that leaders be generous creates useful incentives. In the modern world, certainly elections for local officials assist in making them accountable. Requirements that information be available to everyone also helps make leaders accountable, in that they cannot act in private. But reciprocity as practiced on the Northwest Coast created many other ways for leaders to be accountable, as well as addressing justice.

In an electoral system, leaders have been known to pay off their supporters by providing jobs and other benefits; such care for their supporters is often decried as corruption of the electoral process. These leaders are being generous; but actually they are completing a transaction: in return for support in getting out the vote, particular people obtain jobs and benefits. Publicly elected leaders, however, are not the only leaders who would be involved in a system of side payments as existed on the Northwest Coast: all important people controlling resources would be responsible for generous distribution of the output of their lands and factories. With the territory system, all territory had someone who was supposed to care for the land, and be generous with the products of that land.

Because leaders had to be generous, they were accountable both to the members of their house and to leaders of other houses. Titleholders could lose their title, or fail to be promoted into full leadership if they proved unable to fulfill the duties of their position. They also had to prove themselves able to fulfill the role in order to be placed in the new position. Even though birth order initially guided the qualifications for inheriting titles, with oldest sons and daughters having priority, one generation trained their children, and if the training was not successful other, more able, people would be installed in the named positions.

Although the ruling class was able to hold on to power in the Northwest Coast System, they were not able to hold on to all of the wealth. The societies' requirements that leaders distribute and share wealth assured all but the slaves of support.

I argued in Chapter 7 that, had the industrial economy of the Pacific Northwest had to comply with the original rules for admission of new activities to the system, the feast system would have added 'cross-scale' or 'cross-sector' linkages. Operators in the forest would come to recognize the impacts of their actions on fisheries. Operators of mines would need to recognize the effects of their operations on other sectors. The logic of the feast system was that such linkages would be built into the financial organization of a region. The CEOs of each industry would be evaluated by the CEOs of other industries.

Once one accepts the idea that the profits of a particular regional economic activity should be shared with every other economic activity that could negatively or positively affect it, then it is possible to address the need for 'cross-scale and cross-level linkages' as discussed in the resilience literature. But these types of link are not explored in the literature.

The territoriality system

All of the resilience literature accepts with little question the fundamental notion of 'property' that has been spread from Europe, especially England, around the world as the modern market system has spread. Even the commons literature, until recently, has kept the word 'property,' simply pointing out that property can be classified into three types: private property, state property, and common property. The change in category of property indicates a change in the characteristic of the owner of the property. The fundamental idea of 'property' remains, in that the owner can both control the property and keep all of residual or surplus – the profit and rent. In 2008, the International Association for the Study of Common Property changed its name to the International Association for the Study of the Commons. After much discussion, the members agreed that a common pool resource was different from a property regime such as common property. The commons can refer either to the common pool nature of a resource, or to any of many territorial systems that assign roles and responsibilities in the management of a resource. The Association thus expanded the scope of its studies.

Close examination of the Northwest Coast system shows that the words 'property' and 'owner,' although commonly used to explain the system, actually do not adequately capture the fundamental characteristics of the territory systems on the Northwest Coast. I have labeled them 'proprietorship' systems. I could also have used the term 'trusteeship' systems.

The importance of this point can be understood, in part, by examining the types of position that are defined in the Northwest Coast system. The position of 'owner' did not exist. The titleholding positions might be known today as 'trustees': people who are responsible for taking care of the assets of the beneficiaries. The beneficiaries were those people who had become members of a house, plus members of neighboring houses who had a share in the return on the assets through the system of side payments. The head titleholder was the head trustee. He or she was assisted by lesser titleholders, one of whom was in training to become the head trustee-titleholder. Women had important titles and assisted the titleholder, particularly in the training of his successor.

The entire landscape was assigned to one or another trustee-titleholder. There was no land or body of water near land without a person clearly responsible for it. Most persons were born with a connection to part of the landscape, both through their mother's and their father's clan. Depending on whether or not the system was matrilineal or patrilineal, the dominant connection was through either the mother or the father. Some parts of the landscape, the rivers, had multiple trustee-titleholders because they flowed past many titleholders' lands and fishing stations.

Entrance to and exit from the trustee-titleholder positions depended upon demonstration of knowledge about how to carry out the duties of the trustee position. Head titleholders had a probationary period of a year in which they could demonstrate their qualifications by collecting the wealth needed to hold a feast at which final recognition of the title would be given. The titleholder had to know the history of the territory for which he would become responsible. The oral histories of these territories, in principle, extended back to the origin of the relationship between the title and the land. Many in the Resilience Alliance stress the importance of memory in providing humans with the knowledge that they need to deal with crises as well as with day-to-day decision-making. Titleholders had to be able to recite from memory the history of their territory, and be able to witness the demonstration of such knowledge for titleholders of other territories. Should a crisis cause a breakdown of the territorial system, the widespread presence of people with such memories would help in reorganizing the system. While some parts of the history may have been forgotten, because of the death of the titleholders in an epidemic or war, reconstructing the system would still be possible from the fragments that would remain.

Because titleholders were functionally trustees responsible to the other titleholders, the people holding these positions had to be adept at the process of joint decision-making. Aggregation rules describe the rules for decision-making for all the other rules in the system. Chapter 6 dealt with the implementation of the Nuu-chah-nulth protocols for such joint decision-making in the case of the Clayoquot Sound Scientific Panel. That chapter also explained that the consensus-based rules were evident throughout the Pacific Northwest. Some communities were quite clear that the feasting system had been created to solve problems of continual warfare among communities (Fiske & Patrick 2000: 104–5). The feasting system was, for these societies, a peacemaking system. In the process of considering options when major crises occurred, the rules of the system ensured that all important people would be heard. Thus if one person had a proposal that seemed 'far out,' that idea would not be summarily dismissed. This opened the door for innovation and for adaptive response to challenges, another key feature stressed by the Resilience Alliance for systems that have survival capabilities.

I have been interested in observing the interaction of members of the provincial bureaucracies in British Columbia in response to the requirement that they provide 'consultation and accommodation' to the indigenous peoples of the province. This requirement has been imposed on the provincial authorities by the Supreme Court of Canada under the doctrine that the Crown must act honorably. The idea of sharing decision-making power with anyone else does not sit well with provincial bureaucrats. They think that they have the final say in decisions; there is even a rule that people may not 'fetter' the decision-making authority of key officials, especially in the forestry sector. A process of consensus-building among the community, involving achieving approval from every important person, certainly could be seen as fettering the actions of a provincial government official. If the official is operating in the mindset of maximizing sustained yield of fiber production, a mindset that has been shown to be contrary to resilience, increasing the ability of people to fetter him would assist in promoting resilience.

All three types of rule that have been reviewed above, namely position, boundary and aggregation rules, intersect with a key scope rule, which is that all trustee/titleholders need to take care of the territories for which they are responsible. This concern for future generations was supported on the Northwest Coast by widespread beliefs in reincarnation. People who would live in the future would be concerned about the condition of the land. This could directly motivate titleholders, believing they were taking care of the land for themselves. It would indirectly motivate titleholders because everyone else would also be concerned. This concern promotes resilience by motivating people to address the implications of any major disturbances that threatened to reduce system productivity. It produces a concern for cumulative effects. Certain independent actions might not seem, by themselves, to have a system-wide impact. But if such impacts become evident, through inter-actions that are described as cumulative effects in the environmental impact litera-ture, then the scope rule that holds titleholders responsible for system caretaking would force the titleholders to take action regarding cumulative impacts.

Several of the rule types combine to provide strong incentives for social learn-ing. Because of the payoff rules, everyone benefits when the productivity of any one portion of the landscape improves, just as everyone is hurt if the landscape productivity decreases. Sharing in returns makes secrecy less important. When sharing is not present, individuals who learn how best to make the system work are assisted by keeping that information private, for their benefit. With side payments ubiquitous, private knowledge serves the public through the reciprocity system, and the reason for secrecy is removed. The rules for public discussion of deci-sions also would work to reveal information and knowledge. When new ideas have passed the tests involved in public discussion and become part of the deci-sion-making processes, rules that require leaders to demonstrate their knowledge would serve to assist in making the social learning permanent.

One of the great frustrations for Northwest Coast leaders and holders of tradi-tional knowledge has been the reluctance of the dominant society to be willing to utilize that knowledge. While they respect all sources of knowledge and are will-ing to consider arguments that initially seem to be incorrect, they realize that in the dominant society such open-mindedness is not present among powerful elites. Universities have their standards of peer review to legitimate knowledge. Bureau-cracies have standards of professional action, which derive from many sources. One source is the education offered by universities. Another is the mandate or mission of the bureaucracy, which involves serving particular clientele. Reporting and review of personal actions are strictly hierarchical; bureaucrats react to the opinions of their superiors. These attitudes restrict the ability of persons in those roles to listen to people without credentials or powerful roles.

Within private firms, knowledge is judged by narrow standards: will this infor-mation improve profitability? If it is particularly good information for this result, it will be kept secret. Such secrecy does not promote social learning. As with public bureaucracies, reporting relationships in business firms also place much importance on the views of superiors; workers are expected to take orders. When the strictly hierarchical structure is changed, such organizations can become labeled 'learning organizations.' Peter Senge (2006) has urged organizations to become more open to information from below, even if such information leads to fundamental structural change that weakens managers.

Turning to payoff rules, the potlatch system clearly takes away the full owner-ship of the surplus value produced by an enterprise, requiring that a portion of the generated wealth be distributed to other enterprises in the same system. The argu-ments presented in Chapter 4 address the ways in which such a system addresses two important problems in managing the resilience of a social–ecological system: (1) the dilemmas created by private action can undermine the socially best result for common pool goods such as salmon; and (2) a privately focused economic exchange system fails to recognize links that are financial external effects.

In order to be resilient, a system needs to be able to change as its problems change. A system of trustees managing house territories is relatively inflexible, in that the roles of stewards are set and territories cannot be bought and sold. This contrasts with the ability of a private property system to have rapid change when new parties purchase land or make long-term lease arrangements. I would argue that the extreme flexibility of a private property system allows disturbance to enter the system without adequate review and consultation by everyone involved. A resilient system not only deals with change thrust upon it, it rejects change that will not be desirable.

Present-day relevance

I end this chapter, and the book, by remarking briefly on relevance to today. The Resilience Alliance is very concerned with learning how to create resilience in the modern world. Perhaps its members have not examined the potential contribution of mandated reciprocal exchange or contingent tenure because of an assumption that rules such as potlatch feasts and trusteeship over land are politically infeasible. In Trosper (1998), I proposed that watersheds could be reorganized as systems of ecosystem trusts. In place of houses, a landscape would be divided into trusteeship units, each with a head trustee who would be the CEO of that unit. The watershed as a whole would be governed by a board made up of all CEOs. The feast function would be taken over by an ecosystem trust board. All major strategic decisions by each of the trusteeship units would have to be approved by the trust board. An example of such a strategic decision would be a major capital investment. All trusteeship units would contribute a portion of their net profit to others in the system, as a set of side payments in place of the feasts used on the Northwest Coast.

One of the reviewers of that paper suggested that it be rejected because the proposals were politically infeasible. Fortunately for me, the subject editor for the special issue asked for a third opinion. In my reply, I pointed out that political infeasibility did not disprove the economic feasibility: when externalities are pervasive, rules of actions have to take those externalities into account. Yet the reviewer had a point. Of course a system of mandated gifts would appear strange today. Restrictions on the ability of property owners to buy and sell, and to select their CEOs, would also not be immediately acceptable. Yet these principles were part of a resilient system, which suggests some version of them should be given serious consideration.

When I explain the ways in which reciprocity rules and territoriality rules contribute to resilience, many react by identifying those rules with 'communism' or 'socialism'. The identification is incorrect. Sharing one's profit with one's neighboring enterprises means that specific connections are made. The system is not a general policy of sharing profit, as in the slogan, 'from each according to ability, to each according to need.' Need is not the immediate rationale for creating interdependencies to deal with external effects. But there is an element of general redistribution in the idea that successful titleholders had to be the most generous. Some of their generosity went to everyone. Thus the 'communism' slogan can be used against these ideas; but such redistribution is a small part of the Northwest Coast system. Mostly these proposals advocate tight local control on decision-makers to enforce the trusteeship requirements. These structures don't require a centralized state, and may indeed reduce the power of such states if implemented, another characteristic not generally associated with socialism.

But resilience and sustainability are extremely important. Local communities who wish to reorganize and adopt such approaches can do so through the flexibility offered by modern contract law. The experience of the Northwest Coast suggests that fundamental changes to incorporate reciprocity may be very helpful in creating resilient social–ecological systems.

The purpose of this book has been to explore how social–ecological systems on the Northwest Coast had rules that quite plausibly contributed to the resilience of those systems. That those rules appear 'far out' in comparison with rules acceptable in modern market economies does not mean that lessons cannot be learned. Even such a minor application of contingency as the Section 4(e) rules of the Federal Power Act was able to assist the Confederated Salish and Kootenai Tribes in changing the operations of Kerr Dam, to the benefit of the affected resources on the Flathead Indian Reservation. The public discussion procedures of the National Environmental Policy Act led those affected by the two dams on the Elwha River to be able to persuade the federal government to agree to fund their removal. While the legalistic rules of the environmental impact process can be used to restrict consideration of such extreme measures, those processes of public discussion can also be used to encourage such consideration. The Federal Regulatory Energy Commission was required to consider alternative ways to deal with the impacts of the Lower Elwha and Glines Canyon dams in the process of awarding new licenses. Since hydroelectric licenses in the USA have to be renewed and reviewed every 50 years, those points of review provide the type of public scrutiny that would have been a regular occurrence had rules from the Northwest Coast systems been part of the governance approaches in the affected watersheds.

Of course, these rules are far out. They were incomprehensible to the outsiders who came to the Pacific Northwest. The large potlatch feasts were scandalous. The requirement to seek approval from titleholders for access to their lands was simply not considered. Lands and resources were expropriated. But in British Columbia, the settlers failed to comply with the Royal Proclamation of 1763; now they find that their title to the land has a cloud. It appears to be a weak cloud, able to provide only minor leverage to the aboriginal people. The need to renegotiate the territorial system in British Columbia creates an opportunity to introduce new decision-making rules that would support resilience. Co-management experts exist in aboriginal communities; the titleholders have been trained and can assist the dominant society in changing their organizational rules. As resilience and sustainability become more important, rules such as those used on the Northwest Coast deserve serious examination to determine how they can be incorporated into present day social–ecological systems. Such rules cannot be imposed. People seriously concerned about themselves and future generations could consider how they might adjust current relationships to include more reciprocity in order to have more resilience.

References

Adams, J.W. 1973, *The Gitksan Potlatch: Population Flux, Resource Ownership, and Reciprocity*, Holt, Rinehart & Winston of Canada, Toronto, Montreal.

Ames, K.M. & Maschner, H.D.G. 1999, *Peoples of the Northwest Coast: Their Archeology and Prehistory*, Thames & Hudson, London.

Anderson, E.N. 1994, 'Fish as Gods and Kin' in *Folk Management in the World's Fisheries*, eds C.L. Dyer & J.R. McGoodwin, University Press of Colorado, Niwot, CO, pp. 139–60.

Anderson, E.N. 1996, *Ecologies of the Heart: Emotion, Belief, and the Environment*, Oxford University Press, New York, Oxford.

Anderson, M.K. 2006, *Tending the Wild: Native American Knowledge and the Management of California's Natural Resources*, University of California Press, Berkeley, CA.

Anderson, T.L. 1995, *Sovereign Nations or Reservations? An Economic History of American Indians*, Pacific Research Institute for Public Policy, San Francisco, CA.

Anderson, T.L. 1997, 'Conservation – Native American Style', *Quarterly Review of Economics and Finance*, 37: 769–85.

Andreoni, J.M. & Miller, J.H. 1993, 'Rational Cooperation in the Finitely Repeated Prisoner's Dilemma: Experimental Evidence', *The Economic Journal*, 103 (418): 570–85.

Andreoni, C. & Varian, H. 1999, 'Preplay contracting in the Prisoners' Dilemma', *Proceedings of the National Academy of Sciences, USA*, 96 (19): 10933–38.

Arneil B. 1996. 'The Wild Indian's Venison: Locke's Theory of Property and English Colonialism in America', *Political Studies* XLIV: 60–74.

Arnott, R. & Stiglitz, J.E. 1991, 'Moral Hazard and Nonmarket Institutions: Dysfunctional Crowding Out or Peer Monitoring?', *American Economic Review*, 81: 179–90.

Atleo, E. Richard (Umeek) 2004, *Tsawalk: A Nuu-chah-nulth Worldview*, UBC Press, Vancouver.

Bailey, M.J. 1992, 'Approximate Optimality of Aboriginal Property Rights', *Journal of Law and Economics*, 35 (1): 183–98.

Basso, K.H. 1996, *Wisdom Sits in Places: Landscape and Language among the Western Apache*, University of New Mexico Press, Albuquerque, NM.

Berkes, F. 1999, *Sacred Ecology: Traditional Knowledge and Resource Management*, Taylor & Francis, Philadelphia, PA.

Berkes, F. & Folke, C. (eds) 1998, *Linking Social and Ecological Systems: Management Practices and Social Mechanisms for Building Resilience*, Cambridge University Press, Cambridge.

Berkes, F., Colding, J. & Folke, C. 2000, 'Rediscovery of Traditional Ecological Knowledge as Adaptive Management', *Ecological Applications*, 10: 1251–61.

Berman, J. 2000, 'Red Salmon and Red Cedar Bark: Another Look at the Nineteenth-century Kwakwaka'wakw Winter Ceremonial', *BC Studies*, 125: 53.

Berman, T., Ingram, G.B., Gibbons, M., Hatch, R.B., Maingon, L. & Hatch, C. 1994, *Clayoquot & Dissent*, Ronsdale, Vancouver.

Beynon, W. 2000, 'Potlatch at Gitsegukla: William Beynon's 1945 Field Notebooks' in *Potlatch at Gitsegukla*, eds M. Anderson & M. Halpin, UBC Press, Vancouver.

Binmore, K. 1994, *Playing Fair: Game Theory and the Social Contract, Volume 1*, MIT Press, Cambridge, MA.

Binmore, K. 1998, *Just Playing: Game Theory and the Social Contract, Volume 2*, MIT Press, Cambridge, MA.

Bluestone, B. & Harrison, B. 2000, *Growing Prosperity: The Battle for Growth with Equity in the Twenty-first Century*, Houghton Mifflin, Boston, MA.

Blumm, M.C. & Nadol, V.A. 2001, 'The Decline of the Hydropower Czar and the Rise of Agency Pluralism in Hydroelectric Licensing', *Columbia Journal of Environmental Law*, 26: 81–130.

Boas, F. 1989a [1889], 'The Aims of Ethnology' in *A Franz Boas Reader: The Shaping of American Anthropology 1883–1911*, ed. G. Stocking, Hermann Bartsch, New York, pp. 67–71.

Boas, F. 1989b [1904], 'The History of Anthropology' in *A Franz Boas Reader: The Shaping of American Anthropology 1883–1911*, ed. G. Stocking, Hermann Bartsch, New York, pp. 23–36.

Boas, F. & Hunt, G. 1905, *Kwakiutl Texts*, Memoir of the American Museum of Natural History, 5, New York.

Boas, F. & Hunt, G. 1908, *Kwakiutl Texts, Second Series*, Memoir of the American Museum of Natural History, 10, New York.

Boas, F. & Rohner, R.P. 1969, *The Ethnography of Franz Boas; Letters and Diaries of Franz Boas Written on the Northwest Coast from 1886–1931*, University of Chicago Press, Chicago, IL.

Boehm, C. 1999, *Hierarchy in the Forest: The Evolution of Egalitarian Behavior*, Harvard University Press, Cambridge, MA.

Borrows, J. 1997, 'Wampum at Niagara: The Royal Proclamation, Canadian Legal History and Self-Government' in *Aboriginal and Treaty Rights in Canada: Essays on Law, Equity, and Respect for Difference*, ed. M. Asch, UBC Press, Vancouver, pp. 155–72.

Borrows, J. 2002, *Recovering Canada: The Resurgence of Indigenous Law*, University of Toronto Press, Toronto.

Boston, T. & Morven, S. 1996, *From Time Before Memory*, School District No. 92, New Aiyansh, BC.

Bowles, S. 2003, *Microeconomics: Behavior, Institutions, and Evolution*, Princeton University Press, Princeton, NJ.

Bowles, S. & Gintis, H. 1998, *Recasting Egalitarianism: New Rules for Communities, States and Markets*, Verso, New York.

Boyd, R.T. 1990, 'Demographic History, 1774–1874' in *Northwest Coast*, ed. W. Suttles, US Government Printing Office, Washington, DC, pp. 135–48.

Boyd, R. & Richerson, P.J. 1985, *Culture and the Evolutionary Process*, University of Chicago Press, Chicago, IL.

Boyd, R. & Richerson, P.J. 2002, *The Origin and Evolution of Cultures*, Oxford University Press, New York.

Brubaker, E. 1998, 'The Common Law and the Environment: The Canadian Experience' in *Who Owns the Environment?*, eds P.J. Hill & R.E. Meiners, Rowman & Littlefield, Lanham, MD, pp. 97–118.

Butler, V.L. & Campbell, S.K. 2004, 'Resource Intensification and Resource Depression in the Pacific Northwest of North America: A Zooarchaeological Review', *Journal of World Prehistory*, 18 (4): 327–405.

Callicott, J.B. 1989a, 'American Indian Land Wisdom? Sorting out the Issues' in *In Defense of the Land Ethic: Essays in Environmental Philosophy*, ed. J.B. Callicott, State University of New York Press, Albany, NY, pp. 203–19.

Callicott, J.B. 1989b, 'Traditional American Indian and Western European Attitudes Toward Nature: An Overview' in *In Defense of the Land Ethic: Essays in Environmental Philosophy*, ed. J.B. Callicott, State University of New York Press, Albany, NY, pp. 177–201.

Callicott, J.B. 1994, *Earth's Insights: A Multicultural Survey of Ecological Ethics from the Mediterranean Basin to the Australian Outback*, University of California Press, Berkeley, Los Angeles, London.

Carlson, L.A. 1981, *Indians, Bureaucrats, and Land: The Dawes Act and the Decline of Indian Farming*, Greenwood Press, Westport, CT.

Carpenter, S., Walker, B., Anderies, J.M. & Abel, N. 2001, 'From Metaphor to Measurement: Resilience of What to What?', *Ecosystems* 4 (8): 765.

Cash, D.W., Adger, W.N., Berkes, F., Garden, P., Lebel, L., Olsson, P., Pritchard, L. & Young, O. 2006, 'Scale and Cross-Scale Dynamics: Governance and Information in a Multilevel World', *Ecology and Society* (online), 11 (2), www.ecologyandsociety.org/vol11/iss2/art8

Charness, G., Frechette, G.R. & Qin, C. 2007, 'Endogenous Transfers in the Prisoner's Dilemma Game: An Experimental Test of Cooperation and Coordination', *Games and Economic Behavior*, 60 (2): 287–306.

Chichilnisky, G. 1997, 'What is Sustainable Development?', *Land Economics*, 73: 467–91.

Chichilnisky, G., Heal, G. & Starrett, D. 2000, 'Equity and Efficiency in Environmental Markets: Global Trade in Carbon Dioxide Emissions' in *Environmental Markets: Equity and Efficiency*, eds G. Chichilnisky & G. Heal, Columbia University Press, New York, pp. 47–67.

Christman, J. 1994, *The Myth of Property: Toward an Egalitarian Theory of Ownership*, Oxford University Press, New York.

Cohen, F.G. 1986, *Treaties on Trial: The Continuing Controversy over Northwest Indian Fishing Rights*, University of Washington Press, Seattle, WA.

Cole, D. & Chaikin, I. 1990, *An Iron Hand Upon the People: The Law Against the Potlatch on the Northwest Coast*, University of Washington Press, Seattle, WA.

Confederated Salish and Kootenai Tribes 2000, *FY2001 4(e) Condition Submittals: FWIS, HAP, Annual Report/Workplan*, Confederated Salish and Kootenai Tribes, Pablo, Montana.

Copes, P. & Reid, M. 1995, *An Expanded Salmon Fishery for the Gitksan–Wet'suwet'en in the Upper Skeena Region: Equity Considerations and Management Implications*, Discussion Paper 95, 3rd edn, Institute of Fisheries Analysis, Simon Fraser University, Vancouver, BC.

Costanza, R. & Patten, B.C. 1995, 'Defining and Predicting Sustainability', *Ecological Economics*, 15: 193–96.

Costanza, R., Norton, B.G. & Haskell, B.D. (eds) 1992, *Ecosystem Health: New Goals for Environmental Management*, Island Press, Washington, DC.

Cove, J.J. 1982, 'The Gitksan Traditional Concept of Land Ownership', *Anthropologica*, 24: 3–18.

Crawford, S.E.S. & Ostrom, E. 1995, 'A Grammar of Institutions', *American Political Science Review*, 89: 582–600.

Crawfurd, J. 1859, 'On the Conditions Which Favour, Retard, or Obstruct the Early Civilization of Man', *Transactions of the Ethnological Society of London N.S.*, 1: 154–77.

Daly, R. 2005, *Our Box Was Full: An Ethnography for the Delgamuukw Plaintiffs*, UBC Press, Vancouver, Toronto.

David, P.A. 1998, 'Communication Norms and the Collective Cognitive Performance of "Invisible Colleges"' in *Creation and Transfer of Knowledge: Institutions and Incentives*, eds G.B. Navaretti, P. Dasgupta, K.G. Maler & D. Siniscalco, Springer-Verlag, Berlin, pp. 115–63.

Delcourt, P.A. & Delcourt, H.R. 2004, *Prehistoric Native Americans and Ecological Change: Human Ecosystems in Eastern North America since the Pleistocene*, Cambridge University Press, Cambridge and New York.

Demsetz, H. 1967, 'Toward a Theory of Property Rights', *American Economic Review*, 57: 347–59.

Department of the Interior 1995, *Treatment of Public Comments Section 4(e) Conditions for the Kerr Hydroelectric Project, Montana, October 13, 1995*, Department of the Interior, Washington, DC.

Deur, D. & Turner, N.J. 2005, *Keeping it Living: Traditions of Plant Use and Cultivation on the Northwest Coast of North America*, University of Washington Press/UBC Press, Seattle, WA, and Vancouver.

Donald, L. 1997, *Aboriginal Slavery on the Northwest Coast of North America*, University of California Press, Berkeley, CA.

Dryzek, J.S. 1987, *Rational Ecology: Environment and Political Economy*, Basil Blackwell, Oxford, New York.

Durkheim, E. & Fields, K.E. 1995, *The Elementary Forms of Religious Life*, Free Press, New York.

Echeverria, J.D., Barrow, P. & Roos-Collins, R. 1989, *Rivers at Risk: The Concerned Citizen's Guide to Hydropower*, Island Press, Washington, DC.

Ellingson, T. 2001, *The Myth of the Noble Savage*, University of California Press, Berkeley, CA.

Elmqvist, T., Folke, C., Nystrom, M., Peterson, G.D., Bengtsson, J., Walker, B. & Norberg, J. 2003, 'Response Diversity, Ecosystem Change, and Resilience', *Frontiers in Ecology and the Environment*, 1 (9): 488–94.

Elster, J. & Moene, K.O. 1989, 'Introduction' in *Alternatives to Capitalism*, eds J. Elster & K.O. Moene, Cambridge University Press, Cambridge, pp. 1–35.

Elwha Project Human Effects Team 1995, *Elwha River Restoration Project: Economic Analysis Final Technical Report*, www.nps.gov/archive/olym/elwha/docs/econanaly.htm.

Federal Energy Regulatory Commission, 2001, *Hydropower Projects under Commission License*, www.ferc.gov.

Feeny, D., Hanna, S. & McEvoy, A.F. 1996, 'Questioning the Assumptions of the "Tragedy of the Commons" Model of Fisheries', *Land Economics*, 72: 187–205.

Feit, H.A. 1991, 'The Construction of Algonquian Hunting Territories: Private Property as Moral Lesson, Policy Advocacy, and Ethnographic Error' in *Colonial Situations: Essays on the Contextualization of Ethnographic Knowledge*, ed. G.W. Stocking Jr, University of Wisconsin Press, Madison, WI, pp. 109–34.

Feit, H.A. 2007, 'Myths of Ecological Whitemen: Histories, Science, and Rights in North American – Native American Relations' in *Native Americans and the Environment:*

Perspectives on The Ecological Indian, eds M.E. Harkin & D.R. Lewis, University of Nebraska Press, Lincoln, NE, pp. 52–92.

Fiske, J. & Patrick, B. 2000, *Cis dideen kat = When the plumes rise: The Way of the Lake Babine Nation*, UBC Press, Vancouver.

Fladmark, K.R., Ames, K.M. & Sutherland, P.D. 1990, 'Prehistory of the Northern Coast of British Columbia' in *Northwest Coast*, ed. W. Suttles, US Government Printing Office, Washington, DC, pp. 229–39.

Folke, C. 2006, 'Resilience: The Emergence of a Perspective for Social–Ecological Systems Analyses', *Global Environmental Change*, 16: 253–67.

Folke, C., Carpenter, S., Elmqvist, T., Gunderson, L., Holling, C.S., Walker, B., Bengtsson, J., Berkes, F., Colding, J., Danell, K., Falkenmark, M., Gordon, L., Kasperson, R., Kautsky, N., Kinzig, A., Levin, S., Mäler, K., Moberg, F., Ohlsson, L., Olsson, P., Ostrom, E., Reid, W., Rockström, J., Savenije, H. & Svedin, U. 2002, *Resilience and Sustainable Development: Building Adaptive Capacity in a World of Transformations*, Environmental Advisory Council to the Swedish Government, Stockholm, Sweden.

Folke, C., Colding, J. & Berkes, F. 2003, 'Synthesis: Building Resilience and Adaptive Capacity in Social–Ecological Systems' in *Navigating Social–Ecological Systems: Building Resilience for Complexity and Change*, eds F. Berkes, J. Colding & C. Folke, University of Cambridge Press, Cambridge, pp. 352–87.

Folke, C., Pritchard, L., Berkes, F., Colding, J. & Svedin, U. 2007, 'The Problem of Fit Between Ecosystems and Institutions: Ten Years Later', *Ecology and Society* (Online), 12 (1): 30, www.ecologyandsociety.org/vol12/iss1/art30/.

Foy, P.G. 2008, 'Another Opinion: The Test used by Vickers J. for Proof of Aboriginal Title', *Aboriginal Forestry 2008*, ed. Garton, Billy S. (Chair), Pacific Business and Law Institute, Vancouver, BC.

Fudenberg, D. & Tirole, J. 1991, *Game Theory*, MIT Press, Cambridge, MA.

Furtwangler, A. 1997, *Answering Chief Seattle*, University of Washinton Press, Seattle, WA and London.

Gaspart, F. & Seki, E. 2003, 'Cooperation, Status Seeking and Competitive Behaviour: Theory and Evidence', *Journal of Economic Behavior Organization*, 51 (1): 51–77.

Geisler, C.C. 1995, 'Land and Poverty in the United States', *Land Economics*, 71: 16–34.

Gisday Wa & Delgam Uukw 1992, *The Spirit in the Land: Statements of the Gitksan and Wet'suwet'en Hereditary Chiefs in the Supreme Court of British Columbia, 1987–1990*, Reflections, Gabriola, BC.

Gitxsan Chiefs' Office 2007, *Who We Are: Traditional System*, www.gitxsan.com/html/who/people/trad.htm.

Glavin. T. 1996, *Dead Reckoning: Confronting the Crisis in Pacific fisheries*, Greystone Books, David Suzuki Foundation, Vancouver.

Goldman, I. 1975, *The Mouth of Heaven: An Introduction to Kwakiutl Religious Thought*, Wiley, New York.

Gore, A. 1992, *Earth in the Balance: Ecology and the Human Spirit*, Houghton Mifflin, Boston, MA.

Gottesfeld, Leslie M. Johnson 1994, 'Conservation, Territory, and Traditional Beliefs: An Analysis of Gitksan and Wet'suwet'en Subsistence, Northwest British Columbia, Canada', *Human Ecology*, 22 (4): 443.

Gowan, C., Stephenson, K. & Shabman, L. 2006, 'The Role of Ecosystem Valuation in Environmental Decision Making: Hydropower Relicensing and Dam Removal on the Elwha River', *Ecological Economics*, 56 (4): 508.

Gunderson, L.H. & Holling, C.S. (eds) 2002, *Panarchy: Understanding Transformations in Human and Natural Systems*, Island Press, Washington, DC.

Gunderson, L. & Pritchard, L.J. 2002, *Resilience and the Behavior of Large-Scale Systems*, Island Press, Washington, DC.

Gunderson, L.H., Holling, C.S. & Light, S.S. 1995, *Barriers & Bridges to the Renewal of Ecosystems and Institutions*, Columbia University Press, New York.

Gunderson, L.H., Folke, C., Olsson, P. & Peterson, G.D. 2006, 'Water RATs (Resilience, Adaptability, and Transformability) in Lake and Wetland Social–Ecological Systems', *Ecology and Society* (Online), 11 (1), www.ecologyandsociety.org/vol11/iss1/art16/.

Haggan, N., Turner, N., Carpenter, J., Jones, J., Mackie, Q. & Menzies, C. 2006, *12,000+ Years of Change: Linking Traditional and Modern Ecosystem Science in the Pacific Northwest*, Fisheries Centre, University of British Columbia, Vancouver.

Hann, C.M. 1998, *Property Relations: Renewing the Anthropological Tradition*, Cambridge University Press, Cambridge, and New York.

Hardin, G. 1968, 'The Tragedy of the Commons', *Science*, 162: 1243–48.

Harkin, M.E. 1997, *The Heiltsuks: Dialogues of Culture and History on the Northwest Coast*, University of Nebraska Press in cooperation with the American Indian Studies Research Institute, Indiana University, Bloomington, IN and Lincoln, NB.

Harkin, M. 1998, 'Whales, Chiefs and Giants: An Exploration into Nuu-chah-nulth Political Thought', *Ethnology*, 37 (4).

Harris, D.C. 2001, *Fish, Law, and Colonialism: The Legal Capture of Salmon in British Columbia*, University of Toronto Press, Toronto.

Heal, G.M. 1998, *Valuing the Future: Economic Theory and Sustainability*, Columbia University Press, New York.

Henrich, J.P. (ed.) 2004, *Foundations of Human Sociality: Economic Experiments and Ethnographic Evidence from Fifteen Small-scale Societies*, Oxford University Press, Oxford, New York.

Hewes, G.W. 1973, 'Indian Fisheries Productivity in Pre-contact Times in the Pacific Salmon Area', *Northwest Anthropological Research Notes*, 7 (2): 133–55.

Higgs, R. 1996, 'Legally Induced Technical Regress in the Washington Salmon Fishery' in *Empirical Studies in Institutional Change*, eds L.H. Alston, D.C. North & T. Eggertsson, Cambridge University Press, Cambridge, pp. 247–79.

Hoffman, E., McCabe, K.A. & Smith, V.L. 1998, 'Behavioral Foundations of Reciprocity: Experimental Economics and Evolutionary Psychology', *Economic Inquiry*, 36: 335.

Holling, C.S. & Meffe, G.K. 1996, 'Command and Control and the Pathology of Natural Resource Management', *Conservation Biology*, 10 (2): 328–37.

Horwitz, M.J. 1992, *The Transformation of American Law, 1780–1860*, Oxford University Press, New York.

Hunn, E.S., Johnson, D.R., Russell, P.N. & Thornton, T.F. 2003, 'Huna Tlingit Traditional Environmental Knowledge, Conservation, and the Management of a "Wilderness" Park', *Current Anthropology*, 44: S79–103.

Hunt, R.C. & Gilman, A. 1998, *Property in Economic Context*, University Press of America, Lanham, MD.

Jackson, M.O. & Wilkie, S. 2005, 'Endogenous Games and Mechanisms: Side Payments among Players', *The Review of Economic Studies*, 72 (2): 543–66.

Jennings, F. 1976, *The Invasion of America: Indians, Colonialism, and the Cant of Conquest*, Norton, New York.

Johnsen, D.B. 1986, 'The Formation and Protection of Property Rights among the Southern Kwakiutl Indians', *Journal of Legal Studies*, 15 (1): 41–67.

Johnsen, D.B. 2001, 'Property Rights, Knowledge Accumulation, and Salmon Husbandry among Northwest Coast Tribes', *New York University Environmental Law Journal*, 10 (1): 1–69.

Johnson, A.W. & Earle, T.K. 2000, *The Evolution of Human Societies: From Foraging Group to Agrarian State*, 2nd edn, Stanford University Press, Stanford, CA.

Ju, Y. & Born, P. 2008, 'Externalities and Compensation: Primeval Games and Solutions', *Journal of Mathematical Economics*, 44 (3/4): 367–82.

Kan, S. 1989, *Symbolic Immortality: The Tlingit potlatch of the Nineteenth Century*, Smithsonian Institution Press, Washington, DC.

Keesing, R. 1989, 'Creating the Past: Custom and Identity in the Contemporary Pacific', *Contemporary Pacific*, 1.

Kew, J. E. Michael 1990, 'History of Coastal British Columbia Since 1846' in *Northwest Coast*, ed. W. Suttles, US Government Printing Office, Washington, DC, pp. 159–79.

Kolm, S. 2000a, 'Introduction: The Economics of Reciprocity, Giving and Altruism' in *The Economics of Reciprocity, Giving and Altruism*, eds L. Gerard-Varet, S. Kolm & J. Mercer Ythier, Macmillan, London, pp. 1–46.

Kolm, S. 2000b, 'The Economics of Reciprocity' in *The Economics of Reciprocity, Giving and Altruism*, eds L. Gerard-Varet, S. Kolm & J. Mercer Ythier, Macmillan, London, pp. 115–41.

Krech III, S. 1999, *The Ecological Indian: Myth and History*, W.W. Norton, New York.

Krech III, S. 2007a, 'Beyond *The Ecological Indian* ' in *Native Americans and the Environment: Perspectives on the Ecological Indian*, eds M.E. Harkin & D.R. Lewis, University of Nebraska Press, Lincoln, NB, pp. 3–31.

Krech III, S. 2007b, 'Afterword' in *Native Americans and the Environment: Perspectives on the Ecological Indian*, eds M.E. Harkin & D.R. Lewis, University of Nebraska Press, Lincoln, NB, pp. 343–53.

Laffont, J.J. 1989, 'Externalities' in *The New Palgrave: Allocation, Information, and Markets*, eds J. Eatwell, M. Milgate & P. Newman, W.W. Norton, New York, pp. 112–16.

Lane, B. 1973a, *Political and Economic Aspects of Indian–White Culture Contact in Western Washington in the Mid-19th Century*, Expert Testimony for US v. Washington, US District Court, Seattle, No. 9213.

Lane, B. 1973b, *Makah Economy Circa 1855 and the Makah Treaty: A Cultural Analysis*, Expert Testimony for US v. Washington, US District Court, Seattle, No. 9213.

Lane, B. 1973c, *Anthropological Report on the Identity, Treaty Status and Fisheries of the Skokomish Tribe of Indians*, Expert Testimony for US v. Washington, US District Court, Seattle, No. 9213.

Lane, B. 1973d, *Anthropological Report on the Identity, Treaty Status and Fisheries of the Lummi Tribe of Indians*, Expert Testimony for US v. Washington, US District Court, Seattle, No. 9213.

Langdon, S.J. 2007, 'Sustaining a Relationship: Inquiry into the Emergence of a Logic of Engagement with Salmon among the Southern Tlingits' in *Native Americans and the Environment: Perspectives on the Ecological Indian*, eds M.E. Harkin & D.R. Lewis, University of Nebraska Press, Lincoln, NB, pp. 233–73.

Latour, B. 2004, *Politics of Nature: How to Bring the Sciences into Democracy*, Harvard University Press, Cambridge, MA.

Lears, T.J. Jackson 1985, 'The Concept of Cultural Hegemony: Problems and Possibilities', *American Historical Review*, 90 (3): 567.

Lebel, L., Anderies, J.M., Campbell, B., Folke, C., Hatfield-Dodds, S., Hughes, T.P. & Wilson, J. 2006, 'Governance and the Capacity to Manage Resilience in Regional Social–Ecological

Systems', *Ecology And Society* (Online), 11 (1): 19, www.ecologyandsociety.org/vol11/iss1/art19/.

Lertzman, D.A. 2006, *Bridging Traditional Ecological Knowledge and Western Science in Sustainable Forest Management: The Case of the Clayoquot Scientific Panel*, Haskayne School of Business, University of Calgary, Calgary, Alberta.

Lichatowich, J. 1999, *Salmon without Rivers: A History of the Pacific Salmon Crisis*, Island Press, Washington, DC.

Link, M.R. & English, K.K. 2000, 'Long-term, Sustainable monitoring of Pacific Salmon Populations Using Fishweels to Integrate Harvesting, Management, and Research' in *Sustainable Fisheries Management: Pacific Salmon*, eds E.E. Knudsen, C.R. Steward, D.D. MacDonald, J.E. Williams & D.W. Reiser, CRC Press/Lewis Publishers, Boca Raton, FL, pp. 667–74.

Loomis, J.B. 1996, 'Measuring the Economic Benefits of Removing Dams and Restoring the Elwha River: Results of a Contingent Valuation Survey', *Water Resources Research*, 32 (2): 441.

Mabee, H.S. & Hoberg, G. 2006, 'Equal Partners? Assessing Comanagement of Forest Resources in Clayoquot Sound', *Society and Natural Resources*, 19 (10): 875.

MacFarlane, A. 1998, 'The Mystery Of Property: Inheritance and Industrialization in England and Japan', in *Property Relations: Renewing the Anthropological Tradition*, ed. C.M. Hann, Cambridge University Press, Cambridge and New York, pp. 104–23.

Macho-Stadler, I., Perez-Castrillo, D. & Wettstein, D. 2007, 'Sharing the Surplus: An Extension of the Shapley Value for Environments with Externalities', *Journal of Economic Theory*, 135 (1): 339–56.

Mankiw, N.G. 2007, *Principles of Microeconomics*, 4th Canadian edn, Thomson Nelson, Toronto.

Marglin, S.A. 2008, *The Dismal Science: How Thinking Like an Economist Undermines Community*, Harvard University Press, Cambridge, MA.

Masco, J. 1995, 'It is a Strict Law that Bids us Dance': Cosmologies, Colonialism, Death, and Ritual Authority in the Kwakwaka'wakw Potlatch, 1849 to 1922', *Comparative Studies in Society and History*, 37 (1): 41.

Mauss, M. 1967, *The Gift: Forms and Functions of Exchange in Archaic Societies*, W.W. Norton, New York.

Mauze, M. 1994, 'The Concept of the Person and Reincarnation among the Kwakiutl Indians' in *Amerindian Rebirth: Reincarnation Belief among North American Indians and Inuit*, eds A. Mills & R. Slobodin, University of Toronto Press, Toronto, pp. 177–91.

McClellan, C. 1975, *My Old People Say: An Ethnographic Survey of the Southern Yukon Territory*, National Museum, Ottawa.

McDonnell, J.A. 1991, *The Dispossession of the American Indians, 1887–1934*, Indiana University Press, Bloomington, IN.

McEvoy, A. 1998, 'Markets and Ethics in US Property Law' in *Who Owns America? Social Conflict over Property Rights*, ed. H.M. Jacobs, University of Wisconsin Press, Madison, WI, pp. 94–113.

McKay, B. 1982, *Anhluu'ukwsim Xkwsdaksa'askwhl Nisga'a: The Treasured Legacy of the Nisgha (Social Stucture)*, School District 92 (Nisgha), Terrace, BC.

McNeary, S.A. 1994, *Where Fire Came Down: Social and Economic Life of the Nisga̱'a*, Wilp Wilxo'oskwhl Nisga'a, New Aiyansh, BC.

Mills, A. 1994a, *Eagle Down is our Law: Witsuwit'en Law, Feasts, and Land Claims*, UBC Press, Vancouver.

Mills, A. 1994b, 'Rebirth and Identity: Three Gitksan Cases of Pierced-Ear Birthmarks' in *Amerindian Rebirth: Reincarnation Belief among North American Indians and Inuit*, eds A. Mills & R. Slobodin, University of Toronto Press, Toronto, pp. 211–41.

Mills, A. (ed) 2005, *'Hang Onto These Words': Johnny David's Delgamuukw Evidence*, University of Toronto Press, Toronto.

Mills, A. & Slobodin, R. (eds) 1994, *Amerindian Rebirth: Reincarnation Belief among North American Indians and Inuit*, University of Toronto Press, Toronto.

Mitchell, D. 1990, 'Prehistory of the Coasts of Southern British Columbia and Northern Washignton' in *Northwest Coast*, ed. W. Suttles, US Government Printing Office, Washington, DC, pp. 340–58.

Montana Power Company 1999, *Joint Application for Approval of Disposition of Jurisdictional Facilities and Approval of Related Agreements*.

Nadasdy, P. 2002, "'Property' and Aboriginal Land Claims in the Canadian Subarctic: Some Theoretical Considerations', *American Anthropologist*, 104 (1): 247.

Nadasdy, P. 2003, *Hunters and Bureaucrats: Power, Knowledge, and Aboriginal–State Relations in the Southwest Yukon*, UBC Press, Vancouver.

Nadasdy, P. 2005, 'Transcending the Debate over the Ecologically Noble Indian: Indigenous Peoples and Environmentalism', *Ethnohistory*, 52 (208): 291–331.

National Park Service 2005, *Elwha River Ecosystem Restoration Implementation: Final Supplement to the Final Environmental Impact Statement*, www.nps.gov/olym/naturescience/upload/All_Chapters.pdf (last update July 2005).

Newell, D. 1993, *Tangled Webs of History: Indians and the Law in Canada's Pacific Coast Fisheries*, University of Toronto Press, Toronto.

Nisga'a Lisims Government 2002, *A Land Use Plan for Nisga'a Lands*, Land Department, New Aiyansh, BC.

Nisga'a Tribal Council 1995, *Lock, Stock and Barrel: Nisga'a Ownership Statement*, Nisga'a Tribal Council, New Aiyansh, BC.

Oberg, K. 1973, *The Social Economy of the Tlingit Indians*, J.J. Douglas, Vancouver.

Olsson, P., Gunderson, L.H., Carpenter, S.R., Ryan, P., Lebel, L., Folke, C. & Holling, C.S. 2006, 'Shooting the Rapids: Navigating Transitions to Adaptive Governance of Social–Ecological Systems', *Ecology and Society* (Online), 11 (1): 18. www.ecologyandsociety.org/vol11/iss1/art18/.

Olympic National Park 2008, *Freeing the Elwha: Restoration in Olympic's Largest Watershed*, www.nps.gov/olym/naturescience/upload/elwharestoration.pdf (last update 18 April 2008).

O'Neill, J. 2007, *Markets, Deliberation and Environment*, Routledge, London, New York.

Ostrom, E. 1990, *Governing the Commons: The Evolution of Institutions for Collective Action*, Cambridge University Press, Cambridge.

Ostrom, E. 2001, 'Reformulating the Commons' in *Protecting the Commons: A Framework for Resource Management in the Americas*, eds J. Burger, E. Ostrom, R.B. Norgaard, D. Policansky & B.D. Goldstein, Island Press, Washington, DC, pp. 17–41.

Ostrom, E. 2005, *Understanding Institutional Diversity*, Princeton University Press, Princeton, NJ.

Ostrom, E., Gardner, R. & Walker, J. 1994, *Rules, Games, and Common-Pool Resources*, University of Michigan Press, Ann Arbor, MI.

Otis, D.S. 1973, *The Dawes Act and the Allotment of Indian Land*, University of Oklahoma Press, Norman.

Penner, J.E. 1997, *The Idea of Property in Law*, Clarendon Press, Oxford, New York.

Peters, P.E. 1998, 'The Erosion of Commons and the Emergence of Property: Problems for Social Analysis' in *Property in Economic Context*, eds R.C. Hunt & A. Gilman, University Press of America, Lanham, MD, pp. 351–78.

Pettigrew, R.M. 1990, 'Prehistory of the Lower Columbia and Willamette Valley' in *Northwest Coast*, ed. W. Suttles, US Government Printing Office, Washington, DC, pp. 518–29.

Piddocke, S. 1965, 'The Potlatch System of the Southern Kwakiutl: A New Perspective', *Southwestern Journal of Anthropology*, 21: 244–64.

Pinkerton, E. 1998, 'Integrated Management of a Temperate Montane Forest Ecosystem through Wholistic Forestry: a British Columbia Example' in *Linking Social and Ecological Systems*, eds F. Berkes & C. Folke, Cambridge University Press, Cambridge, pp. 363–89.

Pinkerton, E. & Weinstein, M. 1995, *Fisheries that Work: Sustainability through Community-based Management*, The David Suzuki Foundation, Vancouver, BC.

Pyne, S.J. 1982, *Fire in America: A Cultural History of Wildland and Rural Fire*, Princeton University Press, Princeton, NJ.

Ranco, D.J. 2007, 'The Ecological Indian and the Politics of Representation: Critiquing *The Ecological Indian* in the Age of Ecocide' in *Native Americans and the Environment: Perspectives on the Ecological Indian*, eds M.E. Harkin & D.R. Lewis, University of Nebraska Press, Lincoln, NB, pp. 32–51.

Raunet, D. 1996, *Without Surrender, Without Consent: A History of the Nisga'a Land Claims*, Douglas & McIntyre, Vancouver.

Resilience Alliance 2000, *A Consortium Linking Ecological, Economic and Social Insights for Sustainability*, www.resalliance.org.

Resilience Alliance 2008a, *Research on Resilience in Social Ecological Systems – A Basis for Sustainability*, www.resalliance.org.

Resilience Alliance 2008b, *Resilience Assessment*, www.resalliance.org/3871.php.

Richerson, P.J. & Boyd, R. 2002, *Not by Genes Alone: How Culture Transformed Human Evolution*, University of Chicago Press, Chicago, IL.

Ridley, M. 1996, *The Origins of Virtue: Human Instincts and the Evolution of Cooperation*, Viking, New York.

Rigsby, B. 1998, 'A Survey of Property Theory and Tenure Types' in *Customary Marine Tenure in Australia*, eds N. Peterson & B. Rigsby, University of Sydney, NSW, pp. 22–46.

Rose, A. 2000, *Spirit Dance at Meziadin: Chief Joseph Gosnell and the Nisga'a Treaty*, Harbour Publishing, Madeira Park, BC.

Rosman, A. & Rubel, P. 1971, *Feasting With Mine Enemy: Rank and Exchange among Northwest Coast Societies*, Columbia University Press, New York.

Rousseau, J. 1984 [1755], *A Discourse on Inequality*, Penguin, London.

Russell, P.H. 2006, *Recognising Aboriginal Title: the Mabo Case and Indigenous Resistance to English-settler Colonialism*, UNSW Press, Sydney.

Rynard, P. 2000, "Welcome In, But Check Your Rights at the Door': The James Bay and Nisga'a Agreements in Canada', *Canadian Journal of Political Science*, 33 (2): 211–43.

Sah, R.K. & Stiglitz, J.E. 1988, 'Committees, Hierarchies and Polyarchies', *Economic Journal*, 98: 451–70.

Sah, R.K. & Stiglitz, J.E. 1991, 'The Quality of Managers in Centalized Versus Decentralized Organizations', *Quarterly Journal of Economics*, CVI: 289–95.

Sahlins, M. 1993, 'Goodbye to *Tristes Tropes* : Ethnography in the Context of Modern World History', *Journal of Modern History*, 65 (1): 1–25.

Sahlins, M. 1996, 'The Sadness of Sweetness: The Native Anthropology of Western Cosmology', *Current Anthropology*, 37 (3): 395–428.

Sax, J.L. 1971, 'Takings, Private Property and Public Rights', *The Yale Law Journal*, 81 (2): 149–86.

Sax, J.L. 1993, 'Property Rights and the Economy of Nature: Understanding Lucas v. South Carolina Coastal Council', *Stanford Law Review*, 45 (5): 1433.

Schalk, R.F. 1986, 'Estimating Salmon and Steelhead Usage in the Columbia Basin before 1850: The Anthropological Perspective', *Northwest Environmental Journal*, 2: 1–29.

Schlager, E. & Ostrom, E. 1992, 'Property-Rights Regimes and Natural Resources', *Land Economics*, 68 (3): 249–62.

Scientific Panel for Sustainable Forest Practices in Clayoquot Sound 1994a, *Report of the Scientific Panel for Sustainable Forest Practices in Clayoquot Sound*, Clayoquot Scientific Panel, Victoria, BC.

Scientific Panel for Sustainable Forest Practices in Clayoquot Sound 1994b, *Progress Report 2 – Review of Current Forest Practice Standards in Clayoquot Sound*, Clayoquot Scientific Panel, Victoria, BC.

Scientific Panel for Sustainable Forest Practices in Clayoquot Sound 1995a, *Report 3 – First Nations' Perspectives Relating to Forest Practices Standards in Clayoquot Sound*, Clayoquot Scientific Panel, Victoria, BC.

Scientific Panel for Sustainable Forest Practices in Clayoquot Sound 1995b, *Report 4 – A Vision and its Context: Global Context for Forest Practices in Clayoquot Sound*, Clayoquot Scientific Panel, Victoria, BC.

Scientific Panel for Sustainable Forest Practices in Clayoquot Sound 1995c, *Report 5 – Sustainable Ecosystem Management in Clayoquot Sound: Planning and Practices*, Clayoquot Scientific Panel, Victoria, BC.

Scott, J.C. 1998, *Seeing like a State: How Certain Schemes to Improve the Human Condition have Failed*, Yale University Press, New Haven, CT.

Senge, P.M. 2006, *The Fifth Discipline: The Art and Practice of the Learning Organization*, revised and updated edn, Doubleday/Currency, New York.

Sensiba, C.R. 1999, 'Who's in Charge Here? The Shrinking Role of the Federal Energy Regulatory Commission in Hydropower Relicensing', *University of Colorado Law Review*, 70: 603–40.

Shein, B. & Wheeler, D. 1975, *POTLATCH: A Strict Law Bids Us Dance*, Canadian Filmmakers Distribution West, Alert Bay, BC.

Singleton, S. 1998, *Constructing Cooperation: The Evolution of Institutions of Comanagement*, University of Michigan Press, Ann Arbor, MI.

Smith, C.L. 1979, *Salmon Fishers of the Columbia*, Oregon State University Press, Corvallis, OR.

Smith, C.L. 2005, 'Low-Level Food Production and the Northwest Coast' in *Keeping It Living: Traditions of Plant Use and Cultivation on the Northwest Coast of North America*, eds D. Deur & N. Turner, University of Washington Press/UBC Press, Seattle, Vancouver, Toronto, pp. 37–66.

Stephenson, I. 1994, 'Cultural Patterns in Cases Suggestive of Reincarnation among the Tlingit Indians of Southeastern Alaska' in *Amerindian Rebirth: Reincarnation Belief among North American Indians and Inuit*, eds A. Mills & R. Slobodin, University of Toronto Press, Toronto, pp. 242–62.

Sterritt, N.J., Marsden, S., Galois, R., Grant, P.R. & Overstall, R. 1998, *Tribal Boundaries in the Nass Watershed*, UBC Press, Vancouver.

Stewart, H. 1977, *Indian Fishing: Early Methods on the Northwest Coast*, University of Washington Press, Seattle, WA.

Stiglitz, J.E. 1994, *Whither Socialism?* MIT Press, Cambridge, MA.

Suttles, W. 1960, 'Affinal Ties, Subsistence, and Prestige among the Coast Salish', *American Anthropologist*, 62: 296–305.

Suttles, W. 1987, *Coast Salish Essays*, University of Washington Press, Seattle, WA.

Suttles, W. (ed) 1990, *Northwest Coast*, Handbook of North American Indians, Vol. 7, US Government Printing Office, Washington, DC.

Tainter, J.A. 1988, *The Collapse of Complex Societies*, Cambridge University Press, Cambridge.

Taylor, J.E. 1999, *Making Salmon: An Environmental History of the Northwest Fisheries Crisis*, University of Washington Press, Seattle, WA.

Tennant, P. 1990, *Aboriginal Peoples and Politics: The Indian Land Question in British Columbia, 1849–1989*, University of British Columbia Press, Vancouver.

Trosper, R.L. 1974, 'The Economic Impact of the Allotment Policy on the Flathead Indian Reservation', PhD, Harvard University.

Trosper, R.L. 1995, 'Traditional American Indian Economic Policy', *American Indian Culture and Research Journal*, 19 (1): 65–95.

Trosper, R.L. 1998, 'Incentive Systems that Support Sustainability: A First Nations Example', *Conservation Ecology* (Online), 2: 11, www.consecol.org/vol2/iss2/art11/.

Trosper, R.L. 2002, 'Northwest Coast Indigenous Institutions that Supported Resilience and Sustainability', *Ecological Economics*, 41: 329–44.

Trosper, R.L. 2003, 'Resilience in Pre-contact Pacific Northwest Social Ecological Systems', *Conservation Ecology* (Online), 7 (3), www.consecol.org/vol7/iss3/art6/.

Trosper, R.L. 2007, 'Indigenous Influence on Forest Management on the Menominee Indian Reservation', *Forest Ecology and Management*, 249: 134–39.

Turchin, P. 2006, *War and Peace and War: The Life Cycles of Imperial Nations*, Pi Press, New York.

Turner, NJ 2005, *The Earth's Blanket: Traditional Teachings for Sustainable Living*, Douglas & McIntyre, Vancouver.

Turner, NJ, Smith, R. & Jones, J.T. 2005, "A Fine Line Between Two Nations': Ownership Patterns for Plant Resources among Northwest Coast Indigenous Peoples' in *Keeping It Living: Traditions of Plant Use and Cultivation on the Northwest Coast of North America*, eds D. Deur & N. Turner, University of Washington Press, UBC Press, Seattle, WA Vancouver, Toronto, pp. 151–78.

Turney-High, H.H. 1941, 'Ethnography of the Kutenai', *Memoirs of the American Anthropological Association*, 56.

Umeek (E. Richard Atleo) 2004, *Tsawalk: A Nuu-chah-nulth Worldview*, UBC Press, Vancouver.

Varian, H.R. 1994, 'A Solution to the Problem of Externalities when Agents are Well-Informed', *American Economic Review*, 84 (5): 1278–93.

Varian, H. 1995, 'Coase, Competition, and Compensation', *Japan and the World Economy*, 7 (1): 13–27.

Walens, S. 1981, *Feasting with Cannibals: An Essay on Kwakiutl Cosmology*, Princeton University Press, Princeton, NJ.

Walker, B., Holling, C.S., Carpenter, S.R. & Kinzig, A. 2004, 'Resilience, Adaptability and Transformability in Social–Ecological Systems', *Ecology and Society* (Online), 9 (2): 5, www.ecologyandsociety.org/vol9/iss2/art5.

Walker, B., Anderies, J.M., Kinzig, A.J. & Ryan, P. 2006a, 'Exploring Resilience in Social–Ecological Systems through Comparative Studies and Theory Development: Introduction to the Special Issue', *Ecology and Society* (Online), 11 (1): 12, www.ecologyandsociety.org/vol11/iss1/art12/.

Walker, B., Gunderson, L., Kinzig, A., Folke, C., Carpenter, S. & Schultz, L. 2006b, 'A Handful of Heuristics and Some Propositions for Understanding Resilience in Social–Ecological

Systems', *Ecology and Society* (Online), 11 (1): 13, www.ecologyandsociety.org/vol11/iss1/art13/.

Walters, C. 1997, 'Challenges in Adaptive Management of Riparian and Coastal Ecosystems', *Conservation Ecology*, 1 (2): 1.

Webster, G.C. 1991, 'The Contemporary Potlatch' in *Chiefly Feasts: The Enduring Kwakiutl Potlatch*, ed. A. Jonaitis, University of Washington Press, Seattle, WA, pp. 227–48.

Weinstein, M.S. 1994, 'The Role of Tenure and the Potlatch in Fisheries Mangement by Northwest Pacific Coast Aboriginal Societies', *First Nations Fisheries Workshop*, American Fisheries Society.

Weinstein, M. & Morrell, M. 1994, *Need is Not a Number: Report of the Kwakiutl Marine Food Fisheries Reconnaissance Survey*, Kwakiutl Territorial Fisheries Commission, Campbell River, British Columbia.

Wessen, G. 1990, 'Prehistory of the Ocean Coast of Washington' in *Northwest Coast*, ed. W. Suttles, US Government Printing Office, Washington, DC, pp. 412–321.

White, L.J. 1967, 'The Historic Roots of our Ecological Crisis', *Science*, 155: 1203–06.

White, R. 1998, 'Using the Past: History and Native American Studies' in *Studying Native America: Problems and Prospects*, ed. R. Thornton, University of Wisconsin Press, Madison, WI, pp. 217–43.

Williams, Robert A. Jr. 1997, *Linking Arms Together: American Indian Treaty Visions of Law and Peace, 1600–1800*, Oxford University Press, New York.

Wilson, D.S. 2007, *Evolution for Everyone: How Darwin's Theory can Change the Way We Think About Our Lives*, Delacorte Press, New York.

Worl, R. 1990, 'History of Southeast Alaska Since 1867' in *Northwest Coast*, ed. W. Suttles, US Government Printing Office, Washington, DC, pp. 149–58.

Index

Printed in the USA/Agawam, MA
August 9, 2013

578744.019